STUDIES IN
NATIONAL ECONOMIC ACCOUNTING

Collection of National Accounts Studies (1)

STUDIES IN NATIONAL ECONOMIC ACCOUNTING

BY

YOSHIMASA KURABAYASHI

ECONOMIC RESEARCH SERIES
NO. 16
THE INSTITUTE OF ECONOMIC RESEARCH
HITOTSUBASHI UNIVERSITY

KINOKUNIYA BOOK-STORE CO., LTD.
Tokyo, Japan

Printed in 1977

Printed by
Kenkyusha Printing Co., Ltd.
Tokyo, Japan

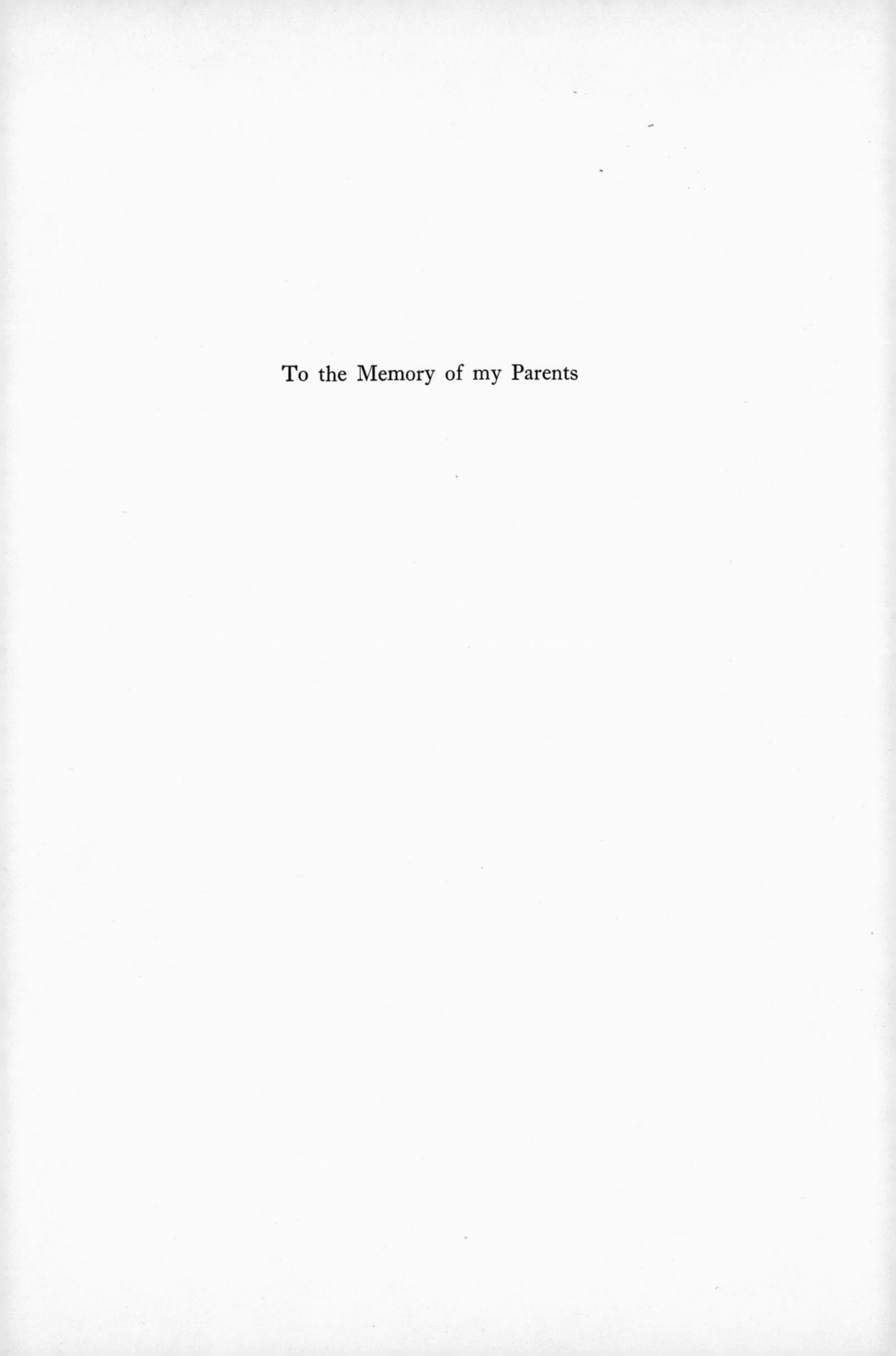

To the Memory of my Parents

PREFACE

This book constitutes the first of the collection of my works on national economic accounting and its related topics which I plan to publish consecutively. As the scope and the contents of the book are summarized in the introductory article, it is only necessary here to add a few marginal remarks. It is intended in this book that the vast scope of the contemporary studies of national economic accounting and their multiplicity should broaden as wide as possible through the articles that I have collected in this volume. While it is hoped that in the book I have paid tribute to the major topics of these contemporary studies it has not been possible to cover all of the topics, and still less to discuss all of them with equal emphasis. In particular, it must be recognized that those on the monetary aspects of national economic accounting are virtually left untouched in this book. Nobody can deny the importance of the monetary aspects that bear on the structure of national economic accounts, in view of the fact that monetary instruments form a basic intermediary of both real and financial flow on which the national economic accounting framework rests. It is hoped that the topics will be thoroughly discussed in the coming volumes.

The remaining part of the preface should be devoted to express my indebtedness to people who have influenced this book. All of the works contained in the book have been distilled in the ideal intellectual environment that obtains at Hitotsubashi University. My interest in national economic accounting was first aroused by an introductory seminar course on Sir J. R. Hicks' *The Social Framework* with Professor Ichiro Nakayama when I was an undergraduate at Hitotsubashi University more than two decades ago, and I have continuously received encouragements from him since then. My debt to Professor Chotaro Takahashi, who was my predecessor at the Institute of Economic Research, Hitotsubashi University, is great. I learnt much from his precious philosophical insight which led me the essence of the idea of national economic accounting underlying the surface of accounting techniques. My indebtedness to Professor Kazushi Ohkawa is also immense. It is he who has taught me the realities of national income measurement and introduced me to the International Association for Research in Income and Wealth. It is also my pleasant duty to extend my indebtedness to my colleagues at Hitotsubashi, too numerous to mention here.

I have benefited immensely from general conferences of the International Association for Research in Income and Wealth since my joining it in 1967. A number of articles contained in the book were originally presented on several occasions of the general conferences and I received valuable comments from the members of the Association. Some of these are mentioned in each of the articles included in the book, still there are many people whose names it is not possible to list here. Among them, my particular indebtedness is due to Professor Morris A. Copeland and Dr. Petter J. Bjerve to whom my studies in national economic accounting were essentially owed when I studied at Cornell and in Oslo almost a decade and half ago.

Finally, my thanks are due to Mr. Gerard Jacquemier whose assistance was considerable in reshaping my English, to Mr. Atsuo Yatsuka who read a part of the draft of the book and gave valuable comments and to Professor Yukihiko Kiyokawa of the Institute of Economic Research by whose arrangements the publication of the book was made possible. But, I must conclude the preface with saying that none of these gentlemen are to be held responsible for the errors and shortcomings that may be contained in this work.

Y. Kurabayashi
Institute of Economic Research
Hitotsubashi University, March 1977

Acknowledgements

My thanks are due to the editorial boards of the following journals that granted me permission to reprint my articles in this book:

Review of Income and Wealth

(i) The Impact of Changes in Terms of Trade on a System of National Accounts: An Attempted Synthesis.

(ii) Terms of Trade Effect, Productivity Change and National Accounts in Constant Prices—Reply and Further Comment.

(iii) Problems of National Accounts Data Adjustments for Developing Countries.

Behaviormetrika

Demographic Factors in the Distribution of Earned Income and the Economic Status of the Old Aged Dependents.

Hitotsubashi Journal of Economics

(i) The Structure of Income Redistribution within an Extended System of National Accounts.

(ii) Use of National Accounts as a Basis of Economic Data System.

Most of the articles are reprinted in this book with corrections, alterations and enlargements. They are indicated in due places of each of the articles.

CONTENTS

I.

INTRODUCTION

THE SCOPE AND METHODS OF STUDIES IN NATIONAL ECONOMIC ACCOUNTING: AN INTRODUCTION AND SUMMARY

1. Scope of the Book

This book is composed of eight essays, most of which have been either published in some academic journals or read at international meetings for reasearch in income and wealth during the past decade. The selection of topics dealt with in these essays was primarily governed by the interest and motivation to satisfy my intellectual curiosity, with only secondary regard to their relevance to current economic issues to which a large number of economists address themselves, or to their use for policy orientation. As these essays are independent in their origin and the time and places of publication, they can be read in any order with readers' interest. Yet, it may be of some help for the readers to address some remarks about what is the scope of the book and in what manner these essays are put into arrangement in the book before summary accounts of each of them are given.

It has often been contended that contemporary studies of national economic accounting started with the end of the second World War. It is true that the rudiments of the idea of national economic accounting had already been implanted in national income studies, both theoretical and empirical, before and during the second World War by Anglo-American and Scandinavian economists including such great names as J. R. Hicks, R. Stone, S. Kuznets, E. Lindhal and R. Frisch.[1] But, the impetus to develop a system of national accounts with the international cooperation of economists and national income statisticians of wide range has essentially been given since the end of the second World War by the initiation of international standards of a system of national accounts by international organizations such as the United Nations and the Organization for European Economic Cooperation and by the activities of the International Association for Research in Income and Wealth. In particular, the publication of two typical international standards of a system of national accounts by the United Nations and OEEC both under the guidance of Professor R. Stone has virtually broken a way through contemporary studies of national economic accounting.[2] I said that the systems of national accounts proposed by the United Nations and OEEC are typical international standards, because it is readily seen that there

1) Even the name of J. M. Keynes might be included in this list. Indeed, his thoughtful accounts of national budgets for financing the War (Keynes [1940]) still full of insight for the development of a system of national accounts. For the literature of the earlier works of national income studies, consultation for Studenski [1961] is particularly recommended.

2) It should be noted that the reference to the United Nations system of national accounts be made to the United Nations [1953], which is referred as old SNA. Old SNA should be distinguished from new SNA which will be referred later. There are three versions of OEEC's system of national accounts. What is referred to is OEEC [1959]. For a system of national accounts that corresponds to case (i) below, see OEEC [1961].

are, in principle, three alternative possibilities for designing a system of national accounts. They are:

(i) a system of national accounts on the basis of domestic concepts,
(ii) a system of national accounts on the basis of national concepts,
(iii) a system of national accounts on the basis of the mixture of domestic and national concepts.

The United Nations system of national accounts corresponds to the case (iii), whereas OEEC's system corresponds to the case (ii).

It appears that contemporary studies of national economic accounting have reached one of their culmination in the publication of the new or revised SNA. As has been widely recognized, a system of national economic accounting is considered to be made up of following component sub-systems:

(i) a system of national accounts in the proper sense,
(ii) the input-output tables,
(iii) the flow of funds accounts,
(iv) sector and national balance sheets,
(v) balance of payments tables.

Having established a firm footing in a system of national economic accounting, the exploration of those component sub-systems has made remarkable progress after the mid-fifties in line with the development of a system of national accounts (in the proper sense). For example, both theoretical and empirical studies in input-output tables have shed a new light on the structural interdependence of production sectors in market economies as well as centrally planned economies. Similarly, the development of the flow of funds accounts has had an onward march into the exploration of the structure and composition of the flow of purchasing power, particularly the flow of financial claims and liabilities, channelling through various sectors of the economy. The estimates of sector and national balance sheets have provided valuable information on the structure and distribution of the stocks of assets and liabilities by sectors and the economy as a whole. The balance of payments table have assumed a unique role in the component sub-systems of national economic accounting, building a bridge over regions which are connected by the flow of goods and services and of financial claims.

Looking through the course of developments in the studies of national economic accounting leading to the publication of new SNA, it is my impression that the style in the continental studies, particularly in Scandinavian countries, of national economic accounting has been governed by the spirit different from that prevailing in the United States. A typical example is those studies which have been achieved by Norwegian economists including P. J. Bjerve, O. Aukrust and P. Sevaldson.[3] Among their studies, the works of Aukrust are especially pertinent to our consideration. His approach to construct a system of national accounts in the works is firmly founded on an axiomatic basis by postulating a set of axioms which are required for deriving basic concepts of national accounts such as value added, net investment, net financial investment, saving and disposable income. His work became one of pioneering studies in national economic accounting. It is interesting to see that an attempt to enlarge his idea in the light of the proposed

3) Earlier works which provide the information on Norwegian national accounts are Aukrust [1949], [1955], Bjerve [1959] and Frisch [1961]. An illuminating summary account of the development of the studies in national accounting in Scandinavia is also found in Ohlsson [1953]. Stuvel's works are, among other things, represented by Stuvel [1965]. For the work of Bénard, see Bénard [1972].

system of the new SNA has been revived by the French economist J. Bénard. Although following somewhat different vein of thought, the works made by the Dutch economist, G. Stuvel may be considered as the one of the most important contribution that falls into the category of characteristic continental studies. Against the continental approach, the tone and the style of the studies in national economic accounting by American economists and national income statisticians are determined by their preference to accumulate empirical data concerning national accounts aggregates, placing relatively less importance on the logical framework of a system of national accounts.[4] Needless to say, the leading economist who represents the style of American studies is S. Kuznets.

Nobody can deny that the new SNA has made a great step towards the integration of the component sub-systems of national economic accounting proposing a detailed blue-print for the integrated system. It is remarkable to note that a large number of countries, including Japan and those in Europe, tend to adapt their own system of national accounts to the new SNA. It is true that there exists some prominent economists who dispute against the straightforward and universal application of new SNA to individual national systems,[5] but it appears that we are not necessarily much convinced of the proposed alternatives by which new SNA can be replaced. In this place, I do neither insist that the new SNA proves to be faultless nor contend that it is absolutely immune from any obscurity of terminology or some of vague presentation in the system. It should be also stressed that some important points

4) The point had already been noted by National Bureau of Economic Research in the occasion of giving an extensive review of national economic accounts of the United States. See, National Bureau of Economic Research [1958].

5) As a few examples of works that are critical about SNA, Ruggles and Ruggles [1970] and Geary [1973] should be noted.

are left unsolved in the new SNA in order to reach its full elaboration, as it is correctly indicated in the end of its introductory chapter. In spite of these shortcomings or unsolved problems, the progress of the new SNA towards a complete and comprehensive system of national economic accounting will not be stopped. Indeed, further extension of the scope of new SNA has been attempted in several directions. First, an attempt to develop a detailed system of the distribution of consumption, income and wealth should be mentioned. The attempt attracts our attention for the reason that the system contains in embryo a novel idea of structuring the accounting of micro-economic agents such as individual households and business enterprises. Second, the structure of the stocks of assets and libilities, both tangible and intangible, has received thorough consideration so as to frame the idea of sector and national balance sheets. Third, a system of price and quantity indexes which are directly separable from the values of commodity flow has been viewed in the light of the new SNA with its special reference to the derivation of value added in constant values, the weighting system, shifts of base years, seasonal adjustments and quality changes in commodities.[6)]

We cannot conclude, perhaps, a brief outline of the developments and dissemination of the new SNA without referring to a recent important project which is represented in an attempt to develop a System of Social and Demographic Statistics (SSDS for short) by the United Nations.[7)] A grand design of SSDS encompasses a wide variety of the fields of social statistics so as to draw up an integrated system which describes quantitatively all aspects of social and community life. Moreover, SSDS endeavours

---

6) Some of these activities are documented in the United Nations [1972], and the United Nations [1973], [1974].

7) Reference to SSDS should be made to the United Nations [1975].

to establish an effective link with SNA so that the system of social statistics may be geared into the circuit of economic transactions. It is admitted beyond all doubt by a growing number of economists that such endeavours to develop a system of social statistics gives a fresh and powerful impetus to quantitative studies of contemporary economic issues, which are increasingly complicated by entangled interrelations between economic and social aspects of social life.

It is these developments in contemporary studies in national economic accounting that provides a background for my central concerns in the essays contained in this volume. Broadly speaking, they are grouped into three categories of subjects. The first three essays are devoted to theoretical studies of national economic accounting dealing with some selected topics raised on the occasion of the refinement of a system of national accounts or with the intention of seeking further elaboration of SNA. The three next essays of the volume are essentially about the application of a system of national accounts. In these essays, I have made efforts to show that a system of national accounts, mainly following the line of thoughts presented in SNA, provides an effective apparatus for sorting out necessary statistical information from a disorganized collection of statistical data. I have also taken the issue of the international comparison of national accounts aggregates in developing countries in one of the essays, making a point that a number of subtle problems for data adjustments are confirmed by statistical analysis. In the final two essays, attempts are made to extend the scope of national economic accounting to the field of social statistics. Demographic factors receive thorough consideration in both essays to show that they should predominate over the consideration of the advent of the 'old-aged society' in Japan as well as most of industrialized countries. Numerical examples mostly taken from actual statistical figures, both national and international, are given in some of my essays. They are simply for illustrative purpose and are not given for policy orientation. I hope the reasoning and conclusions drawn from the statistical analysis of the numerical examples tell something true. Still, my feeling is that it is too premature to apply hastily and unconditionally the conclusions drawn from the statistical analysis to realities, disregarding a number of factors, standing for complex interrelationships between economic, social and political interests.

2. Summary Accounts of the Collected Essays

Having outlined the scope of this volume in relation to contemporary studies in national economic accounting in the foregoing section, I shall present, in this section, summary accounts of the essays contained in the volume which might furnish a convenient guide for readers.

1. The first essay is entitled "A Generalized Technology Assumption in the Doubly Classified Input-output Model of SNA by Commodity and Industry". As I have noted in the preceding section, it is generally recognized by applied economists and national income statisticians that the proposed system of national accounts of the new SNA has opened the way anew for the integration of component sub-systems of national economic accounting. Especially, an attempt to integrate the input-output table into the proposed system of national accounts and the special feature of the design of input-out table have significantly attracted their attention. A remarkable feature of the design of input-output table in the integrated system of national accounts in SNA is that the flow of intermediate products and output is governed by the two-way classification by the type of commodities and the category of industries.

Commodities are considered in the system of national accounts in SNA one of the major objects of production activities, whereas industries are those agents who are responsible for carrying out the production activities and are constituted by a variety of establishments. The two-way classification leads us to the matrix of intermediate inputs by commodity$\times$industry and the matrix of outputs by industry$\times$commodity respectively. The generation of the matrices of intermediate inputs and outputs creates apparent dissimilarity in the design of input-output table with the conventional one of Leontief type in that each industry in SNA can produce different categories of products including both characteristic and secondary products. Against this form of presentation in SNA, it is assumed in the conventional input-output model of Leontief type that only one category of products is produced by each industry. Putting it in other words, it is implied in the input-output table of SNA that the emergence of joint products which are completely excluded from the scope of the conventional input-output model of Leontief type is the typical case.

So-called technology assumptions are introduced in the input-output model of SNA to cope with the unique feature of the input-output relation. The technology assumptions in SNA are made by a pair of relations which represent the input-output relation between intermediate inputs and outputs on the one hand and the composition of product-mix on the other. Two kinds of technology assumptions called the *commodity technology* and the *industry technology* respectively are introduced in the input-output model of SNA as possible extremes. It is the anomalies of reasoning for the working of the input-output model of SNA resulting from vague conception of the technology assumptions that I take up in the first essay at the issue. Making a point that the commodity technology and the industry technology of SNA do in no sense constitute the alternative assumptions in the sense that one is excluded from the other, I proceed to propose a more generalized technology assumption called F technology which proves to be a more general and relevant production correspondence between a set of inputs and a set of outputs for the case of joint production. The idea of generalized inverse is introduced in order to deal with the non-singularity of the coefficients matrix of F technology. It is shown that the determination of the output vector, both of commodities and of industries, is substantially simplified by the introduction of F technology and that the meaning of the determination is much clarified. The theoretical structure of F technology is further explored in the appendix of the essay. In the appendix, the structure of F technology is constructed on a firm and logical basis fully recognizing the unique characteristics of the input-output model of SNA that are essentially represented by the production of joint products by each industry. It is shown that our F technology rests on a particular input structure called NOSLIS (a non-substitutable and linear input structure) and that F technology assumption is derivable from the structure as a special case of a generalized Leontief input function. As a corollary of these reasonings, it is also discovered that the constant input-output coefficients matrix of SNA may be regarded as a type of a generalized Leontief input function which is reduced to our F technology assumption with specific constraints. In the last section of this essay, the workability of our F technology assumption is numerically tested. Taking numerical examples out of those shown in SNA, the computation of the coefficient matrices derived from F technology assumption is carried out. The results of computation provide reasonable figures in their comparison with those which are obtained from the application of different technologies of SNA. A case of mixed technology based on our F technology assumption is experimented. It is interesting to see that the numerical result of this experiment proves to be identical to what is expected from theoretical manipulation. These results are of some interest for those who are interested in going through the technology assumptions of SNA discovering that our F technology assumption is sufficiently workable.

2. In the second and third essays, which are entitled "A System of National Accounts in Constant Prices " and " Further Considerations of National Accounts in Constant Prices " respectively, my attention is turned to the presentation of a system of national accounts in constant prices. The topic was originally taken up by R. Stone and was developed independently by G. Stuvel and R. C. Geary. The question is basically like this: Is it always possible to construct a consistent system of national accounts in constant prices only knowing the price and quantity information, both of base and of current years, on those entries which represent the commodity-flow? The commodity-flow entries are defined here as those entries whose values can be decomposed into price and quantity terms. Stone opened a debate by showing that the presntation of a consistent system of national accounts in constant prices under the condition is not always possible. Geary and Stuvel treated the problem from an entirely new angle. Granting appropriate deflators concerning the commodity-flow to deflate the non-commodity flow entries and introducing balancing item for each of accounting relations, Geary concluded that a consistent system of national accounts in constant prices can be well-defined with the discovery that the resulting balancing items denote trade gains or losses arising out of changes in terms of trade. Stuvel offered a solution for the problem following a vein of thoughts similar to Geary's and showed that trade gain or loss emerging from the trade with the rest of the world is eventually absorbed into trade gains raised in

domestic accounts ensuring the zero-sum constraint of balancing the relationships between the external trade gains (or losses) and the internal trade losses (or gains).

It is at this moment of the debate that R. Courbis came on the stage proposing his ingenious theory. In his theory he attempted to generalize the theories by Geary and Stuvel referring to the following points:

(i) an invention of the deflator applied to the non-commodity entries of the rest of the world account,
(ii) the disaggregation of a system of national accounts in constant prices into the sector accounts in constant prices,
(iii) the proposition of a system of national accounts in constant productivity in association with a system of national accounts in constant prices.

The central theme of my second essay is centred on the point (i) with taking note of the point (iii). In the essay, it is shown that a new formula of the deflator for the non-commodity flow entries which is substituted for Courbis's formula leads us to the balancing entry of the rest of the world account in constant prices, which, in turn, is expressed as the weighted average of trade gains (or losses) caused by changes in terms of trade in two extreme cases indicated in Geary's theory. My argument further goes on contending that similar sorts of trade gains (or losses) due to changes in terms of trade may arise in domestic economic activities if suitable deflators for the non-commodity flow entries that appear in domestic accounts are applied and that the external trade gains (or losses) caused by changes in terms of trade completely resolve themselves into the domestic trade gains (or losses) attaining the zero-sum restraint of the balancing entries of national accounts in constant prices. In the last part of the essay, attempts to establish an effective link between changes in terms of trade in broad sense and productivity changes considering sector production account in constant prices. Subject to changes in quantities of inputs, both of intermediate products and of labour, relative to outputs, my argument maintains that the terms which express productivity changes be introduced for formulating the sector production account. The argument is concluded with showing that a meaningful relationship which connects the term with trade gains (or losses) due to changes in relative prices of inputs and outputs can be established.

The article was again favoured with opportunities of receiving comments by Courbis after its publication on September, 1971 issue of *Review of Income and Wealth*. In one of his notes, he succeeded in making more explicit of the link which exists between trade gains and factor productivity gains following the line of thought offered in my essay. In the light of this development, the second essay is supplemented by additional remarks on the development as my after-thought.

The formulation of value added in constant prices (or real value added) has been implicitly implied in the discussion of the second essay, particularly in connection with the presentation of a sector production account in constant prices. It has often been argued by applied economists that one of the most ideal method to derive the value added by production sectors or industries, whatever they may be called, is the double deflation method. But, the double deflation method has long been recognized by national income statisticians as one of the major stumbling blocks in the derivation of actual figures of national accounts aggregates in constant prices, albeit the neatness and elegance of the method, because of often default of obtaining consistent time series in constant prices. Facing with the failure in the empirical application of the double deflation method, some economists argue for the adoption of a much simplified method without paying regard for the basic fact underlying in the derivation of the value added by production sectors in constant prices. The fact is that the consistent derivation of the constant values of value added by production sectors is closely associated with and constrained by the formulation of the sector production accounts in constant prices as is hinted in the discussion of the second essay. In the third essay of this volume my efforts are directed to clarify the nature of the double deflation method, making comparison of it with the method of single deflation. In the comparison, I make a point that the intrinsic weakness of the double deflation method lies in the fact that the effect of changes in relative prices between inputs and outputs should necessarily be incorporated in the derivation of value added in constant values. Then, in order to overcome this weakness, I proceed to show that the incremental quantum index for value added by production sectors is formulated on the basis of the sector production accounts in constant prices and that the formulation is decomposed into (i) the incremental index of the quantum of the value added obtained from the single deflation and (ii) the weighted sum of the incremental index for the relative prices between intermediate inputs and output. Moreover, it is uncovered by some mathematical manipulation of the formulation that the double deflated quantum index of the value added by production sectors is virtually reduced to a form of Divisia index that is constituted by the single deflated quantum index for value added by production sectors with the correction of the terms of trade caused by changes in relative prices between intermediate inputs and outputs. Having noted recent discussions by economists on the nature of Divisia index of real value added and its meaning, it is contended that the translation of the quantum index for real value added by production sectors into the form of Divisia index possibly opens a new way of looking in that the derived quantum index for value added by production sectors may be interpreted as the true economic index not merely as the statistical index. This point has a special relevance to the derivation of value added in constant prices by production sectors within the framework of a system of national accounts. In the foregoing discussions on quantum and price indexes built on a system of national accounts, they have simply been regarded as the statistical index, as the arguments in the chapter on the system for quantity and price comparison of new SNA clearly indicate. Our formulation to derive the value added in constant prices by production sectors in the form of Divisia index allows us to interpret the derived value added in constant prices from the Divisia quantum index of value added by production sectors as one possible case of the true economic index. It is hoped that my attempts in this essay will be considered as one preliminary work for building a bridge spanning over two independent approaches of index numbers, which are usually termed the economic (functional) and the statistical (atomistic) approaches.

3. In the fourth and fifth essays, which are entitled " The Structure of Income Redistribution within an Extended System of National Accounts " and " Use of National Accounts as a Basis of Economic Data System " respectively, I am concerned with one aspect of the uses of a system of national accounts termed the *instrumental uses* by new SNA. Those uses of a system of national accounts which are concerned with " our ability to collect and process information " are called the instrumental uses.

In the fourth essay, the structure of income redistribution composed of the market sectors at large and the public sector is considered. Noting the growing role of government activities in industrialized societies, their scope is briefly reviewed to distinguish their genuine role. Broadly speaking, the major functions performed by a variety of government agencies are grouped into three categories. They are: (i) the supply of public goods and services, (ii) the redistribution of income by the enforced and/or contracted transfer of income for administering the economic and social policies for the advancement of the well-being of the public and (iii) taking the leading role for shaping the economy's fiscal and financial policies. The extent of those government agencies which form the body of government authorities as a group may differ in what categories of government activities are considered. The concept of the *general government* is especially used, in this essay, for specifying the categories of functions (ii) and (iii). A set of government agencies which are primarily concerned with the category of functions (i) is called the *producers of government services* and is distinguished from the general government. The remaining resident agents are grouped so as to compose the *market sector at large*. It is seen that the activities associated with the market sector at large are sharply contrasted with those which refer to what is termed the *public sector* that is consitututed by the producers of government services and the general government. The breakdown of the economy into the market sector at large and the public sector provides an appropriate sectoring for the analysis of the process of income redistribution. In the light of the sectoring, a system of extended national accounts specifically designed shedding light on the process of the redistribution of income, channelled its way from the publict sector to the market sector at large and vice versa, is shown in a matrix form. For the convenience of more detailed analysis, the market sector at large is broken down into sub-sectors: (1) non-financial business enterprises, (2) financial institutions, (3) households and (4) private non-profit institutions serving for households. It is important for the analysis of the process of income redistribution that the primary distribution of factor income is clearly distinguished from its redistribution. Then, the process of income redistribution is displayed by a series of generated sub-matrices on the extended system of national accounts. The series of the generation of the sub-matrices starts with the factor income originated in the market sector at large, transforming it into the sub-matrix of the factor income received by the market sector at large which, in turn, is subject to the sub-matrices of income transfers between the market sector at large and the public rector, and finally reaches the sub-matrix of the disposable income of the market sector at large. Along the way of generating the sub-matrices, principles to classify the recipients of income and groups of households are discussed. The important role of demographic factors for the grouping of households is one of the points stressed in this essay. As the concept of income transfer plays the decisive part in the generation of the sub-matrices of income transfer between the market sector at large and the public rector, our discussion goes on clarifying its nature and its classification. For the illustration of these matrices, numerical examples of the matrices produced on the basis of valuable studies by Ichikawa and Sengoku are given. It is suggested that the introduction of demographic factors into the generated sub-matrix for the disposable income of the market sector at large has special relevance for the contemporary studies of the distribution and redistribution of income, because, facing with the coming of the so-called 'old-aged society' in Japan, it is foreseeable that the conflict of interests between generations would be the centre of issues on the redistribution of income. Our discussion in this essay is concluded with an appendix, in which the structure of the redistribution of income receives thorough consideration for its use in connection with theoretical basis of the measurement of income inequality.

In the lines spelling out the instrumental uses of a system of national accounts, SNA places special stress on the increasing role of computers for the collection and processing information. The lines deserve to be quoted here:

> The increasing use of computers, whose efficient operation demands an exact understanding of the simple connections between innumerable bits of information, sets a rising premium on a coherent framework in which every bit is seen to have its place.
> (United Nations, *A System of National Accounts*, New York 1968, section 1. 74.)

It is the vigour of establishing a coherent framework for systematized collecting and processing of statistical information that guides the fifth essay of this volume. Starting with a brief review of the availability and reporting of economic data current in Japan, the classification of economic data according to sources and purposes of data collection is given. It is shown by this classification that the consideration of economic data in this essay is limited to what is termed the data for general purposes. The structure of the economic data for general purposes available in Japan is then displayed in the tabulation. It is indicated by the tabulation that the Japanese structure of economic data is characterized by a decentralized system of data reporting and collection. It is argued that the lack of coordination and the redundant duplications of the reporting often observed in Japanese economic data are basically caused by the decentralized system of data reporting and collection. It immediately follows from these shortcomings that the accurate information will not be accumulated unless we grasp the full meaning of the complex conceptual framework underlying the real and financial transactions on which the focus of the proposed economic data system is placed. The economic data system, EDS for short, is composed of three major component systems that are mutually interrelated. They are: (i) the major system, (ii) the supporting system and (iii) the sub-system. A system of national accounts which is particularly represented in the development of new SNA serves the purpose of designing EDS, especially for the major system of EDS. The structure of the major system is built on two aspects of a system of relations: (1) the form of relation and (2) the content of relation. The major system matrix is derived from these aspects of a system of relations. The scope of the major system matrix is further expanded by the breakdown of its elements so as to form a link with the supporting system of EDS that supplements the major system. Sub-matrices for its elements are generated as a result of the breakdown they serve the component elements of the supporting system. Examples of the generated sub-matrices are illustrated, paying special regard to Japanese experiences of their application. It is shown, in conclusion, that the construction of EDS has special relevance to work out a system of economic data in Japan, with anticipation that the design of EDS proposed here will provide an opportunity to review the extent and contents of various statistical surveys currently carried out in Japan in a systematic perspective and to remove unnecessary information and redundant duplications.

4. In the sixth essay entitled " Problems of National Accounts Data Adjustments for Developing Countries ", I experiment with data adjustments of national accounts aggregates for developing countries, particularly of GDP by expenditure and by industry origin, on a consistent basiss. The necessary data are collected from United Nations' *Yearbook of National Accounts Statistics* for the decade between 1958 and 1967 with the intention that the data collected from the source may cover as many developing coun-

tries as possible and be adjusted on the uniform basis of 1960 constant values. For the purpose, attempts are made to make the most of the capacities of computers in that the processing of data and their adjustments are carried out on the computers minimizing the manual works for their adjustments. The period of the experiments is fixed on the ground that it broadly corresponds with the First Development Decade. The results of the processing and the adjustments of GDP series are shown in a tabulated form in Table 2. Observation of Table 2 discloses the facts: (i) that the availability of data greatly differs by regions, (ii) that the data in current values are generally more available than those in constant values and (iii) that the data by expenditure components are generally more available than those by industry origin. The types of national accounts data adjustments that I have met in the processing of the series of data are broadly itemized under the headings: (1) the adjustments due to changes in estimates, (2) those due to changes in base years, (3) conceptual adjustments and (4) the adjustments in the case of missing observation. Taking up these points one after another, I point out the nature of problems and show how I solve them.

In the sections that follows the discussion of national accounts data adjustments in general, numerical exercises on two specific topics are made on selected Latin American countries. As far as compilation and use of national accounts statistics are concerned, Latin America belongs to one of the most developed areas among developing countries. Enormous amounts of work and experience have been accumulated in developing the methodology and measurement of national account by both national and international agencies. In particular ECLA studies of national accounts aggregates have received wide recognition by the students of national accounts statistics. The topics of the experiments are: (1) the reconcilation of foreign trade statistics with national accounts and (2) the inter-country comparison of GDP by expenditure. Concerning the topic (1), a question is often raised about the comparability of foreign trade statistics with national accounts statistics because of their conceptual difference. Generally speaking, the foreign trade statistics refer to exports and imports of merchandise, whereas exports and imports in national accounts statistics include those of goods and services. If the two sources of data are perfectly consistent, the conceptual difference should be reduced to exports and imports of services. Estimates of the ratio of imports of goods and services (excluding investment income) to imports of merchandise (including freight and insurance on merchandise) are made on the basis of data taken from IMF, *Balance of Payment Yearbook*. The estimates allow us to give approximate size of the importance of services in exports and imports. Knowing the estimates, I proceed to compare the imports of goods taken from national accounts with the imports of goods taken from IMF, *International Financial Statistics*, both of which are expressed in c.i.f. in current values of national currency unit, for a selection of five Latin American countries. It is discovered by the comparison that the gap of the two magnitudes is within the margin of 10% of the imports of goods taken from IMF's IFS. An impression created from the comparison is that national accounts statistics are tolerably consistent with foreign trade statistics.

Turning to the second topic, the inadequacy of official exchange rates for inter-country comparisons of GDP and related aggregates has long been recognized by the pioneering works of Kravis and Gilbert in OEEC publications. Following their idea and applying the purchasing power equivalent for the conversion of GDP components in local currency unit into U.S. dollars, Braithwaite has carefully examined the quality of the converted figures of GDP aggregates and has drawn interesting conclusions from the examination. Yet, his examination is limited to the figures of 1960 without making the examination over time. Taking up the point at issue, I compare per-capita GDP by expenditure components in 1960 prices, converted into U.S. dollars using the official exchange rates, with the corresponding components computed by Braithwaite for a selection of 15 Latin American countries. The following features are discovered from the comparison:

(1) The Braithwaite estimates of per-capita GDP in U.S. dollars exceed the corresponding estimates by myself for most of 15 Latin American countries with the only exception of Brazil. In this exceptional case, it appears that the case has been largely caused by the overstatement of the official exchange rate relative to the purchasing power equivalents of private consumption and gross fixed capital formation.

(2) The comparison of the purchasing power equivalent of private consumption with the official exchange rate for each individual countries does not seem to lead to the results as definite as is the case of GDP.

(3) The remarkable undervaluation of the official exchange rate relative to the purchasing power equivalent of government consumption is observed for each of 15 Latin American countries. The result correctly supports the conjecture that was set forth by Braithwaite.

(4) For one third of 15 Latin American countries the official exchange rate indicates an overstatement relative to the purchasing power equivalent of gross fixed capital formation. Against this, the official rates of the remaining two third turn out to be undervalued in relation to the purchasing power equivalent of gross fixed capital formation. It should also be noted that the degree of

undervaluation is generally less than the degree of overvaluation in two different groupings of cases. In order to separate the differential effect of the uses of the conversion factors of individual GDP components relative to the official exchange rates between countries from the effect of those between different years, a statistical testing is experimented by the analysis of variance. The results of the computation is displayed in Table 8. The following conclusions are drawn from the results.

(1) It is likely that the use of purchasing power equivalents for the conversion GDP components into U.S. dollars produces significant deviation from what is converted by the use of the official exchange rate.

(2) On the average of 15 Latin American countries as a whole, it appears that the use of the purchasing power equivalents for the conversion of GDP and government consumption into U.S. dollars produces significant deviation from what is converted by the use of the official exchange rate. But, this is not necessarily the case for private consumption and gross fixed capital formation.

As some Latin American countries adopt the system of free exchange rates for external trade, it is interesting to see whether the adoption of free exchange rates alters the picture drawn from the application of the official exchange rate. The following conclusions may be formed by the experiment of the analysis of variance similar to the case of the official exchange rate applying for selected 7 Latin American countries.

(1)′ It easily turns out that GDP conversion by the application of free exchange rates generally undervalues it in relation to the application of the purchasing power equivalent of GDP.

(2)′ The conversion of private and government consumption by the application of free exchange rates relative to the application of purchasing power equivalents leads to their undervaluation.

It is likely that the degree of their undervaluation is comparatively amplified by taking free exchange rates for conversion in place of official rates. A general impression following from this observation is that free exchange rates are inappropriate as a substitute for the purchasing power equivalent of respective GDP components.

(3)′ In the comparison over time of the relative variation of GDP components, it is observed that the magnitude of the relative variation of the components is rising, although it is not appreciably high. This suggests that the degree of undervaluation caused by the application of free exchange rates as conversion factors is growing conspicuous in the early sixties.

4. In the last two essays, my attention is especially directed to the vast and sweeping structural changes both of economic and social, in our society experienced in the past decade. Having achieved a remarkable economic growth, more than doubling the GNP in the decade, Japan has emerged from the ruins of defeat as one of the industrial giants of the world. In the course of this development, her industrial structure has been subject to enormous changes, moving its weights from agriculture to manufacturing and services, from light industry to heavy industry and from traditional industry to modernized industry. Her demographic structure has also been changed. Caused by a sharp declining of the birth-rate, decrease of the death-rate and extended life-expectancy, she stands now at the threshold of the so-called old-aged society. The structure of man-power has been transformed in the decade from the stage of labour surplus to the one of labour shortage. In parallel with the structural changes in her economy and demography, her social structure has also experienced vast transformations. The progress of urbanization caused by her economic growth has widened the gap in community life between the congested urban area and the isolated rural area.

In spite of the material progress of our society, the quality of urban life has suffered from various kinds of disamenity such as air and water pollution and congestion of people and trafic arising from the material progress. It is true that the income distribution statistics of Japan in the past decade clearly indicate a remarkable decrease of the measure of income inequality. But, it appears that none of us is so naive as to be able to contend from the measurement of income inequality that unequal opportunities could be entirely rooted out by such decrease of income inequality. Hence, it is important from the view point of social justice to investigate what factors contribute to and what causes determine unequal opportunities, which often plant the root of social discontent in the people.

All the issues raised here urgently call upon sufficient amounts of statistical information. It is such statistical needs that I intend in the seventh essay entitled "A Socio-economic Statistical System for Measuring a Society's Social and Economic Performance " to respond them. As the social and economic activities in any of the industrialized societies including Japan are closely interwoven, it is necessary for the collection and compiling of statistical information that their statistical design should be drawn in a system such that its components prove to be mutually interconnected. A few examples of the attempts to draw up the statistical design deserves to be noted in this connection. First, the United Nations' proposal for a System of Social and Demographic Statistics (SSDS), exactly makes the point at issue, contending that the purpose of the proposed SSDS is to provide a connected information system for social and demographic statistics which will be useful for description, analysis and policy making in the different fields of social life. Second, another approach that should be noted here is the project that has been undertaken by the National Bureau of Economic Research under the guidance of Professor R. Ruggles. In the methodology of the project, the emphasis is particularly placed on relating social indicators and social statistics directly to the national economic accounts, insisting that the hard-core of the problem is the linkage between economic and social information.

It is intended at the beginning section of the seventh essay to present an alternative and synthetic approach for the measurement of economic and social performance of an industrialized society. The approach is illustrated as a system of socio-economic statistics (SESS) in a flow-chart in Diagram 1. The approach is proposed as an alternative to aforementioned examples in that it is primarily designed to provide a system framework for the measurement of economic and social performance of an industrialized society that is subject to rapid social and economic transformations like Japan. Moreover, the approach claims to be synthetic approach in that it attempts to build a bridge between the United Nations system and the National Bureau of Economic Research Project. Our approach is common to the United Nations system in that a mutually interlocked system is designed for the collection and compilation of requisite statistics. Our approach has also something in common with the emphasis placed on the project of the National Bureau of Economic Research. In this respect, the section that presents a fairly exhaustive account of the *Basic Survey of Social and Community Life* which is currently initiated by Bureau of Statistics of the Prime Minister's Office of the Japanese Government indicating that it provides a suitable data-base for SESS has special relevance to the aim of the National Bureau of Economic Research Project. The seventh essay is concluded with the exposition of the structure of man-power balance which constitutes a sub-system of SESS illustrated with actual figures taken from Japanese statistics. It is disclosed by the structure of man-power balance that vast changes in man-power occurred in the mid-sixties are vividly displayed in the figures.

In the final essay, the focus of the work is primarily directed to demographic factors in the explanation of the distribution of earned income and their implications for the economic status of the old aged. In doing this, I attempt to fully exploit the precious information obtained from *Sample Survey of Recipients of Health Insurance*, which has been unduly ignored as a statistical source for the analysis of size distribution of earned income. By presenting the distribution of earned income cross-tabulated according to different schemes of health insurance, sex, income and age groups, it is shown that demographic factors such as sex and age contribute to the formation and the pattern of size distribution of earned income. Following this observation, I proceed to take up the economic status of the old aged dependents over 65. Few attempts have been made so far to explore the economic status of the old aged dependents in relation to economic and demographic characteristics of those who support them largely because of the meagre statistical sources. Processed out of the statistical source mentioned before, the distribution of the old aged dependents is tabulated again according to income and age groups of those who support them, by different sex and categories of health insurance schemes. It is discovered from the statistical analysis of variance applied to the tabulation that the variation of the distribution for the old aged dependents is largely explained by the age effect of those who support them with the implication that the income effect of those who support them plays less essential part. These findings seem to have a definite significance for the policy making of social welfare, in that the advent of the " old aged society " should make it necessary to collect exhaustive quantitative information on the old aged dependents in relation to those who support them. The attempts made in this essay will be a step forwarding in this direction.

I have left one important point unexplained as far as I reach the end of a somewhat lengthy introduction. The point is this: Someone may wonder whether contemporary studies of national economic accounting are really qualified to face contemporary social and economic issues? In order to respond to this grave question, readers may allow me to invite the monologue of Marschallin from Hugo von Hofmannsthal's *Der Rosenkavalier:*

> " Das alles ist geheim, so viel geheim. Und man ist dazu da, dass man's ertragt. Und in dem " Wie " da liegt der ganze Unterschied ".

REFERENCES

(References concerning each essays are indicated at the end of respective essays.)

Odd Aukrust, "On the Theory of Social Accounting", *Review of Economic Studies*, 1949/50.

Odd Aukrust, *Nasjonalregnskap: Teoretiske prinsipper*, Oslo 1955.

Odd Aukrust, "An Axiomatic Approach to National Accounting. An Outline", *Review of Income and Wealth*, September 1966.

Jean Bénard, *Comptabilité nationale et modèles de politique économique*, Paris 1972.

Petter J. Bjerve, *Planning in Norway*, Amsterdam 1959.

Ragner Frisch, "The Oslo REFI Interflow Table", *Bulletin de l'Institut International de Statistique*, 33e Session, Paris 1961.

R. C. Geary, "Reflections on National Accounting", *Review of Income and Wealth*, September 1973.

J. M. Keynes, *How to Pay for War*, London 1940.

National Bureau of Economic Research, *The National Economic Accounts of the United States*, Washington D. C. 1958.

OEEC, *A Standardized System of National Accounts*, 1958 edition, Paris 1959.

OEEC, *Systems of National Accounting in Africa*, Paris 1961.

Ingvar Ohlsson, *On National Accounting*, Stockholm 1953.

Nancy Ruggles and Richard Ruggles, *The Design of Economic Accounts*, New York 1970.

Paul Studenski, *The Income of Nations*, New York 1961

G. Suvel, *Systems of Social Accounts*, Oxford 1965.

United Nations, *A System of National Accounts and Supporting Tables*, New York 1953.

United Nations, *A System of National Accounts*, New York 1968.

United Nations, A Draft System of the Distribution of Income, Consumption and Accumulation, E/CN. 3/425, 1972.

United Nations, One Dimensional Statistics of Tangible Assets, CES/WP. 22/45, 1973.

United Nations, Draft International Guidelins on the National and Sector Balance Sheet and Reconcilation Accounts of the SNA, E/CN. 3/460, 1974.

United Nations, *Towards a System of Social and Demographic Statistics*, New York 1975.

II.

THEORETICAL ASPECTS OF NATIONAL ECONOMIC ACCOUNTING

1

A GENERALIZED TECHNOLOGY ASSUMPTION IN THE DOUBLY CLASSIFIED INPUT-OUT MODEL OF SNA BY COMMODITY AND INDUSTRY

1. Introduction

The publication of the revised United Nations system of national accounts, which is usually called SNA for short, has attracted considerable attention of national income statisticians as well as applied economists. In particular, their attention is directed to an attempt to incorporate the input-output model into an integrated system of national accounts and to a particular feature of the proposed input-output model, which is doubly classified by commodity and industry. In the proposed system of national accounts in SNA, the commodities are considered one of the major objects of production activities and they are defined by SNA as including those goods and services which are normally sold on the market at a price which is intended to cover the costs of production. The agents responsible for carrying out the production activities are called industries in SNA, whose core is made up of establishments. The flow of intermediate products and outputs which characterize the production activities in the input-output model is met by the two-way classification of commodities and industries. The flow of outputs is classified according to commodities and industries so that the characteristic products of a particular industry may be clearly distinguished from its secondary products. The latter category of products is further subdivided in SNA by subsidiary products and by-products. Subsidiary products, according to the definition in SNA, refer to such products, for example, as aeroengines produced by the motor-car industry whose scale of production is unrelated to the level of production for the industry's characteristic products. On the other hand, by-products, such as gas made by the coke industry, are those which are produced only on a scale which is fairly closely related to the industry's characteristic production. The two-way classification of the flow of outputs creates apparent dissimilarity with the conventional input-output model of Leontief type in that each industry in SNA can produce different categories of products including both characteristic and secondary products. Against this assumption of SNA, it is assumed in the conventional input-output model of Leontif type that only one category of products is produced by each industry. It is disclosed to us a furthher dissimilarity that the flow of outputs in SNA is described in the array of matrix doubly classified by commodities and industries, whereas the conventional input-output model the flow of outputs is expressed by a vector arranged according to industries implicitly implying that there exists strict one-to-one correspondence between the categories of commodities and industries.

The two-way classification according to different categories of commodities and industries is similarly applied to the flow of intermediate products in SNA. It follows from the two-way classification that the flow of intermediate products in SNA is described as the absorption of a specific commodity for the usage of intermediate input in a particular industry. The input-output coefficients which connect the flow of intermediate inputs with the flow of outputs have two different aspects. First, they are looked at as the production correspondence between commodity inputs and commodity outputs. The correspondence represents the technological relations for the production of commodities by the usage of commodity inputs. In the second place, the input-output coefficients may be considered the production correspondence by which the outputs by industries are related to the industries' inputs. In the case, the correspondence specifies the technological relations that prevail over industries. Two alternative assumptions referring to a commodity technology and an industry technology in SNA are a device for distinguishing these two different aspects of the production correspondence.[1)]

It is intended in this article to show that two technology assumptions proposed in SNA are not necessarily compatible alternatives insisting that one of them is implied of the other. Having dealt with anomalies resulting from the technology assumptions, a more generalized technology assumption that enable to remove them is introduced. It is shown that the technology assumption is general in the sense that the input-output coefficients matrix by commodities transforms itself into a similar matrix of input-output coefficients by industries and that the converse is also the case. Some mathematical exercises are carried out to show that manipulations performed in the mathematical annexes of chapters III and IV of SNA can be greatly simplified by the adoption of the gen-

1) Throughout this article, reference of SNA should be made to United Nations [1968]. A brief account of the structure of SNA is given in Stone's collected essays [1970].

eralized technology assumption. In the last section of this carticle, the workability of our technology assumption is verified by giving numerical examples of input-output coefficient matrices. It is of some interest for the readers of SNA to see that the result of numerical examples experimented by the hypothetical figures taken from the input-output tables exhibited in chapter III of SNA suggests that our technology assumption be sufficiently workable and a useful alternative to the technology assumptions of SNA.

2. Notations, Assumptions and Conceptual Framework

Our discussion starts with the conceptual framework displayed in Figure 1 with the notations defined below:

Figure 1. The Input-output Framewerk

		P		NP	Σ
		COM	IND		
P	COM	·	U	e	q
	IND	V	·	·	g
NP		·	y'	·	η
Σ (sum)		q'	g'	η	

In the basic conceptual framework of Figure 1 the row and column of *P* stand for the production activity, whereas the row and column of NP indicate the non-production activity. The rows and columns corresponding to COM and IND distinguish the categories of commodities and industries respectively.

In the notations used in Figure 1 the capital Roman letters are used for indicating matrices and the small Roman letters are for vectors. The Greek letter denotes a scalar and a prime superscript stands for the transposing of either matirx or vector. Thus, we can give the following definitions:

U: matrix of the flow of intermediate products, whose element u_{ij} stands for the flow of i-th commodity absorbed by j-th industry for the intermediate use of production;

V: a matrix of the flow of outputs, whose element v_{kl} denotes the flow l-th commodity produced by k-th industry;

e: a vector of the flow of final products, whose element e_i represents the flow of i-th commodity;

q: a vector of the flow of outputs, whose element q_i denotes the flow of output of i-th commodity;

g: a vector of the flow of outputs, whose elements g_j distinguishes the flow of output originated from j-th industry;

y: a vector of the flow of value added, whose element y_j represents the flow of value-added originated from j-th industry;

η: the total of the value-added.

It is noted here that vectors are represented by column vectors.

The following assumptions are made before we proceed with the discussions of the input-output model of SNA.

(Assumption 1) Neither undesirable output nor non-marketable output is produced in any production activity.

(Assumption 2) The number of commodities is not necessarily equal to that of industries. For convenience, it is assumed here that m is not less than n, m and n being the number of commodities and industries respectively.

The first assumption states that the production activity in the basic conceptual framework is confined to the production of desirable commodities excluding from its scope those goods and services which are undesirable or non-marketable. Non-marketable goods and services are such that their production is not intended to cover at least the cost of production. Their typical example is public services which are essentially taken care of by the activities of government agencies at various levels. Those goods and services which are not freely disposed of, such as the disamenities in the environment, are termed undesirable output.

The second assumption exactly conforms to the practice of SNA. From a practical view point for compiling the input-output tables, it is reasonable to assume that the number of commodities supersedes the number of industries. We shall come back the point in the later stage of discussions insisting that the assumption is sufficiently meaningful and relevant for our discussions.

3. The Input-Output Model and Technology Assumptions in SNA

In this section the input-output model and technology assumptions in SNA will be summarized utilizing the basic conceptual framework. In order to grasp clearly the characteristics of our generalized technology assumption, it is important to give a summary account of the input-output model of SNA. Its accounting relations are denoted by

(3. 1) $q = Ui + e$,

(3. 2) $q = V'i$,

(3. 3) $g = Vi$.

In the relations, i stands for a summation vector all of whose elements are unity. The production technology of the input-output model of SNA is constituted by (i) constant input-output coefficients and (ii) the constant composition of product-mix. The relationship of constant input-output coefficients is written by

$$U = B\hat{g}\,, \tag{3.4}$$

where $\hat{g}$ is a diagonal matrix whose diagonal elements are occupied by the elements of g and B is a matrix of constant input-output coefficients. It may be worthy to note that B should not be confounded with the matrix of conventional input-output coefficients of Leontief type, because in B intermediate inputs by commodities are related with fixed proportions to output by industries.

There are two alternative assumptions to formulate the constant composition of product-mix. They are:

$$V' = C\hat{g}\,, \tag{3.5}$$

where C is a matrix of constant coefficients. And

$$V = D\hat{q}\,, \tag{3.6}$$

where D is also a matrix of constant coefficients. Putting it in other words, an alternative assumption of (3.5) states that the composition of output by commodities is kept constant for each industry, whereas the assumption of (3.6) implies that the composition of output by industries is constant for each commodity.

If (3.4) is combined with (3.5), the production technology of the input-output model in SNA is reduced to what is called the assumption of a commodity technology as indicated below:

$$U = (BC^{-1})V' \tag{3.7}$$

It is readily seen that the derived matrix BC^{-1} with which the intermediate inputs U are associated with outputs V is a matrix constituted of commodity rows and commodity columns. Let A stand for

$$A = BC^{-1}$$

and write in a vector form

$$(3.8) \qquad A = (a^1, \ldots, a^m).$$

Without loss of generality, it is assumed that in the aigument (3.8) there are m commodities. An element a^i in A denotes a column vector of intermediate inputs that are required for the production of unit output of i-th commodity regardless of any industry it is produced. With a^i constant, (3.8) postulates the assumption of a commodity technology, meaning that a commodity has same input structure in whatever industry it is produced. But, if we write B in a vector form as

$$(3.4)' \qquad B = (b^1, \ldots, b^n),$$

then an element b^j of B is a column vector whose element are written by

$$b_{ij} = \frac{u_{ij}}{g_j},$$

where u_{ij} is an element of U. It is noted that (A.2) is assumed in the derivation of (3.4)′. In (3.4)′, b^j denotes a column vector of intermediate inputs that are required for the production of unit output of j-th industry regardless of the industry's output composition of commodities. Note that b^j is a vector of constants. Then, (3.4)′ necessarily implies the statement that an industry has the same input structure whatever its product mix. The statement is nothing but an expression of the assumption of an industry technology put forth in SNA. Thus, it follows from the preceding reasoning that the production technology embodied in (3.7) and (3.8) is, in fact, based upon not only the assumption of a commodity technology but also the assumption of an industry technology. But, in the light of the construction of technology assumptions in SNA, it is apparent to us that the two technology assumptions are alternatives, which are mutually exclusive. The argument of the technology assumptions in SNA seems to fall into inconsistency in that the assumption of a commodity technology assumes, as a matter of fact, the assumption of an industry technology.[2]

A few anomalies in the argument of the technology assumptions in SNA deserves to be noted here. First, in the production technology of (3.7) and (3.8) B must be a square matrix, because the non-singularity of C is necessary in the operation of (3.7). If A of (3.8) is replaced by the following relation

$$A = BD, \tag{3.9}$$

which is obtained by combining an input coefficient matrix with an output coefficient matrix in which the elements represent the proportion of each commodity which is produced by the various industries. SNA states that effect can be given to the assumption of an industry technology by (3.9). In the case, B is not necessary to be a square matrix as the construction of A in (3.9) indicates. Second, q is determined by combining (3.1), (3.2) with (3.7)

$$q = (I - BC^{-1})^{-1}e. \tag{3.10}$$

On the other hand, in the case of the usage of (3.9) q is written by

$$q = (I - BD)^{-1}e. \tag{3.11}$$

The inverse matrices appeared in (3.10) and (3.11) represent the direct and indirect requirements of outputs which are necessary for meeting a given vector of final demand e. An anomaly arises

2) As we shall make a point in the subsequent section, the reasoning of technology assumptions in SNA is blurred because of the ambiguity of the meaning of technology. The significance of the technology can only be made clear by the rigorous formulation of the input structure and the output structure and the derivation of production correspondence from them. We shall be concerned with the point in the appendix of this article.

in the determination of the output vector q, because the usage of different technology assumptions results in different levels of outputs for the same final demand. In the following section, a more generalized technology assumption which provides a proper remedy for the striking anomalies will be proposed and add a few comments on the meanings that underlie the assumption.

4. A Generalized Technology Assumption and its Meanings

Let $v_{(i)}$ and $v^{(c)}$ stand for vector forms of the output matrix V denoting $v_{(i)}$ the vector of outputs by industry and $v^{(c)}$ the vector of outputs by commodity. Assuming the assumption (A.2), the vectors are written by

$$(4.1) \qquad v_{(i)} = (v_1, \ldots, v_m), \quad \text{where} \quad v_j = \begin{pmatrix} \vdots \\ v_{jk} \\ \vdots \end{pmatrix},$$

and

$$(4.2) \qquad v^{(c)} = (v^1, \ldots, v^n), \quad \text{where} \quad v^i = \begin{pmatrix} \vdots \\ v_{hi} \\ \vdots \end{pmatrix},$$

In (4.1) an element v_j stands for the composition of outputs by commodity produced by j-th industry and is derived from the transposing of V, whereas an element v^i of $v^{(c)}$ in (4.2) expresses the output composition of i-th commodity originated from various industries. Consider a matrix of constants which has the dimension of commodity$\times$commodity,

$$(4.3) \qquad F = [f_{ij}],$$

supposing that

$$(4.4) \qquad \sum_j f_{ij} v_j = u_j .$$

u_j in (4.4) denotes the input structure of j-th industry which is obtained from j-th column of the input matrix U. (4.4) shows the linear production correspondence of i-th commodity produced by various industries. In a matrix form (4.4) may be written by

$$(4.4)' \qquad FV' = U.$$

As an alternative assumption of technology, (4.4)′ is substituted for (3.4) which displays some anomalies in combining it with (3.5) or (3.6). It is interesting to exhibit the hidden meanings that underlie the more generalized technology assumption of (4.4) or (4.4)′.

It becomes immediately apparent to us that the assumption of (4.4)′ is more general than that of (3.4), if the former is compared with the latter. In particular, $\hat{g}$ of (3.4) is compared with $v_{(i)}$ of (4.1) writing $\hat{g}$ in a vector form

$$(4.5) \qquad \hat{g} = (v_1', \ldots, v_n'), \quad \text{where} \quad v_j' = \begin{pmatrix} 0 \\ \vdots \\ v_{j.} \\ \vdots \\ 0 \end{pmatrix},$$

and

$$v_{i.} = \sum_j v_{ij}$$

Then, (3.4) may be written by

$$(3.4)' \qquad \sum_j b_{ij} v_j' = u_j,$$

which is directly comparable with (4.4). (3.4)′ and (4.4) have the same form when they are considered as a form of the linear production correspondence. But, the contents of the vector outputs by industry greatly differ. All elements of v_j in (4.4) are non-negative, whereas in the case of (3.4)′ v_j' is occupied by null elements except the j-th element which denotes the total output of j-th industry.

It is discovered from the meanings of F technology that the structure of technologies which yield a variety of different joint products for a given input vector is implicit in the technology.

They form a striking contrast with what is implied in the technology of the conventional input-output model of Leontief type in that the emergence of joint products is excluded from the technology of the conventional input-output model. One of the essential features of SNA is exhibited in its new approach to cope with the input-output model breaking through the limitation of conventional approach. We shall show in the appendix of this article how the assumption of F technology is formulated on the input structure and the output structure. In doing this, it will be shown that our F technology rests on a particular input structure called NOSLIS (a non-substitutable and linear input structure) and that the assumption of F technology expressed in (4.4) is derivable from it as a special case of a GL input function (a generalized Leontief input function). The assumption of constant input-output coefficients B made by SNA in (3.4) may be regarded as a type of GL input function which is reduced to the assumption of F technology if each industry has the same input structure, i.e.

$$b_{ij} = b_j, \quad \text{for all } i \text{ and } j.$$

The condition supports our reasoning advanced in the preceding section to the effect that alternative technology assumptions of SNA are not necessarily tenable.

In place of the formulation of technology assumptions in SNA combining either (3.4) with (3.5) or (3.4) with (3.6), it seems appropriate to use (3.5) and (3.6) completely independent of the technological structure of input and output regarding them as the cases of product-mix. In what follows we shall refer to the case of product-mix represented by (3.5) as *Case: I* and to the case of product-mix represented by (3.6) as *Case: II*.

Another point that should be considered for the formulation of (4.4) (or (4.4)′) is how the determination of variables in the input-output model is affected by our generalized technology assumption. In the next section I shall take up the point and show interesting properties arising out of the determination of the level of outputs. In doing this, a matrix F defined by (4.3) and (4.4) will be referred to as F technology matrix in subsequent discussion. In connection with the terminology of F technology matrix, it will often be the case in what follows that our generalized technology assumption be termed the assumption of F technology.[3)]

5. A Generalized Inverse of $(I-F)$ and its Transformation

A great advantage gained from the use of the F technology assumption is that the determination of the level of outputs vector in the input-output model of SNA is substantially simplified. In order to see that, it is necessary to introduce the concept of generalized inverse of a matrix. Following the idea of Moore and Penrose, we shall introduce the concept and discuss its properties as the preliminary of discussion in what follows.[4)]

(Definition) Let A stand for a matrix consisting of m rows and n columns. A Moore-Penrose inverse of A is defined as a solution of the following matrix equations,

(5.1) (i) $ABA = A$, (ii) $BAB = B$,

(iii) $(AB)' = AB$, (iv) $(BA)' = BA$,

where B is the solution having the dimension of n rows and m columns.

---

3) The idea of F technology is originally hinted by Mr. Sakuma for streamlining matrix algebra of the input-output model in SNA. It appears that little attention is directed to explore the particular features of technology that SNA confronts by economists and national income statisticians, though they take the structure of SNA as granted.

4) The idea to use the generalized inverse of a matrix is suggested by Dr. Kariya. A basic reference of it is Penrose [1955].

It is readily seen that the solution is determined uniquely. Letting A^+ stand for a B matrix that satisfies the Definition, the following properties hold for A^+:

$$(5.2)\qquad \text{(v)}\ (A')^+ = (A^+)', \qquad \text{(vi)}\ (A'A)^+ = A^+(A^+)',$$
$$\text{(vii)}\ R(A) = R(A^+) = R(AA)^+ = \text{tr}\, AA^+,$$

where $R(A)$ and tr A are the rank and trace of A.

The following lemma is due to Penrose.

(Lemma) Let P and Q be orthogonal matrices having dimensions of $m \times n$ and $n \times m$ respectively, Then, there exists a matrix A having the dimension of $m \times n$ such that

$$(5.3)\qquad PAQ = \begin{bmatrix} \lambda_1 & & & 0 \\ & \ddots & & \\ & & \lambda_r & \\ 0 & & & 0 \end{bmatrix}$$

where $r = R(A)$ and $\lambda_i = (\gamma_i)^{1/2}$ whose $\gamma_i (i = 1, 2, \ldots, r)$ are characteristic roots of AA'.

Recalling (5.3), we note that

$$(5.4)\qquad A = P' \begin{bmatrix} \lambda_1 & & & 0 \\ & \ddots & & \\ & & \lambda_r & \\ 0 & & & 0 \end{bmatrix} Q'.$$

Let B, whose dimension is $n \times m$, be defined by

$$(5.5)\qquad B = Q \begin{bmatrix} 1/\lambda_1 & & & 0 \\ & \ddots & & \\ & & 1/\lambda_r & \\ 0 & & & 0 \end{bmatrix} P.$$

Then, it is easy to see that B satisfies properties (i)–(iv) of (5.1). Being B determined uniquely, B is a Moore-Penrose inverse of A. Here, it is noted that AB and BA are idem-potent, i.e.

$$(5.6)\qquad \text{(viii)}\ (AB)^2 = AB, \qquad \text{(ix)}\ (BA)^2 = BA.$$

Indeed, note that

(5.7) $AB = P'\begin{bmatrix} I_r & 0 \\ 0 & 0 \end{bmatrix}P$ and $BA = Q\begin{bmatrix} I_r & 0 \\ 0 & 0 \end{bmatrix}Q'$

(viii) and (ix) of (5.6) immediately follows.

The following propositions are established by the definition and properties of the Moore-Penrose inverse matrix.

(Proposition 1) The necessary and sufficient condition that the equation

$$Ax = a$$

has a solution is

$$r = R(A) = R([A, a]),$$

whence the solution can be expressed in the form that

(5.9) $x = A^+a + (I_n - A^+A)z$,

z being an arbitrary vector of dimension $n \times 1$.

(Proposition 2) The necessary and sufficient condition that the matrix linear equation

$$AX = C$$

has a solution is

(5.10) $AA^+C = C$,

whence the solution is given by

(5.11) $X = A^+C + (I_n - A^+A)Z$,

Z being an arbitrary matrix of dimension $n \times l$.

Consider a matrix A having the dimension of $m \times n$ supposing that $R(A) = n$, being $m \geqq n$. It is easy to see that B in (5.5) is transformed into

(5.12) $B = Q\begin{bmatrix} 1/\lambda_1 & 0 & \\ & \vdots & 0 \\ 0 \cdots\cdots & 1/\lambda_r & \end{bmatrix}P.$

(5.13) immediately follows from the transformation.

(5.13) (x) $BA = A^{+}A = I_n$

Having briefly reviewed the concept of generalized inverse of a matrix and its properties, we shall come back to the determination of output vectors in the input-output model of SNA. In the first place, we shall take up the determination of the vector of commodity outputs. From (3.1), (3.2) and (4.4)$'$ q is written by

$$(5.14) \qquad q = FV'i + e = Fq + e\,.$$

Two possibilities arise in the determination of q in (5.14). First, it is apparent to us that q is solved in terms of e if $(I-F)^{-1}$ exists, i.e.

$$(5.15) \qquad q = (I-F)^{-1}e\,.$$

Second, if the existence of $(I-F)^{-1}$ is not the case, then Proposition 1 can be applied resulting in q as the solution of (5.14)

$$(5.16) \qquad q = (I-F)^{+}e + (I-(I-F)^{+}(I-F))z\,.$$

Recalling (5.13) and noting that $e=0$ is implied by $V=0$, hence being $q=0$, it is easily seen that

$$(5.17) \qquad q = (I-F)^{+}e\,.$$

Here, (5.17) also indicates that the vector of commodity outputs is solved interms of e and a generalized inverse of $(I-F)$. It becomes clear from the comparison of (5.15) or (5.17) with (3.10) and (3.11) that the commodity outputs vector q is uniquely determined under the assumption of F technology making a striking contrast with the fact that the determination of q in SNA essentially depends upon the choice of the output set, i.e. the choice of technology in the linear production correspondence. It is readily seen that an F technology matrix acts the same part as an input coefficients matrix does in the conventional input-output model of Leontief type.

Turning our attention to the determination of the vector of industry outputs g, it turns out that two possibilities arise in the determination which corresponds with two cases of the formulation of the output sets that is referred to in the foregoing section. Indeed, from (3.1), (3.2), (3.3), (3.5) and (4.4)$'$, as for *Case: I*,

$$\begin{aligned} q &= FV'i+e\,, \\ V'i &= FV'i+e\,, \\ C\hat{g}i &= FC\hat{g}i+e\,, \\ Cg &= FCg+e\,, \\ (I-F)Cg &= e\,. \end{aligned} \tag{5.18}$$

Analogous to the determination of q, two cases are considered. First, suppose the inverse of $(I-F)$ exists. Noting that

$$Cg=(I-F)^{-1}e$$

and recalling Proposition 1, g can be solved in the form of

$$g=C^{+}(I-F)^{-1}e+(I-C^{+}C)e\,. \tag{5.19}$$

Observe that $g=0$ is implied by $e=0$ and (5.13). Then, we have

$$g=C^{+}(I-F)^{-1}e\,. \tag{5.20}$$

It is interesting to note that additional manipulation of (5.20) helps us to shed light on the usefulness of an F technology matrix. By the pre-multiplication of (5.18) by C^{+},

$$(C^{+}C-C^{+}FC)g=C^{+}e\,,$$

and recalling again (5.13), g is expressed as either

$$g=(I-C^{+}FC)^{-1}C^{+}e \quad \text{or} \quad g=(I-C^{+}FC)^{+}C^{+}e\,. \tag{5.21}$$

Second, if the existence of $(I-F)^{-1}$ is not the case, g is direct from the application of Proposition 1 to (5.18) resulting in

(5. 20)′ $g = (C - FC)^{+} e$.

It immediately follows from (5.20)′ that (5.21) is the case for g given by (5.20)′. Similarly, it is easy to show the determination of the vector of industry outputs for the *Case: II.* In fact, for the case of the existence of $(I - F)^{-1}$

(5. 22) $g = D(I - F)^{-1} e$.

If the existence of $(I - F)^{-1}$ is not the case, then we have

(5. 22)′ $g = D(I - F)^{+} e$.

In the derivation of (5.22) and (5.22)′ the following relation is essential:

$$D(I - F)q = De.$$

Note that

$$g = Dq.$$

Then, corresponding with (5.21), it is not difficult to see that one of the following relations holds, i.e.

(5. 23) $g = D(I - F)^{-1} D^{+} De$ or $g = D(I - F)^{+} D^{+} De$.

The expression of (5.23) can be further reformulated by means of the properties of Moore-Penrose inverse as indicated below:

(5. 23)′ $g = (I - DFD^{+})^{-1} De$ or $g = (I - DFD^{+})^{+} De$.

(5.21) and (5.23)′ are directly comparable with the determination of the vector of industry outputs that is carried out in SNA and expressed by

(5. 24) $g = (I - C^{-1} B)^{-1} C^{-1} e$,

for *Case: I*, and by

(5. 25) $g = (I - DB)^{-1} De$

for *Case: II.* It is seen in the comparison that (5.24) and (5.25) are reduced to more generalized expressions of (5.21) and (5.23)′ replacing $C^{-1}B$ and DB by $C^{+}FC$ and DFD^{+} respectively. Thus, the comparison naturally leads to Proposition 3.

(Proposition 3) Under the assumption of F technology, the direct and indirect requirements of outputs for meeting a given vector of final demand from which the vector of industry outputs is derived are generated from a generalized similar transformation of F and are expressed in a form of Moore-Penrose inverse.

As a special case of Proposition 3, the following corollary immediately follows.

(Corollary) Suppose the number of commodities is equal to the number of industries in the assumption of F technology. Then, under the assumption of F technology, the direct and indirect requirements of outputs in Proposition 3 are generated from a similar transformation of F and the Moore-Penrose inverse is reduced to a regular inverse.

Indeed, if $(I-F)$ is non-singular, it is easy to see that

$$(I-F)^{+} = (I-F)^{-1}.$$

Noting that F^{+} is reduced to F^{-1}, the Corollary immediately follows.

Proposition 4 in what follows deserves to be noted for the derivation of a non-negative solution of the vector of industry outputs.

(Proposition 4) $(I-C^{+}FC)^{-1}$ and $(I-DFD^{+})^{-1}$ in (5.21) and (5.23)′ are non-negative if $(I-F)^{-1}$ and $C^{+}FC$ or DFD^{+} are non-negative.

In order to show Proposition 4, it is sufficient to show that the Frobenius root of either $C^{+}FC$ or DFD^{+} is not greater than that of F. Let

$$|I-\lambda C^{+}FC| = 0,$$

and $\lambda(F)$ denotes the Frobenius root of F. C is written by

$$C = PDQ,$$

where P and Q are square matrices having the dimension of $m \times m$ and $n \times n$ respectively. Then, we have

$$C^+ = Q'D^+P', \quad \text{where} \quad D = \begin{bmatrix} d_1 & & \\ & \ddots & \\ & & d_n \\ & 0 & \end{bmatrix}.$$

Hence,

$$C^+FC = Q'D^+P'FPDQ.$$

Denoting $\mu(F)$ a characteristic root of F,

$$\mu(C^+FC) = \mu(D^+P'FPD).$$

Putting $F^* = P'FP$, it is demonstrated that

$$\lambda(D^+F^*D) \leqq \lambda(F^*).$$

Because, decomposing F^* into

$$F^* = \begin{bmatrix} F^*_{11} & F^*_{12} \\ F^*_{21} & F^*_{22} \end{bmatrix}$$

and putting

$$D^+ = \begin{bmatrix} 1/d_1 & & & \\ & \ddots & & 0 \\ & & 1/d_n & \end{bmatrix} \quad \text{and} \quad \tilde{D} = \begin{bmatrix} d_1 & & \\ & \ddots & \\ & & d_n \end{bmatrix},$$

we have

$$D^+F^*D = \tilde{D}^{-1}F_{11}D.$$

But,

$$\lambda(F_{11}) \leqq \lambda(F^*).$$

Hence, Proposition 4 holds.

The following Corollary immediately follows as a special case of Proposition 4, in which the number of commodities is equal to the

number of industries, noting that the characteristic roots of a matrix are same as those of its similar transformation.
(Corollary) $(I-C^{-1}FC)^{-1}$ and $(I-DFD^{-1})^{-1}$ are non-negative if and only if $(I-F)^{-1}$ is non-negative.

As I have noted before, most of mathematical manipulations that are carried out in annexes to chapters III and IV of SNA are greatly simplified by the introduction of the assumption of F technology. As an example of the simplification, it is simply shown that a value added vector by commodity z is obtained from the linear transformation of a value added vector by industry y assuming that the transformation is undergone in the output set by the formulation of *Case: II* in the foregoing section. The argument refers to the section 4.96. of the annex to chapter IV of SNA. As z is defined by the relation,

$$\begin{aligned} q &= z+\hat{q}F'i \\ &= z+\hat{q}V^{-1}U'i. \end{aligned}$$

By the premultiplication of D on both sides,

$$\begin{aligned} Dq &= Dz+D\hat{q}V^{-1}U'i \\ &= Dz+U'i. \end{aligned}$$

Noting that

$$g = y+U'i,$$

and

$$Dq = D\hat{q}i = Vi = g,$$

it immediately follows that

$$y = Dz. \tag{5.26}$$

6. The Workability of the Assumption of F Technology

It has been noted in section 4 that the assumption of F technology is meaningless unless an F matrix is non-negative. But, the existence of a non-negative F matrix is not necessarily ensured by foregoing assumptions, when an F is supposed to be derived from U and V by (4.4)′. It is a matter of empirical test whether an F satisfies the requirement of a non-negative matrix depending upon the structure of U and V, both of which are supposed to be non-negative. We shall proceed to make some experimental tests for the workability of the assumption of F technology utilizing numerical figures of U and V. In the absence of the actual figures in the form of U and V taken from Japanese input-output tables, hypothetical figures of U and V taken from SNA are employed.

The figures of U and V matrices are displayed in the input-output tables of SNA in chapter III. In particular, the information of V matrix is incorporated in Table 3.1, whereas the information of U matrix is screened out of Table 3.2. Our experimental works are greatly facilitated by the structure of tables 3.1 and 3.2 which is so arranged that the number of commodities may be identical with that of industries. According to the assumption (A.1), the services of general government and nonprofit private institutions in Table 3.1 are excluded from the scope of our experiment. Using (4.4)′ an F matrix is expressed in terms of U and V as

$$(6.1) \qquad F = U(V')^{-1},$$

assuming that V is non-singular. The result of computation is exhibited in Table 1. In Table 1, all elements are non-negative except one that is located in the intersection of row 1 and column 12. In view of its magnitude, the negative element arises out of rounding errors and is regarded as a null element. It follows from the experiment that the derived F matrix satisfies the requirements for non-negative F matrix.

The derived F matrix is directly comparable with the commodity×commodity input-output coefficient matrices which are shown in SNA as Tables 3.3, 3.4 and 3.5 respectively. The production of the commodity×commodity input-output coefficient matrices is based upon a variety of alternative procedures for transferring inputs and outputs, as SNA puts it. Table 3.3 of SNA illustrates the case of transferring outputs alone for the derivation of a commodity×commodity input-output matrix on the premise that each output can be interpreted either as a commodity output plus the subsidiary production of the industry of which that commodity is the characteristic product or as an industry output plus the output of that industry's characteristic product by other industries. Tables 3.4 and 3.5, on the other hand, illustrate the cases of adopting the assumptions of a commodity technology and an industry technology respectively. Hence, a commodity×commodity input-output coefficient is written as BC^{-1} for the case of the assumption of a commodity technology, whereas the one based upon the assumption of an industry technology is given by BD. Let a_{ij} stand for the element of i-th row and j-th column of the commodity×commodity input-output coefficient matrices displayed in Tables 3.3, 3.4 and 3.5 of SNA. The comparison of the matrices with our F matrix is given in a form of relative deviation around f_{ij}, which is defined by

$$(6.2) \qquad r_{ij} = \frac{(a_{ij}-f_{ij})}{f_{ij}},$$

r_{ij} are tabulated for different alternative assumptions of transferring inputs and outputs in Tables 2, 3 and 4 below. It is easy to see that the deviation becomes the smallest in magnitude in the comparison between the matrix based upon the assumption of a commodity technology of SNA and the derived F matrix. The fact that some a_{ij} dc not coincide with f_{ij} leaving some non-zero r_{ij} accounts for the argument that the assumption of a commodity technology of SNA does not necessarily embody the pure production correspondence for the production of commodity output in the output set in the sense that the assumption depends, in fact, on the assumption of an industry technology, as the argument of section 3 proceeds. A great deal of discrepancy occurs in the comparison of remaining cases. It appears that the magnitude of the discrepancy is greater in the comparison between a_{ij}, which is based upon the assumption of the transfer of outputs alone and f_{ij}, than the comparison between a_{ij} based upon the assumption of an industry technology and f_{ij}. Table 5 shows $(I-F)^{-1}$, which is non-negative as it is expected.

The assumption of F technology is also applicable to the case of mixed assumptions to which SNA refers, particularly, in section 3.87 et seq. Suppose a V matrix is decomposed into two submatrices as

$$V = V_1 + V_2, \tag{6.3}$$

where V_1 is an output matrix whose elements are constituted by characteristic products and subsidiary products and is distinguished from V_2 which is constituted only by by-products. The production correspondence between inputs and outputs for V_1 and V_2 is formulated by the following assumption.

(Assumption 3) The linear production correspondence which connects V_1 with U is written by

$$F^1 V_1' = U, \tag{6.4}$$

implying that the assumption of F technology is made for the production of V_1. The production of V_2 is dependent on the production V_1 and is expressed by the relation

$$V_2 = V_1 E, \tag{6.5}$$

where E is a matrix of constants having the dimension of commodity×commodity.
Rewriting (6.4) and (6.5) in a matrix form,

$$\begin{bmatrix} V_2' \\ U \end{bmatrix} = \begin{bmatrix} E' \\ F^1 \end{bmatrix} [V_1'] . \tag{6.6}$$

Let e_{kl} stand for the element of k-th row and l-th column of E and $v_{ij}^{(1)}$ for the element of i-th row and j-th column of V_1. It is easy to see from (6.6) that the production of i-th commodity as by-product induced by the production of the corresponding commodity as characteristic product by j-th industry, i.e.

$$v_j^1 = (v_{j1}^{(1)}, \dots, v_{jl}^{(1)}, \dots, v_{jn}^{(1)}) ,$$

is given by

$$\sum_h v_{jh}^{(1)} e_{hi} . \tag{6.7}$$

It should be borne in mind for the formulation of Assumption 3, particularly for the relation (6.5), that the decomposition of V_2 is compatible with the definition of by-products which is given in the introductory section. A mixed technology assumption in our case means that the assumption of F technology prevails in the production of characteristic products including subsidiary products, whereas it also implies that the production of by-products linearly depends on an industry's capacity production of a particular commodity as the characteristic product.

The determination of a commodity output vector q which is associated with V in (6.3) is easily made under the Assumption 3. Indeed, noting (3.1) and (6.4), we have

$$\begin{aligned} q &= Ui+e \\ &= F^1 V_1' i+e . \end{aligned}$$

From (6.3) and (6.5),

$$V' = V_1' + E'V_1'$$
$$= (I+E')V_1'.$$

And, assuming the non-singularity of $(I+E')$,

$$V_1' = (I+E')^{-1}V'.$$

Then, it is easy to see that

$$(6.8) \qquad q = F^1(I+E')^{-1}V'i + e$$
$$= F^1(I+E')^{-1}q + e$$
$$= [I - F^1(I+E')^{-1}]^{-1}e.$$

The non-singularity of $[I-F^1(I+E')^{-1}]$ is assumed in the operation of (6.8). In this connection, it may be of some interest to note that the following proposition is made.

(Proposition 5) Suppose an F technology prevails in the production of V and $(I-F)^{-1}$ is non-negative. Then, $[I-F^1(I+E')^{-1}]^{-1}$ is non-negative in the characteristic production of V_1 for the decomposition of V by (6.3).

Note that

$$F^1(I+E')^{-1} = U(V_1')^{-1}[V'(V_1')^{-1}]^{-1}$$
$$= U(V')^{-1}.$$

By the corollary of Proposition 3, for the production of V

$$FV' = U,$$

and

$$(I-F)^{-1} \geqq 0.$$

Then, in the characteristic production of V_1 under the condition of (6.3) $[I-F^1(I+E')^{-1}]$ is reduced to $[I-F]$. And, Proposition 5 holds.

Proposition 5 is again confirmed by the following numerical

experiment, whose numerical example is taken from what is indicated in SNA. In section 3.38 of SNA, a numerical example for the decomposition of V into V_1 and V_2 according to (6.3) which illustrates the consequences of mixing the assumptions of a commodity technology and an industry technology is given. Using the numerical example and making the Assumption 3, E and F^1 are numerically determined. Hence, $[I-F^1(I+E')^{-1}]^{-1}$, which is displayed in Table 6, is calculated. It is apparent by the comparison of Table 6 with Table 5 that Proposition 5 is numerically confirmed with the observation that

$$[I-F^1(I+E')^{-1}]^{-1} = (I-F)^{-1}.$$

A General Note to the Classification of Commodities

Following the classification of SNA, the categories of commodities are given below:

1. Agriculture, forestry and fishing
2. Mining
3. Food, beverages and tobacco
4. Textiles, wearing apparel and leather
5. Rubber, chemicals and petroleum products
6. Basic metals
7. Metal products, machinery and equipment
8. Manufacturing n.e.c.
9. Gas, electricity and water
10. Construction
11. Transport and communication
12. Distribution
13. Services

Table 1 The

1	1	2	3	4	5	6
1	45.00	0.00	176.00	73.00	0.00	0.00
2	1.00	19.00	5.00	8.00	62.00	41.00
3	166.00	0.00	130.00	1.00	3.00	0.00
4	5.00	6.00	3.00	384.00	21.00	1.00
5	103.00	33.00	38.00	73.00	266.00	59.00
6	0.00	29.00	2.00	1.00	7.00	304.00
7	43.00	45.00	24.00	21.00	33.00	31.00
8	5.00	30.00	34.00	13.00	28.00	10.00
9	7.00	21.00	7.00	9.00	28.00	43.00
10	30.00	47.00	3.00	6.00	5.00	5.00
11	40.00	37.00	22.00	21.00	38.00	43.00
12	32.00	20.00	14.00	19.00	18.00	45.00
13	33.00	19.00	27.00	27.00	38.00	40.00

Note: Figures are magnified by 10^3 times.

Table 2 A matrix of r_{ij} in the case

	1	2	3	4	5	6
1	−2.22	*	−2.84	−2.74	*	*
2	100.00	0.00	20.00	0.00	−1.61	2.44
3	−1.20	*	−3.08	0.00	300.00	*
4	0.00	0.00	0.00	−2.08	0.00	0.00
5	−0.97	6.06	47.37	1.37	−9.40	−1.69
6	*	−3.45	0.00	0.00	57.14	−6,58
7	0.00	−2.22	0.00	4.76	6.06	109.68
8	40.00	13.33	−2.94	23.08	7.14	10.00
9	0.00	4.76	0.00	0.00	117.86	−2.33
10	0.00	0.00	0.00	0.00	0.00	0.00
11	0.00	−2.70	−4.55	0.00	−5.26	−4.65
12	0.00	0.00	50.00	47.37	0.00	−6.67
13	0.00	0.00	0.00	−3.70	−5.26	−5.00

Note: * inaicates the cases of $f_{ij}=0$.

derived F Matrix

7	8	9	10	11	12	13
0.00	0.00	0.00	0.00	0.00	−1.00	0.00
2.00	33.00	223.00	11.00	12.00	2.00	1.00
0.00	1.00	0.00	0.00	10.00	1.00	0.00
7.00	22.00	0.00	2.00	5.00	19.00	3.00
35.00	57.00	54.00	30.00	40.00	31.00	15.00
167.00	4.00	11.00	64.00	4.00	1.00	0.00
263.00	35.00	60.00	52.00	65.00	20.00	29.00
30.00	249.00	12.00	147.00	10.00	53.00	62.00
12.00	19.00	69.00	2.00	2.00	22.00	14.00
3.00	4.00	2.00	175.00	18.00	30.00	13.00
19.00	32.00	36.00	25.00	202.00	25.00	7.00
14.00	33.00	18.00	17.00	17.00	23.00	9.00
37.00	51.00	19.00	38.00	23.00	31.00	12.00

of the adjustment of outputs Alone (unit: %)

7	8	9	10	11	12	13
*	*	*	*	*	*	*
50.00	3.03	−13.90	0.00	0.00	0.00	0.00
*	100.00	*	*	0.00	100.00	*
0.00	9.09	*	0.00	0.00	21.05	0.00
2.86	8.77	98.15	0.00	0.00	0.00	0.00
−56.89	100.00	336.36	−1.56	25.00	0.00	*
−3.04	20.00	−30.00	21.15	1.54	0.00	0.00
10.00	−4.02	41.67	2.04	0.00	−1.89	0.00
0.00	0.00	−13.04	0.00	0.00	0.00	0.00
66.67	125.00	0.00	−2.29	0.00	−3.33	0.00
5.26	−3.13	−8.33	0.00	0.00	0.00	0.00
7.14	−3.03	−11.11	0.00	−5.88	0.00	0.00
2.70	−3.92	0.00	0.00	0.00	0.00	0.00

Table 3 A matrix of r_{ij} in the case of

	1	2	3	4	5	6
1	0.00	*	0.00	0.00	*	*
2	0.00	−5.26	0.00	0.00	1.61	0.00
3	0.00	*	0.00	0.00	0.00	*
4	−20.00	0.00	0.00	0.00	0.00	0.00
5	0.00	3.03	0.00	0.00	0.00	0.00
6	*	−3.45	0.00	0.00	0.00	0.00
7	0.00	0.00	0.00	0.00	0.00	0.00
8	0.00	0.00	0.00	0.00	0.00	0.00
9	0.00	4.76	0.00	0.00	0.00	0.00
10	0.00	0.00	0.00	0.00	0.00	0.00
11	0.00	−2.70	0.00	0.00	0.00	0.00
12	0.00	0.00	0.00	0.00	5.56	0.00
13	0.00	0.00	0.00	0.00	0.00	0.00

Note: See the note of Table 2.

Table 4 A matrix of r_{ij} in the case of

	1	2	3	4	5	6
1	−2.22	*	−2.84	−2.74	*	*
2	100.00	0.00	20.00	12.50	9.68	2.44
3	−1.20	*	−3.08	0.00	100.00	*
4	0.00	16.67	33.33	−2.08	−4.76	100.00
5	−0.97	3.03	13.16	0.00	−8.27	0.00
6	*	−3.45	0.00	0.00	28.57	−4.93
7	0.00	0.00	4.17	4.76	6.06	38.71
8	40.00	3.33	0.00	15.38	3.57	20.00
9	0.00	4.76	14.29	11.11	7.14	−2.33
10	0.00	0.00	0.00	0.00	0.00	0.00
11	0.00	−2.70	0.00	0.00	0.00	−4.65
12	0.00	0.00	7.14	0.00	5.56	−6.67
13	0.00	0.00	0.00	0.00	−2.63	−2.50

Note: See the note of Table 2.

the assumption of commodit Technology (unit: %)

7	8	9	10	11	12	13
*	*	*	*	*	*	*
0.00	0.00	0.00	0.00	0.00	0.00	0.00
*	0.00	*	*	0.00	0.00	*
0.00	0.00	*	0.00	0.00	0.00	0.00
0.00	0.00	0.00	0.00	0.00	0.00	0.00
0.00	0.00	0.00	0.00	0.00	0.00	*
0.00	0.00	−25.00	0.00	0.00	0.00	0.00
0.00	0.00	−8.33	0.00	0.00	0.00	0.00
0.00	0.00	0.00	0.00	0.00	0.00	0.00
0.00	0.00	0.00	0.57	0.00	0.00	0.00
0.00	0.00	0.00	0.00	0.00	0.00	0.00
0.00	0.00	0.00	0.00	−5.88	0.00	0.00
0.00	0.00	0.00	2.63	0.00	0.00	0.00

the assumption of industry technology (unit: %)

7	8	9	10	11	12	13
*	*	*	*	*	*	*
50.00	0.00	−13.45	0.00	*	*	0.00
*	100.00	*	*	0.00	100.00	*
0.00	4.55	*	50.00	0.00	15.79	0.00
2.86	3.51	46.30	0.00	0.00	0.00	0.00
0.00	100.00	109.00	1.56	25.00	0.00	*
−2.66	8.57	−26.67	3.85	1.54	0.00	0.00
6.67	−3.61	25.00	−0.68	0.00	−1.89	0.00
0.00	0.00	−8.70	50.00	0.00	0.00	0.00
33.33	50.00	50.00	−2.29	0.00	−3.33	0.00
5.26	0.00	2.78	0.00	0.00	0.00	0.00
7.14	0.00	5.56	0.00	−5.88	0.00	0.00
0.00	−1.96	15.79	2.63	0.00	0.00	0.00

Table 5 The

	1	2	3	4	5	6
1	1087.00	1.00	221.00	130.00	6.00	1.00
2	25.00	1039.00	23.00	39.00	108.00	93.00
3	209.00	1.00	1193.00	29.00	7.00	2.00
4	21.00	18.00	17.00	1637.00	54.00	16.00
5	189.00	76.00	115.00	205.00	1401.00	151.00
6	33.00	72.00	26.00	29.00	45.00	1470.00
7	101.00	89.00	76.00	85.00	94.00	100.00
8	49.00	68.00	77.00	60.00	77.00	52.00
9	22.00	34.00	20.00	31.00	53.00	81.00
10	49.00	64.00	19.00	26.00	21.00	23.00
11	83.00	66.00	61.00	73.00	87.00	103.00
12	51.00	34.00	35.00	49.00	40.00	80.00
13	64.00	39.00	57.00	70.00	73.00	81.00

Note: Figures are magnified by 10^3 times.

Table 6 The derivation

	1	2	3	4	5	6
1	1087.00	1.00	221.00	130.00	6.00	1.00
2	25.00	1039.00	23.00	39.00	108.00	92.00
3	209.00	1.00	1193.00	29.00	7.00	2.00
4	21.00	18.00	18.00	1637.00	54.00	16.00
5	189.00	75.00	115.00	205.00	1401.00	150.00
6	33.00	72.00	26.00	29.00	46.00	1470.00
7	101.00	89.00	76.00	86.00	94.00	100.00
8	49.00	68.00	77.00	59.00	77.00	52.00
9	22.00	34.00	20.00	31.00	53.00	81.00
10	49.00	64.00	19.00	26.00	21.00	23.00
11	83.00	66.00	61.00	73.00	87.00	103.00
12	51.00	34.00	35.00	49.00	40.00	80.00
13	64.00	39.00	57.00	70.00	73.00	81.00

Note: Figures are manified by 10^3 times.

matrix of $(I-F)^{-1}$

7	8	9	10	11	12	13
2.00	5.00	1.00	2.00	4.00	1.00	1.00
39.00	68.00	261.00	42.00	29.00	19.00	13.00
2.00	4.00	1.00	2.00	15.00	2.00	1.00
27.00	58.00	10.00	22.00	18.00	39.00	12.00
117.00	135.00	116.00	102.00	91.00	67.00	38.00
342.00	38.00	63.00	147.00	44.00	20.00	17.00
1399.00	95.00	127.00	125.00	129.00	50.00	53.00
82.00	1362.00	50.00	263.00	41.00	92.00	94.00
43.00	41.00	1091.00	23.00	13.00	32.00	21.00
16.00	18.00	23.00	1223.00	32.00	42.00	19.00
69.00	76.00	78.00	71.00	1270.00	47.00	20.00
46.00	58.00	36.00	44.00	31.00	1033.00	16.00
82.00	89.00	45.00	81.00	46.00	48.00	1024.00

of $[I-F^1(I+E')^{-1}]^{-1}$

7	8	9	10	11	12	13
2.00	5.00	1.00	2.00	4.00	1.00	1.00
39.00	68.00	261.00	42.00	29.00	19.00	13.00
2.00	4.00	1.00	2.00	15.00	2.00	1.00
27.00	58.00	10.00	22.00	18.00	39.00	12.00
117.00	135.00	116.00	101.00	91.00	67.00	38.00
342.00	38.00	63.00	147.00	45.00	20.00	17.00
1399.00	95.00	127.00	125.00	129.00	50.00	53.00
82.00	1362.00	50.00	263.00	41.00	92.00	95.00
43.00	41.00	1091.00	23.00	13.00	32.00	21.00
16.00	18.00	23.00	1223.00	32.00	42.00	19.00
68.00	76.00	78.00	71.00	1270.00	47.00	20.00
46.00	58.00	36.00	44.00	31.00	1033.00	16.00
82.00	89.00	45.00	81.00	46.00	48.00	1023.00

APPENDIX The Structure of F Technology in the Theory of Production

1. As we have noted in section 4, the essential feature that the assumption of F technology encounters lies in the choice of technologies which yield a variety of different joint products for a given input vector. In what follows of this appendix we shall elucidate the structure of F technology with relation to the theory of production. Throughout the discussion it is assumed that the prices of output and its factor inputs are fixed so that the constants given in the formulation of F technology of section 4 in terms of values may be easily transformed into those in terms of volumes. For example, the matrix of constants F with which the input vector of j-th industry and the output vector of j-th industry are associated is defined in value terms of u_j and v_j in (4.4). The assumption allows us to reformulate F in terms of physical volumes of both inputs and output stating

$$(1) \qquad F: \ \sum f_{ij} v'_j = u'_j,$$

where v'_j and u'_j are vectors of output and inputs in physical volumes of j-th industry. As the assumption is made for brevity of dscussion, formidarable obstacles would not be placed in the way of taking into account price elements jointly in our discussion relaxing the assumption.[5] Keeping in mind that the vectors of inputs and output in the discussion that follows refer to physical volumes by the assumption, we shall refrain from using particular notations for physical volumes for their saving confounding v_j and u_j with v'_j and u'_j respectively.

5) The introduction of price elements into the physical structure of F technology will be touched in Kurabayashi, Sakuma and Yatsuka [1977].

2. The structure of F technology is built on the following primitive concepts:[6)]

i) a commodity space which is constituted of distinct goods and services. Those goods and services which are used as inputs to the technology are called factors of production.

(ii) the set of alternative output vectors, which is defined, for a vector of inputs x and a vector of output v, by

$$P(x) \subset \{v \mid v \geqq 0] = V = R^m_+ . \tag{2}$$

iii) a production correspondence P such that

$$P: \ X \rightarrow V, \quad X = \{x \mid x \geqq 0\}, \quad V = \{v \mid v \geq 0\} . \tag{3}$$

In place of ii) and iii) the following concepts may be used:

ii)′ the set of alternative input vectors, which is defined by

$$L(v) \subset \{x \mid v \in P(x), x \in X\} = R^n_+ . \tag{4}$$

iii)′ the inverse production correspondence L such that

$$L: \ V \rightarrow X, \tag{5}$$

for a $v \in V$ the mapping set $L(v)$ is

$$L(v) = \{x \mid v \in P(x), x \in X\} .$$

In what follows $P(x)$ and $L(v)$ are termed an output set and an input set respectively.

The efficient subset of an output set $P(x)$ is defined by

$$E(x) = \{v \in V \mid w \geq v, v \in P(x) \Rightarrow w \not\ni P(x)\}, x \in X . \tag{6}$$

Returning to a production correspondence, a mapping $P: X \rightarrow V$ of input vectors x into subsets $P(x)$ of output vectors is a production correspondence if

6) For the definition of the primitive concepts, reference should be made to Shephard [1970].

(P1) $P(0) = \{0\}$,

(P2) $P(x)$ is bounded for all $x \in X$,

(P3) $x' \geqq x$ implies $P(x') \supset P(x)$,

(P4) $v \in P(x)$ and $0 \leqq v' \leqq v$ implies $v' \in P(x)$,

(P5) $P(x)$ is convex for all $x \in X$,

(P6) $P(\lambda x + (1-\lambda)y) \supset P(x) \cap P(y)$, for all $x, y \in X$ and $\lambda \in [0, 1]$,

(P7) A graph of P, which is defined by

$$G_P = \{(x, v) \mid v \in P(x), x \in X\},$$

is a closed set on $X \times V$.

Being the properties of production correspondence discussed in detail by Shephard, we need not give full accounts of the properties except for marginal comments. It is implied by (P. 4) that the strong attainability of output is the case for $P(x)$. Moreover, (P. 6) insists that a production correspondence concerned here is quasi-concave.[7]

3. On the basis of the primitive concepts given before, the output structure is further specified by introducing the concept of an intrinsically factor limitational output structure, IFLOS for short: (Definition of IFLOS-A) An output set $P(x)$ is termed an intrincically factor limitational production structure if its efficient subset $E(x)$ is constituted of a single element such that

(7) $E(x) = \{v^*\}$; $x \in X, v^* \in V$.

(Definition of IFLOS-B) An output set $P(x)$ is said to be an intrincically limitational production structure if the maximal element of the output set v is contained in $P(x)$, i.e.

---

7) The following notations are used in the comparison of two vectors x and y.

$$x > y \Rightarrow x_i > y_i \text{ for all } i \in \{1, 2, \dots, m\}$$
$$x \geqq y \Rightarrow x_i \geqq y_i \text{ for all } i \in \{1, 2, \dots, m\}$$
$$x \geq y \Rightarrow x_i \geqq y_i \text{ but } x \neq y .$$

(8) $\exists v^*: \ v^*(x) = \max P(x): \ v \leqq v^* \in P(x)$ for all v.

The two definitions are associated with each other by the following remark.

(Remark 1) Let $P(x)$ be a production correspondence having properties (P1)–(P7), then the definition of IFLOS-A implies that of IFLOS-B.

(Proof) It is sufficient to show that

(9) $P(x) \subset \{v \mid v \leqq v^*\}\ ; \ E(x) = \{v^*\}\ .$

Note that $P(x)$ is a compact set by the definition of a production correspondence. Suppose (9) does not hold. Then, we have

$$\exists v^\circ \in P(x): \ v^\circ \leqq v(x)\,,$$

implying that $v^\circ \notin E(x)$. Hence,

$$\exists \bar{v} \geq v^\circ: \ \bar{v} \in P(x)\,.$$

Denoting that

$$\Omega = P(x) \cap \{v \in V \mid v \geqq v^\circ\}\,,$$

it is easy to show that Ω is compact and that $\bar{v} \in \Omega$. Let $d(v, v^\circ)$ stand for the distance between v and v°. Being Ω compact and $d(v, v^\circ)$ continuous on Ω, it attains maximum on Ω. Let z^* stand for the maximum. Then,

$$d(z^*, v^\circ) = \max_{v \in \Omega} d(v, v^\circ)\,.$$

Consider an arbitrary vector z which satisfies $z \geq z^*$. Apparently, $z \geq v^\circ$, because $z^* \geqq v^\circ$. Noting that $d(z^*, v^\circ) < d(z, v^\circ)$, it is immediate that

$$z \notin P(x), \text{ for all } z \geq z^*\,.$$

Hence, z^* is an element of $E(x)$. Suppose $z^* = v^*$, then we have

$$z^* \geqq v^\circ \Rightarrow v^* \geqq v^\circ ,$$

which contradicts

$$v^* \ngeqq v^\circ . \qquad |$$

Let us consider a vector valued function:

(10) $\phi(x) = \max P(x) , \quad x \in X .$

By Remark 1, the vector valued function

$$\phi: \ X \rightarrow V$$

is well-defined if $P(x)$ has the property of IFLOS. ϕ is termed the IFLOS production function. If an output set generated from IFLOS production function degenerates into a set of scalars such that

$$V \subset R_+ ,$$

denoting V the output set, it is seen that the IFLOS production function is reduced to the 'plant base, factor limitational production function' which has been termed by Ozaki.[8)]

4. As a specific type of an output set having the property of IFLOS, a linear and intrincically factor limitational output structure, LIFLOS for short, may be conceivable. The definition of LIFLOS is given below:

(Definition of LIFLOS) An output set $P(x)$, $x \in X$ is said to have a linear and intrincically factor limitational output structure if a production correspondence P: $X \rightarrow V$ satisfies the following requirements:

(i) $P(x) \subset \{v \in V \mid v \leqq v^*(x)\}$; $v^*(x) = \max P(x)$.

(ii) $P(x+y) = P(x) + P(y)$.

(iii) $P(\lambda x) = \lambda P(x)$, for any scalar $\lambda > 0$.

8) See, in particular, Ozaki [1970].

Supposing LIFLOS in a production correspondence, the counterpart of IFLOS production function is what is called a generalized Leontief production function, whose definition is as follows:
(Definition of GL production function) A vector valued function ϕ: $X \rightarrow V$ defined on a mapping

$$\phi(x) = \max P(x), \quad x \in X,$$

is called a generalized Leontief production function if the following requirements are satisfied:

$$\text{(i)} \quad \phi(x+y) = \phi(x) + \phi(y),$$
$$\text{(ii)} \quad \phi(\lambda x) = \lambda\phi(x), \text{ for any scalar } \lambda > 0.$$

The association of a generalized Leontief production function with a IFLOS production function is clearly spelled out by the following remarks.
(Remark 2) Suppose an output set $P(x)$, $x \in X$ has the property of LIFLOS. Then, its IFLOS production function is a *GL* production function.
(Proof) We note that

$$\max P(x) + \max P(y) \in P(x+y).$$

But, by the definition of max,

$$\max P(x) + \max P(y) \leqq \max P(x+y).$$

On the other hand, as

$$\max P(x+y) \in P(x) + P(y),$$

there exists vectors from the output set which satisfy

$$v^1 + v^2 = \max P(x+y), \quad v^1 \in P(x) \text{ and } v^2 \in P(y),$$

whence we have

$$v^1 \leqq \max P(x) \text{ and } v^2 \leqq \max P(y).$$

Then, it follows that

$$\max P(x+y) = v^1+v^2 \leqq \max P(x)+\max P(y) .$$

Hence,

$$\max P(x+y) = \max P(x)+\max P(y) .$$

By the assumption, it is easily seen that

$$\max P(\lambda x) = \lambda P(x) .$$

Consequently, the IFLOS production function of $P(x)$ is a GL production function. |

(Remark 3) Suppose a vector valued function ϕ: $X \rightarrow V$ is a GL production function, then an output structure constructed by

$$(11) \qquad P_\phi(x) = \{v \in V \mid v \leqq \phi(x)\} , \quad x \in X ,$$

has the property of LIFLOS.

(Proof) It is evident that

$$\max P_\phi(x) = \phi(x)$$

and that

$$P_\phi(\lambda x) = \lambda P_\phi(x) .$$

Accordingly, it is sufficient to show that

$$P_\phi(x+y) = P_\phi(x)+P_\phi(y) .$$

Then, it is possible to decompose v into v^1 and v^2 such that

$$v^1+v^2 = v , \quad v \in P_\phi(x)+P_\phi(y)$$

for any given input vectors x and y. It is seen that

$$v^1 \leqq \max P_\phi(x) = \phi(x)$$

and

$$v^2 \leqq \max P_\phi(y) = \phi(y) .$$

Being ϕ a GL production function, we have

$$v = v^1 + v^2 \leq \phi(x) + \phi(y) = \phi(x+y)\,.$$

Hence,

$$v \in P_\phi(x+y)$$

and

$$P_\phi(x) + P_\phi(y) \subset P_\phi(x+y)\,.$$

On the other hand, noting that

$$\phi(x+y) = \max P_\phi(x+y) \in P_\phi(x+y)$$

and

$$\phi(x) + \phi(y) \in P_\phi(x) + P_\phi(y)\,,$$

it is easy to show that

$$v \leqq \phi(x+y) = \phi(x) + \phi(y) \in P_\phi(x) + P_\phi(y)\,,$$

for any given $v \in P_\phi(x+y)$. Hence, it immediately follows that

$$v \in P_\phi(x) + P_\phi(y)$$

and

$$P_\phi(x+y) \subset P_\phi(x) + P_\phi(y)\,. \quad |$$

It is interesting to see that a GL production function is expressed by the form of linear mapping, which leads to the following remark.
(Remark 4) That a vector valued function $\phi\colon X \to V$ is a GL production function is equivalent to saying that ϕ is expressed by a linear mapping in a form

$$\phi(x) = Gx\,, \tag{12}$$

where G is a matrix having $m \times n$ dimension.
(Proof) As ϕ is a linear mapping which transforms an input vector in R^n_+ into an output vector in R^m_+, (12) immediately follows. |
5. It is also possible to specify the structure of production tech-

nology in terms of an input set in place of an output set. The properties of an input set $L(v)$, $v \in V$ which is generated from the inverse production correspondence $L: V \rightarrow X$ are derived from the parallel properties of the production correspondence $P: X \rightarrow V$. Indeed, it is not difficult to show the properties of the input set, which are itemized below without giving proof.

(Remark 5) If the production correspondence $P: X \rightarrow V$ has the properties (P1)...(P6), an input set generated from the inverse production correspondence $L: V \rightarrow X$ has the following properties:

(L1) $L(0) = X$ and $0 \notin L(v)$ for all $v \geq 0$.

(L2) An infinite amount of output cannot be produced by finite amounts of inputs. Hence,

$$\| x \| < +\infty,\ x \in X \text{ and } \| v \| = +\infty,\ v \in V \Rightarrow x \notin L(v).$$

(L3) $L(v') \subset L(v)$ for $v' \geqq v \in V$.

(L4) if $x' \geqq x$ and $x \in L(v)$, then $x' \in L(v)$.

(L5) $L(v)$ is a convex set for all $v \in V$.

(L6) $L(\lambda v + (1-\lambda)w) \supset L(v) \cap L(w)$, for all $v, w \in V$, $\lambda \in [0, 1]$.

(L7) A graph of L, which is defined by

$$G_L = \{(v, x) \mid x \in L(v), v \in V\},$$

is a closed set on $V \times X$.

In parallel with the specification of the output structure by IFLOS, the input set is specified by a non-substitutable input structure (NOSIS) whose alternative definitions are given below.

(Definition of NOSIS-A) An input set $L(v)$, $v \rightarrow V$ is said to have a non-substitutable input structure if its efficient subset $E(v)$ is constituted of a single element such that

(13) $\hat{E}(v) = \{x^*\}$; $v \in V$.

The efficient subset of an input set $L(v)$ is defined by

(14) $E(v) = \{x \mid x \in L(v),\ y \notin L(v) \text{ if } y \leq x\},\ v \in V$.

(Definition of NOSIS-B) An input set $L(v)$ is said to have a non-substitutable input structure if its minimal element is contained in $L(v)$, i.e.

$$(15) \qquad \exists x(v) \in X: \; x(v) = \min L(v) .$$

The two definitions of NOSIS are associated with each other by the following remark.

(Remark 6) The definition of NOSIS-A is equivalent to the definition of NOSIS-B.

(Proof) It is easy to show that

$$\exists \min L(v) \Rightarrow E(v) = \{x^*\} , \quad x^* = \min L(v) ,$$

leading to the statement that the definition of NOSIS-B implies the definition of NOSIS-A.

On the other hand, by a reasoning analogous to Remark 1, it is immediate to show that the reverse statement also holds. |

A vector valued function which is generated from the input structure having the property of NOSIS is called a NOSIS input function whose definition is given by

$$\phi(v) = \min L(v) , \quad v \in V .$$

6. A specific type of the input structure which has the property of NOSIS is constituted by a non-substitutable and linear input structure if the following requirements are satisfied for $L(v)$; $v, w \in V$:

(i) $L(v) \subset \{x \in X \mid x \geqq x^*(v)\}$; $x^*(v) = \min L(v)$.

(ii) $L(v+w) = L(v) + L(w)$.

(iii) $L(\lambda v) = \lambda L(v)$.

The counterpart of a *GL* production function is a generalized Leontief input function whose definition is given below.

(Definition of GL input function) A vector valued function ϕ: $V \rightarrow X$ defined on a mapping

$$\phi(v) = \min L(v), \quad v \in V,$$

is called a generalized Leontief input function if the following requirements are fulfilled:

$$\text{(i)} \quad \phi(v+w) = \phi(v)+\phi(w).$$

$$\text{(ii)} \quad \phi(\lambda v) = \lambda\phi(v).$$

By a resoning analogous to the one used to derive Remarks 3, 4 and 5, the following remarks are readily made.

(Remark 7) Suppose an input set $L(v)$ has the property of NOSLIS (non-substitutable and linear input structure). Then, its NOSIS input function is a GL input function.

(Remark 8) Suppose a vector valued function ϕ: $V \rightarrow X$ is a GL input function. Then, an input structure constructed on

$$(16) \qquad L_{\phi}(v) = \{x \in X \mid x \geqq \phi(v)\}, \quad v \in V,$$

has the property of NOSLIS.

(Remark 9) That a vector valued function ϕ: $V \rightarrow X$ is a GL input function is equivalent to saying that ϕ is expressed by a linear mapping in a form

$$(17) \qquad \phi(v) = Fv,$$

where F is a matrix having $n \times m$ dimension.

It should be noted that Remark 9 is especially relevant to the formulation of our F technology assumption, as it easily turns out that the F technology assumption can be derived from the remark as its special case.

REFERENCES

Y. Kurabayashi, I. Sakuma and A. Yatsuka, "The Structure of the Input-Output

Model in SNA and Technology Assumptions ", (in Japanese), *Keizai Kenkyu*, April 1977.

Iwao Ozaki, " Economies of Scale and Input-Output Coefficients ", *Applications of Input-Output Analysis*, ed. by A. P. Carter and A. Brody, Amsterdam 1970.

R. Penrose, "A Generalized Inverse for Matrices ", *Proceedings of Cambridge Philosophical Society*, Vol. 51, 1955.

Ronald W. Shephard, *Theory of Cost and Production Functions*, Priceton 1970.

Richard Stone, *Mathematical Models of the Economy and Other Essays*, London 1970.

United Nations, *A System of National Accounts*, New York 1968.

Hukukane Nikaido, *Introduction to Sets and Mappings in Modern Economics*, (translated from Japanese by Kazuo Sato), Amsterdam 1970.

2

A SYSTEM OF NATIONAL ACCOUNTS IN CONSTANT PRICES: AN ATTEMPTED SYNTHESIS

1. Introducion

In this paper the author will be concerned with the presentation of the terms of trade effect within a framework of national accounts. The issue has already been taken up by Professor R. C. Geary, Dr. G. Stuvel and other authors. In the next section, the author presents a system of national accounts in a matrix form, which constitutes a conceptual framework for further discussion. He offers a brief summary of the arguments advanced by Geary and Stuvel. It will be pointed out that the nature of the terms of trade effects which are offered by them is primarily dependent on the rule for selecting the deflators for those items which express the non-commodity flow, such as the net factor income from abroad and the net lending to the rest of the world. Since it becomes apparent that the terms of trade effects introduced by them have further disadvantages, the author proposes a new approach for formulating the deflators of the net factor income from abroad and the net lending to the rest of the world. A generalized form which expresses the terms of trade effect readily follows from this new formulation. It is interesting to see that a synthesis between Geary's and Stuvel's approaches is attained by means of this generalized expression.

In section 3 the author discusses the feasibility of fitting the generalized expression of the terms of trade effect to the system of national accounts expressed in constant prices. Three sorts of gains may be distinguished in our system of national accounts in constant prices if the deflator for saving is explicitly defined. They may be termed the expenditure gains, the external trade gains and internal trade gains, following the terminology adopted by Mr. Broderick. It is illuminating to demonstrate that the external trade gains are distributed into the expenditure gains and internal trade gains respectively if the deflator for saving is appropriately chosen. It is noted that the fact may be considered as an extension of Broderick's argument.

In the last section, the author attempts to link changes in terms of trade with productivity changes. In doing this, the author begins with the formulation of the sector production account in constant prices. Subject to changes in volumes of inputs, both of intermediate products and of labour, relative to outputs, it is maintained that the terms which express productivity changes should be introduced for formulating the sector production account in constant prices. It is also pointed out that the term which may be regarded as terms of trade arising from changes in input prices relative to output price is introduced for balancing the sector production account in constant prices if the deflator which is right for deflating factor incomes is reasonably defined. The author proposes a new formula for the deflator. The article concludes by showing that a meaningful relationship between the terms of trade and productivity changes results from this formula.

2. Terms of Trade Effect and the Rest of the World Account in Constant Prices

For the convenience of subsequent discussion the present analysis opens with the presentation of national accounts in a matrix form. The matrix is presented in Table 1, in which the following notations are used:

Table 1.

Regions		I				II
	No.	1	2	3	4	5
I	1		V	C		X
	2				I	
	3	Q	$-D$			P_r
	4			S		K_r
II	5	M		T_r^f	F	

V, gross domestic capital formation
C, consumers' expenditure on goods and services
X, sales of goods and services to the rest of the world
I, net domestic capital formation
Q, gross domestic products
D, consumption of fixed capital
P_r, net factor income received from the rest of the world
S, saving

K_r, net capital transfer received from the rest of the world
M, purchases of goods and services from the rest of the world
T_r^f, net income transfer paid to the rest of the world
F, net increase of lending to the rest of the world

Regions are divided into two parts in this matrix. They are the domestic economy and the rest of the world which are shown in abbreviated form by the Roman characters I and II respectively. A sub-matrix is constituted by the transactions which emerge from the economic activities carried out within the domestic economy, indicated in the first four rows and columns. They are (1) production, (2) capital formation, (3) formation of income and its consumption and (4) capital financing. It is evident from the construction of the submatrix that the idea of the so-called "real and financial dichotomy" is adopted, because the first two rows and columns refer to real flow of goods and services and the remaining two are concerned with the flow of financial claims as assets or liabilities.

It is well recognized that the rest of the world account is derived from the matrix in Table 1:

$$(2.1) \qquad X+P_r+K_r = M+T_r^f+F$$

It is convenient for the subsequent discussion to restate the account by the following relation:

$$(2.2) \qquad CS+P_r = N$$
$$CS = X-M, \qquad N = T_r^f+F-K_r$$

According to the idea of Professor R. Stone, *CS* represents the commodity flow and the remaining two variables in (2.2) fall into the category of the non-commodity flow.

The rest of the world account in constant prices will not necessarily be maintained if a rule for deflating the non-commodity flow items in (2.2) is formulated. In practice, as Geary has pointed out, the following rule for the deflation of P_r and N yields the imbalance of the rest of the world account in constant prices[1].

(Rule 1) The deflator of X is used for the deflators of P_r and N if $CS>0$. On the other hand, the deflator of M is used for the deflators of P_r and N if $CS<0$.

Under such a circumstance, a correction term must be introduced into the rest of the world account in constant prices in order to maintain the balance of its receipt and expenditure. Let $\bar{T}$ stand for the correction term, the balance of the rest of the world account in constant prices is represented by (2.3).

$$(2.3) \qquad \bar{X}+\bar{P}_r+\bar{T}=\bar{M}+\bar{N}$$

It is easily shown that the correction term $\bar{T}$ stands for the effect arising from changes in terms of trade. In fact, $\bar{T}$ is expressed by

$$(2.4) \qquad \text{(i)} \quad \bar{T}=\frac{M}{p_2}\left(1-\frac{p_2}{p_1}\right)=\bar{M}\left(1-\frac{p_2}{p_1}\right) \quad \text{if} \quad CS>0,$$

$$\text{(ii)} \quad \bar{T}=-\frac{X}{p_1}\left(1-\frac{p_1}{p_2}\right)=-\bar{X}\left(1-\frac{p_1}{p_2}\right) \quad \text{if} \quad CS<0.$$

where p_1 and p_2 are deflators of X and M respectively. $(1-p_2/p_1)$ or (p_1/p_2-1) stands for the unit gain (or loss) due to changes in terms of trade.

Attention is particularly called to the fact that the symmetry is observed between the rest of the world account and the domestic economy whether viewed from the side of the domestic economy or from that of the rest of the world. Noting that the national accounts for the rest of the world can be written in the form of Table 2, its rest of the world account is expressed by (2.5).

1) R. C. Geary [1961].

Table 2.

Regions		I	II			
	No.	1	2	3	4	5
I	1		M_2		T_{r2}^f	F_2
II	2	X_2		V_2	C_2	
	3					I_2
	4	P_{r2}	Q_2	$-D_2$		
	5	K_{r2}			S_2	

(2. 5) $\quad X_2+P_{r2}+K_{r2} = M_2+T_{r2}^f+F_2$

X_2 and M_2 in (2.5) stand for the sales of goods and services to the domestic economy and the purchases of goods and services from the domestic economy respectively. Suffix 2 is used for distinguishing the rest of the world from the domestic economy. Taking note of the fact that

(2. 6) $$CS_2 = X_2-M_2 = M_1-X_1 = -CS_1,$$
$$P_{r2} = -P_{r1},$$

(2.7) easily follows.

(2. 7) $\quad N_2 = -(CS_1+P_{r1}) = -N_1$

where the suffix 1 indicates the domestic economy. Owing to the symmetry observed in N and P_r; the selection of deflators for N_2 and P_{r2} directly follows from the rule 1 as indicated below:

(Rule 1′) p_2 is used for the deflators of N_2 and P_{r2} if $CS_2>0$. On the other hand, p_1 is used for the deflators of N_2 and P_{r2} if $CS_2<0$.

For the rest of the world economy, its rest of the world account in constant prices can be presented in a balancing form as (2.8), if a correction term is introduced:

$$(2.8) \qquad \bar{X}_2+\bar{P}_{r2}+\bar{T}_2=\bar{M}_2+\bar{N}_2$$

where $\bar{T}_2$ is the correction term for the rest of the world. $\bar{T}_2$ is also considered as the gain or loss of the rest of the world due to changes in terms of trade. It is easily proved that the sum total of trade gains in the world as a whole is reduced to zero, i.e.

$$(2.9) \qquad \bar{T}_1+\bar{T}_2=0\,.$$

(2.9) is conveniently termed *the zero-sum condition of trade gains.* In fact, (i) if $CS_1>0$ and $CS_2<0$, then

$$\bar{T}_1=\frac{M_1}{p_2}\left(1-\frac{p_2}{p_1}\right)=\frac{X_2}{p_2}\left(1-\frac{p_2}{p_1}\right),$$

$$\bar{T}_2=-\frac{X_2}{p_2}\left(1-\frac{p_2}{p_1}\right),$$

and we obtain

$$\bar{T}_1+\bar{T}_2=0\,.$$

(ii), conversely, if $CS_1<0$ and $CS_2>0$, then

$$\bar{T}_1=-\frac{X_1}{p_1}\left(1-\frac{p_1}{p_2}\right),$$

$$\bar{T}_2=\frac{M_2}{p_1}\left(1-\frac{p_1}{p_2}\right)=\frac{X_1}{p_1}\left(1-\frac{p_1}{p_2}\right),$$

and we obtain

$$\bar{T}_1+\bar{T}_2=0\,.$$

In the derivation of (2.9) it is taken for granted that the exports of the domestic economy are identical with the imports of the rest of the world and vice versa. On account of inconsistencies observed in statistical measurements among various countries, the condition may not necessarily be guaranteed for actual data. The existence of the discrepancy between the exports of the domestic economy and the imports of the rest of the world will create further complication. The point is ignored in this article so that we may not complicate the matter by unnecessary additions.

The disadvantage of this formulation of terms of the trade effect is that the term is solely dependent on either $\bar{X}$ or $\bar{M}$, aside from the term expressing the unit gain (or loss) due to changes in terms of trade. Stuvel's rule for the selection of deflators of N and P_r aims to surmount the disadvantage.[2] His rule may be expressed as below:

> (Rule 2) All entries of national accounts are deflated by a single deflator, say GDP deflator, which reflects the change in general prices. Thus, GDP deflator is used for the common deflator of both P_r and N.

Although he does not indicate the specific deflator which reflects the change in general prices, it is worth noting the fact that the terms of trade effect which is derived from his argument becomes valid if and only if GDP deflator is chosen as the common deflator for all entries of national accounts. According to his argument, the rest of the world account (for the domestic economy) in constant prices is written as

$$(2.10) \qquad \bar{X}_1+\bar{\bar{P}}_{r1}+\bar{\bar{T}}_1 = \bar{M}_1+\bar{\bar{N}}_1$$

where

$$\bar{\bar{P}}_{r1} = \frac{P_{r1}}{P}, \qquad \bar{\bar{N}}_1 = \frac{N_1}{P}$$

2) G. Stuvel [1959].

letting P stand for GDP deflator. $\bar{\bar{T}}_1$ stands for the correction term which expresses the terms of trade effect as indicated below:

$$\bar{\bar{T}}_1 = \bar{M}_1\left(1-\frac{p_2}{P}\right)-\bar{X}_1\left(1-\frac{p_1}{P}\right). \tag{2.11}$$

But, the formulation of the terms of trade effect in (2.11) creates another difficulty, because (2.11) no longer ensures the zero-sum condition of trade gains. Thus, it is required for overcoming the difficulty that a new rule for choosing the deflators of P_r and N which overcomes the disadvantages indicated before should be sought.

What is proposed by the author to meet the requirement is the following rule.

(Rule 3) P_{r1} and N_1 is deflated by a new deflator p_N which is constructed as a weighted harmonic mean of p_1 and p_2:

$$p_N = \frac{1}{\alpha(1/p_1)+(1-\alpha)(1/p_2)}, \tag{2.12}$$

where $0<\alpha<1$ stands for the weight in (2.12) and is specified by

$$\alpha = \frac{X_1}{X_1+M_1}. \tag{2.13}$$

A correction term $\tilde{T}_1$ must be added so that the rest of the world account in constant prices may be established in the following form,

$$\bar{X}_1+\tilde{P}_{r1}+\tilde{T}_1 = \bar{M}_1+\tilde{N}_1. \tag{2.14}$$

if p_N, defined in (2.12), is applied to P_{r1} and N_1 as their deflators. It is readily shown that the correction term is considered as the effect due to changes in terms of trade and is expressed by[3)]

3) M. R. Courbis has proposed another rule for selecting the deflator of P_{r1} and N_1, in his elaborate article, Courbis [1964]. The deflator he chooses is defined by

(2.15) $$\tilde{T}_1 = \bar{X}_1(1-\alpha)\left(\frac{p_1}{p_2}-1\right)-\bar{M}_1\alpha\left(\frac{p_2}{p_1}-1\right)$$

It is interesting to note that the terms of trade effect obtained in (2.15) is expressed by a weighted average of $\bar{M}_1(1-p_2/p_1)$ and $-X_1(1-p_1/p_2)$, which are the terms of trade effects produced by rule 1. Furthermore, it is recalled that the expression of $\tilde{T}_1$ in (2.15) exhibits symmetry with respect to X_1 and M_1. Owing to this symmetry, the zero-sum condition of trade gains is ensured. Thus, letting $\tilde{T}_2$ stand for the terms of trade effect originating from the rest of the world economy, (2.16) holds:

(2.16) $$\tilde{T}_1+\tilde{T}_2 = 0\,.$$

Replacing P by p_1 or p_2 in (2.11), it may be also noted that the expression of $\tilde{T}_1$ in (2.15) assumes a generalized form of (2.11).

3. Terms of Trade Effect and a System of National Accounts in Constant Prices

So far we have discussed the terms of trade effect only within the scope of the rest of the world account. But, the effect necessarily generates significant impact on other segments of the domestic economy. The issue becomes considerably important as we consider the effect within *a system of national accounts in constant prices* instead of one independent account in constant prices. Noting

---

$$p_N = \alpha p_1+(1-\alpha)p_2,\ \text{where}\ \alpha = \frac{\bar{X}_1}{\bar{X}_1+\bar{M}_1}\,.$$

His choice of p_N gives a somewhat complicated expression of T_1, which has no longer close association with any form of terms of trade effects derived from either rule 1 or rule 2. His derivation of terms of trade effect is written by

$$T_1 = \bar{X}_1\left[\frac{1}{\alpha+(1-\alpha)(p_2/p_1)}-1\right]-\bar{M}_1\left[\frac{1}{(1-\alpha)+\alpha(p_1/p_2)}\right].$$

Table 3.

Regions		I				II
	No.	1	2	3	4	5
I	1		V	C		X
	2				I	
	3	Q	$-D$			P_r
	4			S^*		
II	5	M			N	

the relationship in (2.2), the conceptual framework shown in Table 1 is further simplified as Table 3.

where $S^*=S+K_r-T_r^f$.

Suppose that the GDP deflator and the deflator for net capital formation are implicitly determined by means of the production account and the capital formation account which follow from the matrix in Table 3. The deflators for remaining entries which express non-commodity flow, i.e. P_r, N and S^*, are left indeterminate, unless rules for determining these entries are properly furnished. The rule 4 which will be given below and the rule 3 already given make it possible to produce a system of national accounts in constant prices and to determine appropriate deflators for P_r, N and S.

(Rule 4) The deflator of S is formulated by

$$p_S=\frac{1}{\beta(1/p^*)+(1-\beta)(1/p_C)} \tag{3.1}$$

Where p^* and p_C stand for the implicit NDP deflator and the deflator for consumers' expenditure on goods and services respectively.[4] β stands for a weight and is presented by

$$(3.2) \qquad \beta=\frac{P}{P+C} \quad (0<\beta<1).$$

If these deflators are applied to the constituent entries in the consumption account, a correction term $\bar{\theta}_1$ must be introduced into the consumption account in constant prices so that it may maintain the balance. So we obtain

$$(3.3) \qquad \bar{C}+\bar{S}^*+\bar{\theta}_1=\bar{P}+\tilde{P}_r$$

The correction term can be expressed as (3.4):

$$(3.4) \qquad \bar{\theta}_1=\left[\bar{P}(1-\beta)\left(1-\frac{p^*}{p_C}\right)-\bar{C}\beta\left(1-\frac{p_C}{p^*}\right)\right]+P_r\left(\frac{1}{p_N}-\frac{1}{p_S}\right)$$

$\bar{\theta}_1$ may be termed the expenditure losses, because they account for the use of additional real flow of purchasing power which arises from changes in relative prices. Obviously, it is seen that

$$\bar{\theta}_1>0 \text{ if } p^*<p_C \text{ and } p_S>p_N$$
$$\bar{\theta}_1<0 \text{ if } p^*>p_C \text{ and } p_S<p_N .$$

It is also noted that the expenditure loss is caused not only the relative prices between NDP deflator and the deflator for the consumers' expenditure but also the terms of trade between p_N and p_S.

Similarly, an additional correction term must be inserted in the capital finance account so that it may maintain the balance. Let $\bar{\theta}_2$ stand for the correction term. The capital finance account in constant prices is written by (3.5):

4) The NDP deflator is implicitly defined by the following definitional relation;

$$P=Q-D,$$

if the deflator for Q and D are explicitly defined.

(3. 5) $\bar{I}+\tilde{N}+\bar{\theta}_2 = \bar{S}*$

It can be readily shown that the correction term is expressed by (3.6):

(3. 6) $\bar{\theta}_2 = -(\bar{\theta}_1+\tilde{T})$

$\bar{\theta}_2$, which is analogous to $\bar{\theta}_1$, may be termed the internal trade losses because the term originates from changes in relative prices between the domestic prices and the price of exports and amounts to the internal use of real purchasing power. Thus, the preceding arguments imply far-reaching consequences. Firstly, it is implied that if the rule 3 and rule 4 are formulated for selecting deflators P_r, N and S then a system of national accounts in constant prices can be constructed on the basis of the matrix in Table 3:

(3. 7)
$$\begin{aligned} &\bar{Q} = \bar{V}+\bar{C}+\bar{X}-\bar{M} \\ &\bar{V} = \bar{D}+\bar{I} \\ &\bar{C}+\bar{S}*+\bar{\theta}_1 = \bar{P}+\tilde{P}_r \\ &\bar{I}+\tilde{N}+\bar{\theta}_2 = \bar{S}* \\ &\bar{X}+\tilde{P}_r+\tilde{T} = \bar{M}+\tilde{N} \end{aligned}$$

Secondly, (3.6) implies that the external trade gains are expressed as the sum of the expenditure gains and the internal trade gains, with changes in sign:

(3. 8) $\tilde{T} = -(\bar{\theta}_1+\bar{\theta}_2)$

(3.8) amounts to saying that the gains caused by changes in terms of trade are necessarily distributed into the gains arising from changes in relative prices of the domestic economy.

The issue raised in this section has already been discussed by several authors as Geary, Stuvel and Broderick. In particular, Broderick maintains that a system of national accounts in constant prices can be compiled if a set of deflators for the elements of the system which express the non-commodity flow is properly provided. He also points out that the expenditure gains of households, corporations and public authorities add up to zero. What I have concluded from (3.8) is that his argument can be extended so as to establish explicitly the relationship between the external trade gains, the expenditure gains and the internal trade gains if the rule for selecting the deflators for those transactions which express the non-commodity flow are properly formulated.[5]

4. Terms of Trade Effect between Inputs and Outputs and Productivity Changes

If we note the fact that the terms of trade effect so far discussed is regarded as the effect caused by changes in relative prices between exports and imports, the preceeding argument can be further extended to deal with the terms of trade effect generated by changes in relative prices between inputs and outputs. For the subsequent analysis it is of great help to construct the following table.[6]

In Table 4 the following notations are also employed:

X, outputs

U, the inputs of intermediate products

W, compensation for employees

Y, operating surpluses

Noting the fact that the right hand side of the following production account (in current price),

(4.1) $$Y+W=X-U,$$

5) See J. B. Broderick [1967]. In fact, a similar conclusion to (3.8) is also drawn by Stuvel (G. Stuvel [1959]). But, in his derivation, the entries which stand for the non-commodity flow are uniformly deflated by GDP deflator.

6) A virtually similar table is introduced by Courbis. See R. Courbis [1969].

Table 4.

	1	2	3	4	5	6	7	8
output	X_0	$\bar{X}$	q	$\bar{X}$	q	$\bar{X}$	q	X_1
Intermediate products	U_0	$\tilde{U}$	q	$\bar{U}$	q_u	$\bar{U}$	q_u	U_1
Compensation for employees	$\tilde{W}_0$	$\tilde{W}$	q	$\bar{\bar{W}}$	q_w	W^*	q_y	W_1
Operating surpluses	Y_0	$\tilde{Y}$	q	$\tilde{Y}$	q	Y^*	q_y	Y_1
Gains due to price changes						T		
Gains due to productivity changes				G				
Column total	X_0	$\tilde{X}$		$\bar{X}+G$		$\bar{X}+T$		X_1

Column 1 indicates the base year values in current prices.

Column 2 indicates the current year values in constant prices when the volume of outputs and inputs are kept unchanged.

Column 3 indicates the Laspeyres volume indexes which correspond with entries in column 2.

Column 4 indicates the current year values in constant prices. Intermediate products and labour inputs are deflated by individual deflators.

Column 5 indicates the Laspeyres volume indexes which correspond with entries in column 4.

Column 6 indicates the current year values in constant prices.

Column 7 indicates the Laspeyres volume indexes which correspond with entries in column 6.

Column 8 indicates the current year values in current prices.

T, the adjustment term due to changes in relative prices

G, the adjustment term due to changes in productivity

q, (Laspeyres) volume index of X

q_u, (Laspeyres) volume index of U

q_w, (Laspeyres) volume index of W

q_y, (Laspeyres) volume index of Y. q_y is derived from Y^*/Y_0 which is defined below.

consists of the variables which express the commodity flow, it is reasonable to formulate the deflators for Y and W, which express the non-commodity flow, by the following rule.

(Rule 5) The deflator p_Y defined by

$$(4.2) \qquad p_Y = \frac{1}{\eta(1/p)+(1-\eta)(1/p_u)},$$

where η stands for a weight and is expressed by

$$(4.3) \qquad \eta = \frac{X_1}{X_1+U_1} \qquad (0<\eta<1),$$

is universally used as the deflators for Y_1 and W_1. Here, p and p_u are the deflators of output and the input of intermediate products respectively.

A correction term T for maintaining the balance of production account in constant prices must be introduced, if the rule 5 is applied to column 6 in Table 4 for obtaining W^* and Y^*. Thus,

$$(4.4) \qquad \bar{X}+T = \bar{U}+W^*+Y^*$$

where

$$W^* = \frac{W_1}{p_Y}, \qquad Y^* = \frac{Y_1}{p_Y}.$$

It is easy to see that the correction term in (4.4) is expressed by

$$(4.5) \qquad T = (1-\eta)\bar{X}\left(\frac{p}{p_u}-1\right)-\eta\bar{U}\left(\frac{p_u}{p}-1\right).$$

Obviously,

$$T>0 \text{ if } p>p_u,$$
$$T<0 \text{ if } p<p_u.$$

As $(1-p_u/p)$ indicates the unit gain (or loss) due to changes in relative prices between outputs and intermediate inputs, the correction term in (4.5) indicates the terms of trade effect arising from changes in relative prices. T expresses the gain arising from the terms of trade between output and intermediate products if it is positive, T expresses the loss suffered from corresponding changes in relative prices if it is negative.

It should also be remembered that the following relations are established between the variables in column 2 of Table 4 and those in column 4:

$$\tilde{U}=\frac{q}{q_u}\bar{U}, \qquad \tilde{W}=\frac{q}{q_w}\bar{W}. \tag{4.6}$$

The balancing relation constituted by the variables listed in column 4 will not be maintained unless it is supplemented by a correction term. Let G stand for the correction term, we obtain

$$\bar{X}+G=\bar{U}+\bar{W}+\tilde{Y}. \tag{4.7}$$

Using the relationship in (4.6), the balance for column 2 may be written by

$$\begin{aligned}\bar{X} &= \tilde{U}+\tilde{W}+\tilde{Y} \\ &= \left(\frac{q}{q_u}\bar{U}+\frac{q}{q_w}\bar{W}+\tilde{Y}\right).\end{aligned} \tag{4.8}$$

It is demonstrated by (4.7) and (4.8) that the correction term appeared in (4.7) is broken up into the terms which express the effect of productivity changes in factors of production:

$$G=\left(1-\frac{q}{q_u}\right)\bar{U}+\left(1-\frac{q}{q_w}\right)\bar{W}. \tag{4.9}$$

In fact, the first term appearing in the right-hand side of (4.9) stands for a unit change in productivity arising out of the input of intermediate products. Similarly, the second term in the right-hand side of (4.9) indicates a unit productivity change arising out of labour inputs. Obviously,

$$G>0 \text{ if } q>q_u \text{ and } q>q_w$$
$$G<0 \text{ if } q<q_u \text{ and } q<q_w .$$

If $G>0$, it is called that the effect of productivity changes arising from the decrease of productivity arises.

Substituting X in (4.4) for what is obtained from (4.8), the terms of trade effect originated from changes in relative prices between outputs and the inputs of intermediate products may be expressed by means of the effect of productivity changes:

$$(4.10) \qquad T=\left(1-\frac{q}{q_u}\right)\bar{U}+\left(\frac{q_y}{q_w}-\frac{q}{q_w}\right)\bar{W}+(Y^*-\tilde{Y}).$$

Noting the relation (4.9), it is clear that the effect of productivity changes is associated with the terms of trade effect arising from changes in relative prices which has already been introduced:[7]

$$(4.11) \qquad T=G+(1-\eta)\left(\frac{p}{p_u}-1\right)\tilde{Y}-\left(1-\frac{q_y}{q_w}\right)\bar{W}.$$

---

7) By definition, it is readily seen that

$$Y^*p_Y = Y_1 \text{ and } \tilde{Y}p = Y_1$$

Thus, we obtain

$$(Y^*-\tilde{Y}) = \left(\frac{p}{p_Y}\tilde{Y}-\tilde{Y}\right) = \left(\frac{p}{p_Y}-1\right)\tilde{Y}.$$

Recalling the definition of p_Y in (4.2), $[(p/p_Y)-1]$ is written by

$$\left(\frac{p}{p_Y}-1\right) = (1-\eta)\left(\frac{p}{p_u}-1\right).$$

Accordingly,

$$(Y^*-\tilde{Y}) = (1-\eta)\left(\frac{p}{p_u}-1\right)\tilde{Y}.$$

Noting that G is further restated by[8)]

$$G=\left(\frac{1}{p_u}-\frac{1}{p}\right)[(1-\eta)W_1+U_1], \tag{4.12}$$

it is readily demonstrated from (4.12) that the effect of productivity changes is always positive if and only if the output prices are greater than the the prices of intermediate products. It should be recognized that the terms of trade between inputs and outputs are inseparably associated with productivity changes as I have already shown.[9]

---

8) Replacing T by (4.5), we obtin

$$G=(1-\eta)\left(\frac{p}{p_u}-1\right)(\bar{X}-\tilde{Y})-\eta\left(\frac{p_u}{p}-1\right)\bar{U}$$

$$=(1-\eta)\left(\frac{p}{p_u}-1\right)(\tilde{U}+\tilde{W})-\eta\left(\frac{p_u}{p}-1\right)\bar{U}$$

which results from (4.7). As we can see that

$$p\tilde{W}=W_1,\quad p\tilde{U}=U_1 \quad\text{and}\quad p_u\bar{U}=U_1$$

by definition, G is further written by

$$G=\left(\frac{1}{p_u}-\frac{1}{p}\right)[(1-\eta)W_1+U_1].$$

9) It may be of some interest to remark that the effect of productivity changes indicated above can be written in terms of Divisia indexes which have been widely used by Jorgenson and others for the measurement of the total factor productivity. Let q^D, q_u^D and q_w^D stand for the Divisia quantity indexes of outputs, intermediates inputs and labour inputs respectively. The effect of productivity changes is expressed by

$$G=\frac{1}{1+q^D}[(q^D-q_u{}^D)U+(q^D-q_w{}^D)W].$$

In this expression, the productivity changes reveal themselves as either the difference between outputs and intermediate inputs or the difference between outputs and labour inputs. In connection with the application of Divisia indexes, reference may be made to D. W. Jorgenson and Z. Griliches [1967]; L. R. Christensen and D. W. Jorgenson [1970].

5. Acknowledgements and Additional Remarks

This article is a reproduction of my paper appeared in *Review of Income and Wealth*, September 1971 under the title, " The Impact of Changes in Terms of Trade on a System of National Accounts: An Attempted Synthesis ", with some corrections. The earlier version of it was presented to 11th General Conference of International Association for Research in Income and Wealth, held at Nathanya, Israel in August 1969. I wish to express my deep appreciation for valuable comments and encouragements given to the earlier version by Mr. J. B. Broderick and Dr. Odd Aukrust. Since its publication, I have been afforded opportunities to clarify my arguments by receiving valuable comments from Professor Raymond Courbis. Taking this opprtunity I also wish to express my high appreciation for his comments. As his comments are essential for further clarification of the points raised in the section 4 of this article, additional remarks on his comments are worth making here.[10)]

I shall continue to follow the notations used in the section 4 of this article. Courbis's arguments may be summarized as what follows. Let denote the index of total factor productivity at the current year measured from the base year 0 by π, which is, by definition,[11)]

$$\pi = (\tilde{X}/\tilde{X}_0)/(\tilde{V}/\tilde{V}_0)\,. \tag{5.1}$$

Note that the unit productivity gain (g) is given by

$$1-(1/\pi) = 1-(\tilde{V}/\tilde{V}_0)/(\tilde{X}/\tilde{X}_0)\,. \tag{5.2}$$

10) Courbis [1972, June], [1972, December]. Additional remarks made here refer to Courbis [1972, December].

11) V is defined here as the current value of the total factor inputs.

The productivity gain ($\tilde{G}$) is defined by

$$\tilde{G} = \tilde{X} - \tilde{V}, \tag{5.3}$$

which is rewritten by

$$\tilde{G} = \tilde{X} - (\tilde{U} + \tilde{W} + \tilde{Y}), \tag{5.4}$$

remembering that

$$\tilde{V} = \tilde{U} + \tilde{W} + \tilde{Y}.$$

It should be noted that the productivity gain ($\tilde{G}$) differs from the adjustment term due to changes in productivity (G), which I have introduced in this article, in that

$$G = -\tilde{G}. \tag{5.5}$$

In other words, G indicates the productivity loss if $G>0$ and the productivity gain if $G<0$, as he correctly pointed out. Following his terminology, Y is decomposed into two elements: the first of which is denoted by K and represents the actual cost of physical capital input; the second is denoted by B which is residually determined and represents the pure profit.[12] Then, the productivity gain $\tilde{G}$ is written by

$$\tilde{G} = (\tilde{X}/\tilde{X}_0)[\tilde{U}_0 + \tilde{W}_0 + \tilde{K}_0] - [\tilde{U} + \tilde{W} + \tilde{K}] \tag{5.6}$$

denoting $\tilde{K}$ the constant value of K. Note that by definition

$$X_0 = U_0 + W_0 + K_0 + B_0.$$

(5.6) is reduced to

$$\tilde{G} = (\tilde{X}/\tilde{X}_0)[\tilde{X}_0 - \tilde{B}_0] - [\tilde{U} + \tilde{W} + \tilde{K}]$$

12) The decomposition of Y into K and B is theoretical. From the empirical view point, the determination of B is necessarily subject to the empirical measurement of K. The use of the concept of quasi-rents which I introduce below is entirely free from entangled measurement problems of capital inputs.

or

$$(5.7) \qquad \tilde{G} = \tilde{X} - [\tilde{U} + \tilde{W} + \tilde{K} + (\tilde{B}_0/\tilde{X}_0)\tilde{X}].$$

He contends by (5.7) that the unit margin (B/X) must be left unchanged for the calculation of G if we consider profit as a factor of production. In order to take into account the adjustment term due to changes in terms of trade, he introduce the balancing relation in constant values:

$$(5.8) \qquad \tilde{X} + \tilde{T} = \tilde{U} + \tilde{W} + \tilde{K} + \tilde{B},$$

$\tilde{B}$ being the constant value of B defined by $\tilde{B} = B/p_M$, where p_M stands for the "general price level" whose reciprocal is the real value of money unit. We have

$$(5.9) \qquad T = -\tilde{G} + [\tilde{B} - (\tilde{B}_0/\tilde{X}_0)\tilde{X}]$$

or

$$(5.10) \qquad T = -\tilde{G} + [\tilde{B} - \hat{B}].$$

$\hat{B}$ being the hypothetical benefit of current year with the fixed unit margin at the base year, i.e. $\hat{B} = (\tilde{B}_0/\tilde{X}_0)\tilde{X}$. It immediately follows from (5.10) that T is not necessarily absorbed into $-\tilde{G}$ for the reason that producers do not distribute completely the gains which result from amelioration of factor productivity and of the terms of trade. He also notes that T is not only the terms of trade gain but also incorporates a part of the total productivity gain commenting on (4.11) which is comparable with (5.10).

A new light is further shed on the point by looking upon (4.11) from a different outlook. Remembering (4.7), the quasi-rents in constant values ($\bar{R}$) is defined by

$$(5.11) \qquad \bar{R} = \bar{X} - (\bar{U} + \bar{W}) = \tilde{Y} - G.$$

$\bar{R}$ may be compared with $\tilde{Y}$, which can be regarded as the quasi-rents in constant values under the constant productivity. Then, (5.11) amounts to saying that the productivity gain in Courbis's sense can be measured by the deviation of the quasi-rents in constant values around that under the constant productivity. Note that

$$(1-\eta) = \mu/(1+\mu),$$

where $\mu = U_1/X_1$, which is the input coefficient of intermediate inputs in the current year. Inserting (5.11) and (5.5) into (4.11), it follows that

$$T+[1-(q_v/q_w)]\overline{W} = (1+\omega)\tilde{G}+\omega\bar{R}, \qquad (5.12)$$

where

$$\omega = (\mu/1+\mu)(p/p_u-1).$$

(5.12) states that the terms of trade effect corrected for the adjustment term of the productivity change resulting from labour input is expressed by a linear combination of the productivity gain and the real quasi-rents.[13] It should be remembered by (5.12) that the concept of real quasi-rents is firmly implanted in the measurment of the total productivity gain with which I am concerned in this section.

REFERENCES

J. B. Broderick, " National Accounts at Constant Prices ", *Review of Income and Wealth*, September 1967.

L. R. Christensen and D. W. Jorgenson, " U. S. Real Product and Real Factor Input, 1929–1967 ", *Review of Income and Weath*, March 1970.

---

13) It is interesting to note that the constants in (5.12) are formulated by the relative factor shares (in current values) with the correction for the unit gain or loss due to changes in relative prices between output and intermediate inputs.

M. R. Courbis, " Comptes économiques nationaux à prix constants ", *Etudes et conjoncture*, Juillet 1964.

M. R. Courbis, " Comptabilité nationale à prix constants et a productivité constante ", *Review of Income and Wealth*, March 1969.

M. R. Courbis, " Comment on Y. Kurabayashi: The Impact of Changes in Terms of trade on a System of National Accounts ", *Review of Income and Wealth*, June 1972.

M. R. Courbis, " Terms of Trade Effect, Productivity Change, and National Accounts in Constant Prices—A further comment ", *Review of Income and Wealth*, December 1972.

R. C. Geary, " Problems in the Deflation of National Accounts: Introduction ", *Income and Wealth*, Series IX, London 1961.

D. W. Jorgenson and Z. Griliches, " The Explanation of Productivity Change ", *Review of Economic Studies*, July 1967.

Y. Kurabayashi, " The Impact of Changes in Terms of Trade on a System of National Accounts: An Attempted Synthesis ", *Review of Income and Wealth*, September 1971.

Y. Kurabayashi, " Terms of Trade Effect, Productivity Change and National Accounts in Constant Prices—Reply and further comment ", *Review of Income and Wealth*, September 1972.

G. Stuvel, "Asset Revaluation and Terms of Trade Effects in the Framework of the National Accounts ", *Eco ıomic Journal*, June 1959.

3
FURTHER CONSIDERATIONS OF NATIONAL ACCOUNTS IN CONSTANT PRICES

1. Introduction

The double deflation method has often been recognized by national accounts specialists as one of the major stumbling blocks that impede the derivation of actual figures of constant values in national accounts aggregates albeit the apparent elegance of the method. The double deflation method particularly refers to the derivation of constant values of value added by industry breakdowns which are obtained from the subtraction of output in constant values from the intermediate inputs in constant values. Noting the failure of the empirical application of the method, economists often argue for the adoption of a much more simplified and efficient method. They insist that the single deflation method is superior to the double deflation in its easiness and it provides a proper candidate for the method of deflation. It has been sometimes disregarded by them that the derivation of constant values of value added by industry origins is closely associated with the formulation of production accounts by industries. The link becomes immediately clear if we look at the derivation of value added in constant values within the framework of an input-output table. Let us suppose the following input-output table.

	p	$\bar{p}$
p	q_iM_{ij}	q_iF_i
$\bar{p}$	v_jV_j	

In the input-output table, P and $\bar{P}$ denote the production activity and the rest of economic activities respectively. It is implicit in the table that the following accounting identities hold:

$$\text{(I)}\quad \sum_j q_i M_{ij} + q_i F_i = q_i Q_i \qquad \text{(II)}\quad \sum_i q_i M_{ij} + v_j V_j = q_j Q_j$$

In the input-output table, the following notations are employed:

	Quantum	*Price*
Output of j-th sector	Q_j	q_j
Intermediate inputs from i-th sector to j-th sector	M_{ij}	q_i
Final products of i-th sector	F_i	q_i
Value-added of j-th sector	V_j	v_j

It is noted here that v_j which follows from the double deflation method is implicitly determined.

Denoting that the deflated values are expressed by quantum variables suffixed with *, the derivation of the value-added of j-th sector by the double deflation method is expressed by the equation

(1) as indicated below:

$$(1) \qquad V_j^* = Q_j^* - \sum_i M_{ij}^*$$

Reflection of (1) immediately reveals that (1) expresses the production account of j-th sector in constant values. Indeed, v_j which follows from the double deflation method rests on the existence of the production account of j-th sector in constant values as is indicated in (1).

In what follows of this article the author attempts to clarify the nature of the double deflation method making comparison of it with the single deflation. He will also point out the intrinsic weakness of the double deflation method stating that the effect of changes in relative prices is necessarily incorporated within the derivation of the value-added by sectors which follows from the double deflation method. Then, he will proceed to develop Divisia index of value added by sectors which is derived from sector production accounts in constant prices. The approximate values of Divisia index which is obtainable from the aforementioned formulation yield the approximate value added in constant prices by the derivation. He will furthermore point out that the approximate value added thus derived is decomposed into the single deflated value added and its correction for the change in terms of trade between prices of intermediate inputs and those of primary factors. The article will be concluded with some remarks for the application of the method that the author proposes for the derivation of sector production accounts in constant prices.

2. The Single and Double Deflated Value Added by Production Sector

The sector production account on which (1) rests is written in current values at the base period by

$$(2) \qquad v_j(0)V_j'(0) = v_j(0)V_j''(0) = q_j(0)Q_j(0) - \sum_i q_i(0)M_{ij}(0) = q_j(0)Q_j(0)\cdot[1-\sum_i a_{ij}(0)],$$

where

$$a_{ij}(0) = \frac{q_i(0)M_{ij}(0)}{q_j(0)Q_j(0)}.$$

It is easy to see from (2) that in the base year the single deflated value added is identical with the double deflated value added.

The value added of j-th sector by the single deflation method is expressed by

$$(3) \qquad v_j(0)V_j'(1) = q_j(1)Q_j(1)[1-\sum_i a_{ij}(1)](q_j(0)/q_j(1)),$$

whereas the double deflated value added of j-th sector is written by

$$(4) \qquad v_j(0)V_j''(0) = q_j(0)Q_j(1) - \sum_i q_i(0)M_{ij}(1) = q_j(0)Q_j(1)[1-\sum_i a_{ij}^*(1)],$$

where

$$a_{ij}(1) = \frac{q_i(1)M_{ij}(1)}{q_j(1)Q_j(1)},$$

and

$$a_{ij}^*(1) = \frac{q_i(0)M_{ij}(1)}{q_j(0)Q_j(1)}.$$

It is supposed in the derivation of (3) and (4) that the deflated value added is measured at the period 1. Noting that

$$(5) \qquad a_{ij}^*(1)\frac{q_i(1)}{q_i(0)} = a_{ij}(1)\frac{q_j(1)}{q_i(0)},$$

the deviation of the single deflated value added for j-th sector from the double deflated value added is readily obtained from the following operation:

$$(6) \qquad v_j(0)[V_j'(1)-V_j''(1)] = q_j(0)Q_j(1)[\sum_i a_{ij}^*(1)-\sum_i a_{ij}(1)]$$
$$= q_j(0)Q_j(1)\sum_i [(1-(q_i(1)/q_i(0))/(q_j(1)/q_j(0))a_{ij}^*(1)]$$
$$= q_j(0)Q_j(1)(\sum_i r_{ij}a_{ij}^*(1)),$$

where r_{ij} in (6) stands for the unit gains or losses due to the change in terms of trade between i-th input and j-th ouput with which such national accounts specialists as Geary, Courbis and Kurabayashi have been concerned[1)] in the discussions for the formulation of national accounts in constant prices. It follows from (6) that the single deflated value added for j-th sector apparently deviates from the double deflated value added. The amounts of deviation are decomposed into two parts. They are: (1) constant value of j-th output and (2) j-th column sum of (intermediate) input coefficients (in constant prices) corrected by the unit gains or losses due to the change in terms of trade. Putting it in other words, the amounts of deviation of the single deflated value added from the double deflated value added for j-th sector are measured by the product of the constant value of j-th output by the j-th column sum of input coefficients which is corrected for the unit change in terms of trade. The result suggests that the value added derived either from the single deflation method or from the double deflation method suffers from the effect of changes in terms of trade

1) r_{ij} in (6) is expressed as below:

$$r_{ij} = 1-(q_i(1)/q_i(0))/q_j(1)/q_j(0))$$

The following articles are referred to the formulation of national accounts in constant prices: Geary [1961], Courbis [1964], [1969], and Kurabayashi [1971]. The essential portion of the discussion of these articles is contained in the 2nd essay of this volume.

between intermediate inputs and a sector output.

3. The Divisia Deflated Real Value Added in a Sector Production Account

The association of the value added in constant prices with the changes in terms of trade between intermediate inputs and output which has been pointed out in the preceeding section in fact reflects the change in terms of trade between primary factors and output. Indeed, it is readily seen in the Leontief open model, for an equilibrium set of prices, that unit profits for all production sectors are exactly zero and independent of an exogeneously given vector of final demands. Hence, putting w_0 the price of labour input we have

$$(7) \qquad q_j = \sum_i q_i a^*_{ij} + w_0 a^*_{0j},$$

where

$$a^*_{ij} = \frac{M_{ij}}{Q_j},$$

and a^*_{0j} stands for the coefficient of labour input for j-th sector. (8) immediately follows from (7).

$$(8) \qquad \frac{1 - \sum_i (q_i/q_j) a^*_{ij}}{a^*_{0j}} = \frac{w_0}{q_j}$$

The volume of single deflated value added is readily expressed in terms of a^*_{0j} and w_0/q_j using (8) as indicated below:

$$(9) \qquad V'_j = (1 - \sum_i a^{**}_{ij}) Q_j$$

$$= (1 - \sum_i \frac{q_i}{q_j} a^*_{ij}) Q_j = a^*_{0j} \left(\frac{w_0}{q_j} \right) Q_j \text{ [2]}$$

2) a^{**}_{ij} is defined as $a^{**}_{ij} = a^*_{ij}(q_i/q_j)$, which is directly comparable with a^*_{ij} (0) and a^*_{ij} (1) given in the preceding section.

An incremental index number of the form (10) is obtained from (9),

$$\frac{\Delta V'_j}{V'_j}=\frac{\Delta Q_j}{Q_j}-\frac{\sum_i \Delta(q_i/q_j)a^*_{ij}}{(1-\sum_i (q_i/q_j)a^*_{ij})} \tag{10}$$

Denoting μ_{ij} the ratio of i-th intermediate input to value added of j-th sector,

$$\mu_{ij}=\frac{(q_i/q_j)\,a^*_{ij}}{1-\sum_i (q_i/q_j)\,a^*_{ij}}=\frac{a^{**}_{ij}}{1-\sum_i a^{**}_{ij}}, \tag{11}$$

(10) is further transformed into (12).

$$\frac{\Delta V'_j}{V'_j}=\frac{\Delta Q_j}{Q_j}-\sum_i \frac{\Delta(q_i/q_j)}{(q_i/q_j)}\mu_{ij} \tag{12}$$

As the volume for value added of j-th sector which is obtainable from the double deflation method is expressed by

$$\begin{aligned} V''_j &= Q_j-\sum_i a^*_{ij}Q_j \\ &= (1-\sum_i a^*_{jj})Q_j\,, \end{aligned} \tag{13}$$

it is easy to show that

$$\frac{\Delta V''_j}{V''_j}=\frac{\Delta V'_j}{V'_j}+\sum_i \frac{\Delta(q_i/q_j)}{(q_i/q_j)}\mu_{ij}\,. \tag{14}$$

(14) amounts to saying that the incremental index number of the volume of value added of j-th sector which is derived from the double deflation method is composed of (i) the incremental index number of the volume for value added of j-th sector that is derived from the single deflation method and (ii) the weighted sum of the incremental index number for the relative prices between intermediate inputs and output, where μ_{ij} is used for the weight of i-th

intermediate input for ith output.[3]

Specifically, (14) may be presented in the form of an ordinary differential equation with respect to time, i.e.

$$(15) \qquad (dV_j''/dt)/V_j'' = (dV_j'/dt)/V_j' + \sum_i \mu_{ij}[(d(q_i/q_j)/dt)/(q_i/q_j)]\,.$$

Integration of (15) yields

$$(16) \qquad \frac{V_j''(t)}{V_j''(0)} = \frac{V_j'(t)}{V_j'(0)} \exp \int_0^t \sum \mu_{ij} d[\log (q_i/q_j)]/d\tau \cdot d\tau\,,$$

where $V_j''(0)$ and $V_j'(0)$ stand for the initial values of respective variables. The discrete approximation of (16) for $t=1$ is reduced to

$$(17) \qquad \frac{V_j''(1)}{V_j''(0)} = \frac{V_j'(1)}{V_j'(0)} \prod_i [(q_i(1)/q_i(0))/(q_j(1)/q_j(0))]^{\mu'_{ij}}$$

If the production sectors consist of n sectors, (17) may be expressed in detail by

---

3) Noting that

$$V_j' = (1-\sum_i (q_i/q_j)a_{ij}^*)\Delta Q_j - [\sum_i \Delta(q_i/q_j)a_{ij}^*]Q_j$$

and

$$\sum_i \Delta(q_i/q_j)(q_j/q_i)(q_i/q_j)a_{ij}^* = \sum_i \Delta(q_i/q_j)a_{ij}^*\,,$$

(12) is diret from (10). Similarly, noting that

$$\Delta V_j'' = (1-\sum_i a_{ij}^*)\Delta Q_j$$

the following relation is readily seen:

$$\Delta V_j''/V_j'' = \Delta Q_j/Q_j\,. \qquad (*)$$

(12) and (*) yield (14) immediately. In the derivation of (12) and (14) changes in a_{ij}^* are disregarded for the sake of brevity. The results would not be influenced if the changes in a_{ij}^* were taken into account.

It should be noted that the sum of weights in (14) not necessarily adds up to unity, because

$$\sum_i \mu_{ij} = \sum_i a_{ij}^*/(1-\sum_i a_{ij}^*)\,.$$

$$(17)' \quad I''_V = I'_V[(P_1/P_j)^{\mu'_{1j}}......(P_n/P_j)^{\mu'_{nj}}]$$

where

$$\mu'_{ij} = 1/2\,[\mu_{ij}(0)+\mu_{ij}(1)]\,,$$
$$I''_V = V''_j(1)/V''_j(0), \qquad I'_V = V'_j(1)/V'_j(0)\,,$$
$$P_i = q_i(1)/q_i(0)\,, \qquad P_j = q_j(1)/q_j(0)\,.$$

Reflection of (17)′ shows that the double deflated quantum index for value added of j-th sector is virtually reduced to a form of Divisia index that is constituted by the single deflated quantum index for value added of the same sector with the correction of the terms of trade effect which is indicated by the term within a parenthesis of (17)′. As the derivation of (16) amounts to implying that the process of the double deflation is successively carried out in a fixed time interval of [0, t], the value added in constant prices derived from (16) or (17) is termed here the Divisia deflated real value added.

Using (17) an approximate value of the Divisia deflated real value added for j-th sector is obtained from

$$(18) \quad v_j(0)\,V''_j(1) = v_j(0)\,V''_j(0)\,I'_V[\prod_i (P_i/P_j)^{\mu'_{ij}}]$$
$$= v_j(0)\,V'_j(0)\,I'_V[\prod_i (P_i/P_j)^{\mu'_{ij}}]\,.$$

The product of the first three terms of the right-hand side of (18) denotes the single deflated value added, whereas the term in the parenthesis stands for the correction for the changes in terms of trade to which the reference is made in the preceeding section.

Though I have no intention to go into the detailed properties of Divisia index on which increased attention has been centred by such well-known economists as Roy, Richter, Jorgenson and Griliches, Samuelson and Swamy, Sato and others, some points deserve to be made in connection with the formulation of national accounts in constant prices.[4]

It has been shown by Sato that the Divisia index of real value added is reduced to its unique functional index $X(t)$ which is generated by the following functional relation

$$X(t) = X(Y_1(t), \ldots\ldots, Y_n(t)),$$

associated with

$$y_i(t) = (\partial X(t)/\partial Y_i(t))\lambda(t),$$

where $\lambda(t)$ is independent of i $(=1, \ldots, n)$, being X a generalized homothetic function.[5] Thus, the Divisia deflated value added index derived from (17)′ acquires the property of functional index. The Divisia deflated real value added unfolds a new aspect of national accounts in constant prices by accomodating them with the aspect of the functional index which was left untouched in

4) See, in particular, Roy [1970], Jorgenson and Griliches [1968], Samuelson and Swamy [1974], Sato [1976], Hulten [1973], Sims [1969] and Usher [1974].

5) I owe the point to Professor K. Sato. It is implicit in the construction of the Divisia deflated value added that the primary factors are separable from the intermediate inputs in the underlying production function from which the value added is generated. Apparently, the input-output framework on which our entire analysis rests satisfies the requirement of the separability condition. As has been pointed out by Sato's work, the generalized homotheticity of the production relation allows us to introduce arbitrarily factors of production into the production relation. Letting X and Y_i stand for the output and the factors of production respectively, suppose the factors of production are grouped into the primary inputs and the intermediate products, which are specified by the first m factors of Y_i $(i=I, \ldots\ldots, n$ and $n>m)$. Then, it is interesting to see, under the constraint of the generalized homotheticity of the production relation, that the value added function is generated by

$$X = X(Y_1, \ldots\ldots, Y_m).$$

Consideration of the generalized homotheticity of the production relation also shows that a profit function or the production function with technical change is generated by the specification of inputs that are included in the argument of the production function.

the preceding article.

It is true that the double deflation has its own weakness in that it necessarily incorporates the terms of trade effect emerging from the changes in prices between intermediate inputs and output of a sector, but it should also be noted that the double deflation method has the distinct advantage that it always ensures the internal consistency concerning the GDP=GDE identity in constant prices. One would have to pay a rather heavy cost that could not bear for the valid formulation of national accounts in constant prices if one were forced to renounce the internal consistency. Note that the derivation of the Divisia deflated value added formulated by (17) is under the restraint of (13). Then, it is apparent to us that the Divisia deflated value added is definitely immune from the lack of the internal consistency of national accounts in constant values.

4. The Approximation of the Divisia Deflated Real Value Added

The advantage of using (18) for the derivation of the Divisia deflated value added in constant prices is twofold. First, the approximation estimates the Divisia deflated value added in constant prices without knowing quantum inputs of intermediate products from other production sectors. Second, the approximation takes in its consideration the effect of changes in terms of trade between intermediate inputs and the sector output. It is essential for the approximation that the value of μ'_{ij} is correctly determined. But, it may be not infrequently the case that the terminal value of μ'_{ij}, i.e. $\mu'_{ij}(1)$, is not available at the date of the measurement of constant value. Indeed, to give the terminal value of μ'_{ij} one would demand the information on input-output table at the time of comparison, and the annual compilation of detailed input-output table would require enormous amounts of statistical work. Taking into account the limited availability of the information of input-output table, for the application of (18) it is necessary to replace μ'_{ij} by a reasonable approximation.

The easiest approximation of μ'_{ij} is to assume that μ'_{ij} does not suffer from an intertemporal change. The assumption implies that

$$(19) \qquad \mu'_{jj} = \mu_{ij} .$$

Under the assumption of (19) it particularly deserves to be noted that the production function on which the approximation of the Divisia deflated real value added by (18) rests, is reduced to the following Klein-Rubin type:

$$(20) \qquad Q_i = (V_i)^{1-\Sigma \mu_{ij}} \prod M_{ij}^{\mu_i} .$$

The application of (18) for the derivation of the Divisia deflated value added on the assumption of (19) is straightforward.

In the past decade much sophisticated approach for the approximation has been proposed by R. Stone and his followers. Their method of approximation is often termed by them the RAS or biproportional input-output model. According to the method, the intertemporal change in input-output coefficients is formulated by

$$(21) \qquad a_{ij}^{**}(1) = r_i a_{ij}^{**}(0) s_j ,$$

where r_i and s_j are factors to account for the " substitution effect " between intermediate inputs and the " fabrication effect " for a particular commodity output respectively.[6)]

Denoting

$$(21) \qquad \delta_{ij} = \frac{1}{2}[\mu_{ij}(1) - \mu_{ij}(0)] ,$$

μ'_{ij} is written by

(22) $\mu'_{ij} = \mu_{ij}(0) + \delta_i$.

As an approximation to a_{ij}^{**} (1) it may be reasonable to assume that

(23) $a_{ij}^{**}(1) = ra_{ij}^{**}(0)s_j$.

The assumption (23) implies that the intertemporal change in input-output coefficients is strongly biproportional in the sense that the substitution effect takes place between the groups of intermediate inputs and primary inputs. Putting it in other words, the group of intermediate inputs is, under the assumption of (23), separable from the group of primary inputs in the argument of the production function and the substitution effect is manifested between the two groups of factors of production. Noting that δ_{ij} is written by

$$\delta_{ij} = \frac{1}{2}\left[\frac{a_{ij}^{**}(1)(1-\sum_i a_{ij}^{**}(0)) - a_{ij}^{**}(0)(1-\sum_i a_{ij}^{**}(1))}{(1-\sum_i a_{ij}^{**}(0))(1-\sum_i a_{ij}^{**}(1))}\right],$$

it is easy to show that μ'_{ij} is expressed in terms of the initial value of parameters:

(24) $$\mu'_{ij} = \mu_{ij}(0)\left[1 - \frac{1-rs_j}{2(1-rs_j\sum_i a_{ij}^{**}(0))}\right]$$

It is a matter of empirical testing whether the assumption (23) is effectively applicable for the derivation of the Divisia deflated real value added which is derived from (18). The test will be submitted to further empirical research waiting for the availability of the annual time series data on the input-output tables.

5. Acknowledgements

In writing with this article my deep aprreciation is due to Professor Kazuo Sato who gave me valuable comments on the earlier ver-

6) See, in particular, Bacharach [1970].

sion of this article entitled " The Double Deflation Method, Divisia Index and National Accounts in Constant Prices ", March 1975, mimeographed, which was motivated by my response to his earlier draft of highly stimulating work (Sato [1976]). Needless to say, remaining errors and misstatements in this article are responsible for me.

REFERENCES

M. Bacharach, *Biproportional Matrices and Input-Output Change*, Cambridge 1970.

Raymond Courbis, " Comptes économiques nationaux à prix constants ", *Etudes et Conjoncture*, Juillet 1964.

Raymond Courbis, " Comptabilité nationale à prix constants et à productivité constante ", *Review of Income and Wealth*, March 1969.

R. C. Geary, " Problems in the Deflation of National Accounts: Introduction ", *Income and Wealth*, Series IX, London 1961.

R. C. Geary, " Reflections on National Accounting ", *Review of Income and Wealth*, September 1973.

D. Jorgenson and Z. Griliches, " The Explanation of Productivity Change ", *Review of Economic Studies*, July 1968.

C. R. Hulten, " Divisia Index Numbers ", *Econometrica*, November 1973.

Y. Kurabayashi, " The Impact of Changes in Terms of Trade on a System of National Accounts ", *Review of Income and Wealth*, September 1971.

M. Richter, " Invariance Axioms and Economic Indexes ", *Econometrica*, October 1966.

Rene Roy, *Elements d'économétrie*, Paris 1970.

P. A. Samuelson and S. Swamy, " Invariant Economic Index Numbers as Canonical Duality: Survey and Synthesis ", *American Economic Review*, September 1974.

K. Sato, " The Meaning and Measurement of the Real Value Added Index ", *Review of Economics and Statictics*, November 1976.

C. Sims, " Theoretical Basis for a Double-Deflated Index of Real Value Added ", *Review of Economics and Statistics*, November 1969.

D. Usher, " The Suitability of the Divisia Index for the Measurement of Economic Aggregates ", *Review of Income and Wealth*, September 1974.

III.

APPLICATION OF NATIONAL ECONOMIC ACCOUNTING

4

THE STRUCTURE OF INCOME REDISTRIBUTION WITHIN AN EXTENDED SYSTEM OF NATIONAL ACCOUNTS

1. Introduction

1. In what follows we shall be concerned with the structure of income redistribution between the market sector and the public sector within the framework of an extended system of national accounts. In section 2 the function of government activities will be discussed. The author postulates the sectoring of the market sector at large and the public sector on account of the genuine function of government activities. The discussion in this section ends with the presentation of a system of extended national accounts which provides a basis for the fuller analysis of income redistribution to follow. The structure of income redistribution will receive thorough treatment in section 3. The author points out that the distinction between the primary distribution and the redistribution of factor income is of extreme importance to the structure of income redistribution. He also argues that the struc-

ture of income redistribution is thoroughly exhibited by some important sub-matrices which are derived from the matrix of a system of national accounts presented in section 2. The section is concluded by offering some comments on the classification of transfer concepts. In the appendix, the structure of the redistribution of primary income receives thorough consideration for its use as the theoretical basis of the measures of income inequality.

2. The Function of Government Activities and their Scope

In order to make clear the structure of income redistribution made between the market sector at large and the public sector it is necessary to draw a clear line to distinguish the public sector from the market sector. The scope and definition of the public sector are deeply rooted in the functions performed by various government authorities with which we are concerned at the outset of the discussions that follow in this section. The activities of those government authorities exert many and diverse influences not only on the market sector but also on the economy as a whole, through various channels. Broadly speaking, the functions performed by the government agencies at various levels may be grouped into three major categories. They are: (i) the supply of public goods and services, (ii) the redistribution of income by the enforced and/or contracted transfer of income for administering the economic and social policy aiming at the advancement of well-being of the public and (iii) taking the leading role for shaping and implementing of the fiscal and financial measures. The first function of government activities has long been considered the intrinsic and genuine role of the government. Classical economists were in favour of the cheap government of 'Night Watch State' limiting its intervention into the private economy and its budget to the extent that the people can bear the burden of the cost and tolerate the intervention. In this situation, it naturally follows that the major function of government activities is to provide a minimum supply of public goods and services so as to produce the stable public order for the safety of the people. However, the emergence of the 'Welfare State' and Keynesian economics after the turn of the century has completely changed the picture. The government activities are closely knitted with those activities which are initiated by the market economy, thus necessarily inviting the intervention of government activities into the private economy. The institution of the 'Welfare State' has made it necessary to introduce vast schemes of, and arrangements for, social security which call for deliberate transfer of income by the government, both at the central and at the local levels, to finance these schemes and arrangements. Keynesian economics has supplied us with effective instruments for regulating and controling business cycles creating (or contracting) effective demands channelled through fiscal and financial measures. In this situation, the second and third functions of government activities appear in the centre on the stage. The deficits of the government budget have changed its character transforming them from vice into virtue. The scope of he public sector, which is distinguished from the market sector, varies with these changing functions of government activities which will be explored at some length in what follows.

The genuine role of government activities in the first function lies in the supply of public goods and services which are neither produced nor supplied by private agents. The public goods and services are often defined as those goods and services whose marginal utility for an economic agent is equal to that for others; they are thus essentially for collective use by the public. In other words, the public goods and services may be defined as those goods and services which satisfy the collective wants for the community as a whole. The essential nature of the collective wants is that they cannot split up for the need of one specific individual excluding the satisfaction of other people's need. The examples of such collective wants are the maintenance of justice and order and the security and defense of the community. There exist, of course, some collective wants which fall into border-line cases. The collective wants for health and education may be cited as such cases. In principle the improvement of health and sanitary condition of the community, for example, may be directed to the need of specific individuals. It may be also the case that the health service is conveniently and economically supplied by a private individual. In spite of these possibilities medical cares of the community tend to rely heavily on those services which are organized by the government agencies, as social security schemes are widely introduced by the central and local government. Although the condition is somewhat different in satisfying wants for education, the reliance on the state or local budgets for financing the supply of these educational services by private institutions has become a growing tendency in many countries. Despite the obscurity of such border-line cases it is claimed that the concept of public goods and services remains a useful concept for describing the nature of government activities.

Related to the supply of public goods and services, a few additional comments are worth making. First, as one of the internationally standardized system of national accounts carefully states, these public goods and services are organized by the public authorities 'not normally to sell' for the community. This statement suggests that the supply schedule of the public goods and services may not be aptly explained by the theory of optimum production. One may insist that the public authorities could be looked as if they were the unit of decision making which purports to attain its optimum, because for these public authorities tax rates could play a part similar to the prices of common goods and services. It has been maintained by Lindahl that the community can attain the Pareto optimum provided that the community's tax rates are determined such levels that they may be equitable and acceptable. But the determination of optimum tax rates cannot be explained only by the optimum behaviour of the public authorities. As some economists have already argued, the question of 'powers' of socio-economic groups which constitute the community and the bargaining process between these groups exerts strong influence on the determination of the tax rates.[1] The requirement that the optimum tax rates must be determined exogeneously is a consequence of the non-existence of market for the public goods and services. It may be concluded from this brief discussion that non-marketability of public goods and services bears deep significance on the analysis of government activities. In the publication of the revised SNA non-marketable commodities such as the public goods and services are conceptually distinguished from marketable commodities. This indicates the fact that the nature of public goods and services must attract special attention when fitting them into the conceptual framework of national accounts in an explicit manner.

Second, in view of the fact that the supply of public goods and services for satisfying collective wants is largely financed by tax revenues, their supply exerts strong influence on the income distribution of the community through direct and indirect channels.

1) For the earlier discussions to formulate the optimum tax rates, see Johansen [1965]. Revived interests in exploring the theoretical reformulation of the optimum tax have recently called much attention of economists, particularly Phelps [1973] and Atkinson [1973].

The disposable incomes of both corporations and households are subject to changes brought about by the direct taxes on their primary factor incomes. The income distribution of the community is also influenced by changes in marked prices caused by the incidence of indirect taxes. It should be noted that the effect of the supply of public goods and services on the income distribution of the community is of no less importance for the analysis of government activities.

Placing special emphasis on the first function of government activities, it is contended in the revised SNA that those government authorities which are in charge of the supply of public goods and services be grouped into the category of the producers of government services which is sharply distinguished from the notion of the general government adopted in the old SNA. The concept of the producers of government services, simultaneously introduced, together with the concept of the producers of private non-profit services to households, is invented by the revised SNA for instituting the production structure of non-marketable goods and services into a system of national accounts. More specifically, in the production structure of the producers of government services, the value of their gross output is put to be equal to the costs of producing these services, which, in turn, are composed of outlays on the intermediate consumption of goods and services and of the value added originating from the production.[2] As, theoretically, little is known about the production correspondence of inputs and outputs for the production of such non-marketable commodities as government services, we are compelled to swallow down the assumption that the gross output of such non-marketable commodities is put, as a general rule, to be equal to the costs of pro-

2) See, in particular, the United Nations [1968], section 6.41.

ducing them. It is true that the introduction of the concept of the producers of both government and private non-profit services adds a considerable degree of complication to the production structure of the economy displayed in a system of national accounts, but it must be recognized that the recognition of non-marketable goods and services in the production structure of a system of national accounts undoubtedly makes a definite step towards the new theoretical formulation of the production of non-marketable goods and services.[3)]

The concept of the general government is especially reserved, in this article, for specifying the second and third functions of government activities; it includes those government agencies which actively take part in the second and third functions of government activities within the scope of the public sector. Applying the concept of the general government to actual Japanese institutions, the following classification may be made:

Categories and Sub-categories	*Comments*
(1) Central Government	
(1. 1.) General Accounts	
(1. 2.) Special Accounts	Included here is the Special Accounts for Foreign Exchange, but Postal Saving Special Accounts, Accounts for Governmental Life Insurance and Government Funding Department are excluded. Special Account

3) The critical appraisal of the United Nations system of national accounts with their counter proposal of a system of national economic accounts is given by Ruggles and Ruggles [1970]. It appears that the production structure of non-marketable goods and services attracts less attention in their work than SNA.

		for Food Management is also excluded.
(1. 3.)	Government Special Corporations	Public corporations, Governmental Unincorporated Units and Public Financial Institutions are, as a general rule, excluded here.
(2)	Local Government	
(2. 1.)	Regular Accounts	
(2. 2.)	Public Business Accounts	Those which refer to the supply of gas, electricity and transporation services to the community are excluded, but those which are concerned with the supply of water, medical and hospital services are included.
(2. 3.)	Ancillary Local Agencies	Local Corporations for the Development of Land and Roads and those for the Supply of Housing are excluded.
(3)	Social Security Funds	
(3. 1.)	Special Accounts for Social Insurance	
(3. 2.)	Mutual Assistance Associations	
(3. 3.)	Pension Funds	Welfare Pension Funds and similar institutional Pension Funds such as Farmers Pension Funds, Coal Miners

		Pension Funds etc. are included here.
(3. 4.)	Health Insurance Associations	
(3. 5.)	Welfare Services by Mutual Assistance Association	

The concept of either the producers of government services or the general government is a device for portraying the genuine role of government activities in a system of national accounts clearly distinguishing it from activities that are essentially associated with the market economy at large. In this respect, it seems pertinent to call the group of those economic agents which are essentially associated with the activities of the market economy at large *the market sector at large*. It should be noted that public enterprises and public financial corporations are included in the market sector at large, because their activities are essentially motivated for 'producing goods and services for sale in the market at a price that is normally designed to cover the costs of production'. The activities associated with the market sector at large are contrasted with those which refer to what is termed *the public sector* which incorporate both the producers of government services and the general government. The breakdown of the economy into the market sector at large and the public sector should provide an appropriate conceptual basis for the analysis of income redistribution.

As a point of departure of fitting the government activities into a general conceptual framework of national accounts it is sufficiently meaningful that the pubilc sector be distinguished from the market sector at large. In the light of the sector breakdown, a

Table 1. A system of extended national accounts

			Domestic Economy														Rest of the World
activities			production		formation of income				consumption of income		capital formation		capital financing				
	sector		I	II	I		II		I	II	I	II	I		II		
activities	sector	no. \ no.	1	2	3	4	5	6	7	8	9	10	11	12	13	14	15
Domestic Economy: production	I	1	U^{I}						C^{I}		V^{I}	V^{II}					E^{I}
	II	2		U^{II}						C^{II}							
formation of income	I	3	Q^{I}														Z^{I}
		4			P^{I}			G^{II}									
	II	5		Q^{II}													Z^{II}
		6	T			G^{I}	P^{II}										
consumption of income	I	7				Y^{I}											
	II	8						Y^{II}									
capital formation	I	9	D^{I}											J^{I}			
	II	10		D^{II}												J^{II}	
capital financing	I	11												F^{I}			
		12							S^{I}				N^{I}		K^{I}		K^{I}
	II	13														F^{II}	
		14								S^{II}				K^{II}	N^{II}		K^{II}
Rest of the World		15	I^{I}	I^{II}		G^{I}		G^{II}						B^{I}		B^{II}	

The following notations are used in the table.

- B: net lending to the rest of the world
- C: purchases of goods and services for consumption
- D: capital consumption allowances
- E: sales of goods and services to the rest of the world
- F: flow of financial claims as assets
- G: transfer of factor income
- I: purchases of goods and services from the rest of the world
- J: net domestic capital formation
- K: flow of capital transfer (net)
- N: flow of financial claims as liabilities
- P: net national product at factor income
- Q: net domestic product at factor income S: saving
- T: indirect taxes minus subsidies U: flow of intermediate products
- V: gross domestic capital formation Y: disposable income
- Z: receipts of factor income from the rest of the world

system of extended national accounts specifically designed for focusing on the process of the redistribution of income from the public sector to the market sector at large and in the opposite direction is displayed in Table 1. In the table, the flow of goods and services (real objects) and of financial claims (financial objects) is portrayed on the two parts of territory called *the domestic economy* and *the rest of the world.* It would be quite unnecessary to go into the definition of the terminology of the territory which is given in the internationally acclaimed *Balance of Payments Manual* of the IMF.[4] Four major economic activities are distinguished in the table. They are: (i) production, (ii) consumption, (iii) capital formation and (iv) capital financing. It is in the further breakdown of the consumption activity that we can touch the heart of the redistribution of income, because the process of the redistribution of income occurs in the course of the formation of income and the consumption of income, as we shall see in the next section. The public sector and the market sector at large, into which the economy is subdivided, are denoted by Roman figures for simplification. I stands for the market sector at large and II for the public sector. It may be often required that the market sector at large be further sub-divided into sub-sectors for more detailed analysis. If this may be the case, the following classification may be conceivable, particularly paying regard to the second and third functions of government activities.

(1) non-financial business enterprises
(2) financial institutions
(3) households
(4) private non-profit institutions

4) See, International Monetary Funds [1961].

3. Sub-matrices that Represent The Structure of Income Redistribution

We have noted in the preceding section the significance of the supply of public goods and services from the viewpoint of the income distribution of the community. In order to make the process of income formation and redistribution of income clear, it is extremely useful that the formation of income be subdivided into two stages as we have made in the construction of the matrix in Table 5. The first of these may be termed the primary distribution of factor income which describes the process of distribution of net product to factors of production and formation of factor income. Second of these may be termed the redistribution of factor income, which describes the process of redistribution of factor income between recipients and spending units of factor income. The primary distribution of factor income for the market sector at large and the public sector is represented by the row (and column) 3 and 5 in Table 1 respectively. Similarly, the redistribution of factor income is represented by the rows (and columns) 4 and 6 in the same table.

Suppose that the row (and column) 1 in Table 1 is further subdivided in a number of production sectors and that the row (and column) 3 in the same table is also subdivided according to a number of types of factor income. Then it easily turns out that Q^{I} in Table 1, which stands for the net domestic product originated from the market sector at large, constitutes a rectangular submatrix whose row and column distinguish types of factor income and production sectors respectively. In detail, the matrix is written as indicated in Table 2.

It is generally recognized that the major categories of factor income are formed by (i) the compensation of employees and (ii) the operat-

Table 2. The sub-matrix of the factor income originated in the market sector $[q_{pq}{}^{I}]$

row no. \ column no.		1
row no.	sector	production sectors
3	types of factor incomes	$q_{11}{}^{I} \cdots q_{1q}{}^{I}$ $\vdots \quad \vdots$ $q_{p1}{}^{I} \cdots q_{pq}{}^{I}$

ing surplus. In this regard, the structure of the primary distribution of factor income and its sub-division implies that the concept of property income be classified as a kind of transfer as SNA clearly formulates stating that ' property income may be defined as the actual and imputed transfers of income resulting from the use by one economic agent of the financial assets, land and intangible assets, such as copyrights and patents, owned by another economic agent '.[5)]

The factor income originated from the production sectors are distributed to the recipients of factor income through the process of the primary distribution of factor income. In Table 1 this process is essentially characterized by a transformation of Q^{I} into P^{I}. Formally speaking, the transformation of a matrix Q^{I} into P^{I} may be represented by

$$Q^{I} \cdot \Pi = P^{I} ,$$

5) The United Nations]1968], section 7.46.

Table 3. The sub-matrix of the factor income received by the market sector $[p_{rp}{}^{I}]$

row no.	column no. / sector	3
		types of factor income
4	recipi-ents of income	$p_{11}{}^{I}$ ········· $p_{1p}{}^{I}$ ⋮ ⋮ $p_{r1}{}^{I}$ ········· $p_{rp}{}^{I}$

where Π stands for a permutation matrix.[6] Suppose the row (and column) 4 is further subdivided according to a number of recipients of factor income. As the column 3 is already subdivided into types of factor income, P^{I} is consequently expressed by a sub-matrix whose row and column indicate the classification of factor income according to its recipients and to its types respectively. In detail, the matrix is written as Table 3.

A variety of principles to be applied to the classification of the recipients of factor income is conceivable. It is reasonable and practical to consider that the household constitutes the basic statistical unit of the recipients of factor income. The individual may be considered in his (or her) relation to respective household as one aspect of the statistical unit of the recipients of factor income. Broadly speaking, a set of households is sub-divided into

6) A permutation matrix is such non-negative matrix that has one element of 1 with remaining elements 0 in each row and column.

sub-sets: (i) a set of one-person households and (ii) a set of multi-person households respectively. The sub-division of a set of households according to the size of their constituent members is basic for the analysis of the old-aged households, a considerable portion of which fall into the first category of the sub-division. The sub-division may be subject to further detailed breakdown according to the composition of households. An example of such detailed breakdown is given in the United Nations document of proposing *A Draft System of Statistics of the Distribution of Income, Consumption and Accumulation.*[7]

The grouping of households according to prescribed income classes is one possible principle of popular usage. Two possibilities are, as a general rule, conceivable for counting the income level as the measuring rod of the grouping. First, the total of household income may be used for the determination of the income level. In the second place, the income level of the head of the household may be applicable. In the grouping, the class interval of a number of household groups is formulated on the basis of fractile grouping or on the absolute magnitude of income level. In the case of first possibility, it may be useful to classify the households, particularly of multi-person households, according to the status of earners such that (i) earner, the head of household, (ii) earners, the head of household and his (or her) spouse, (iii) earners, the head of household and other household members except spouse and (iv) earners, the head of household, his (or her) spouse and other household members. The grouping of households doubly classified according to appropriately prescribed income classes and to the earning status of households could add a new dimension to the analysis of the structure of the primary distribution of factor

7) See, the United Nations [1972].

income.[8]

The introduction of demographic factors into the grouping of households further deserves ponderable consideration. In particular, the grouping of households according to the age of the head of the household may be useful. As we shall see in the later articles, the age groups are so constituted that they could distinguish the major turning points in one's personal life cycle.[9] Following classification by age groups may be conceivable.

(i) below 15 years
(ii) 15–19 years
(iii) 20–24 years
(iv) 25–29 years
(v) 30–39 years
(vi) 40–49 years
(vii) 50–54 years
(viii) 55–59 years
(ix) 60–64 years
(x) 65 years and over

The classification of households by size and composition of households also provides valuable information not only for the analysis of the structure of the primary distribution of factor income but

8) The compilation of statistics doubly classified according to income classes and to the earning status of households is available from *National Survey of Family Income and Expenditure* by Bureau of Statistics. The Survey has been introduced in 1959 and carried out every three years to supply the most comprehensive information concerning the structure of households budgets. The most recent Survey (1974) sampled about 53,000 households, among which 3,600 are one-person households. The period of the Survey refers to the three-month period begining with September and ending with November of the year of Survey. See, Bureau of Statistics [1976].

9) The point will be taken up in 7th article of this volume. It should be also recalled that the demographic factors receive thorough consideration in the last article of this volume.

also for the generation of its redistribution, as we shall see later. An example of the grouping of households according to their composition is taken from 1974 *National Survey of Family Income and Expenditure*.

(1) married couple or married couple with unmarried children
(2) married couple with unmarried children and their relatives, excluding their parents
(3) one of parents with unmarried children
    (3. 1.) mother with children below 18 years
    (3. 2.) others
(4) Married couple with their parents or married couple with their children and their parents
    (4. 1.) Husband as the head of household
    (4. 2.) Parents as the head of household
    (4. 3.) Others
(5) Married couple with one of their parents or married couple with children and one of their parents
    (5. 1.) Husband as the head of household
    (5. 2.) Others
(6) Households living with their employees and others

The grouping of households according to the occupation of the household head or so-called socio-economic classes may constitute another possibility of the classification. The classification of households according to the occupation of the head of the household is commonly in use in the family budgets surveys in Japan. The following table (Table 4) shows an example of the classification of households by occupational groups with definition and contents taken from 1974 *National Survey of Family Income and Expenditure*. The classification of households by socio-economic classes has been proposed in the United Nations document (E/CN.3/425). As it is a classification built on the mixture of different social and eco-

Table 4. Classification of occupations

1) Tabulated only for two or more person households.
2) Tabulated only for one-person households.
Note: This classification excludes farmers households mainly engaged in agriculture etc.

Type of Household			Classfication	Definition	Examples
All Households	Workers' Households	Labourers	Regular	Includes manual labourers who are employed in governmental or non-governmental corporations with a long term contract.	Coal sorters, draftsmen, metal finishers, electro-communication operators, driver, crews, conductors, deliverymen, shopmen, sweepers, guards, servants, carpenters, domestic maids, etc.
			Day	Includes manual labourers who are employed in governmental or non-governmental corporations with daily or less than 30 day's contracts.	
		Office workers	Private	Includes wage earners and salaried employees who are employed in non-governmental mines, factories, shops, hospitals, schools, etc. and engaged in clerical, technical or administrative activities.	Typists, telephone operators, nurses, clerks, section chief, physicians, architects, judges, school teachers, policemen, captains, railway conductors, journalists, traveling salesmen, photographers, radio announcers, etc.
			Government	Includes wage earners and salaried employees who are employed in governmental offices, hospitals, schools, etc. and engaged in clerical, technical or administrative activities.	

All Households	Other Households	Individual proprietors	Merchants and artisans	Includes managerial staff of unincorporated or incorporated manufacturing, wholesale, retail or services firms which employ four or less employees.	Cigarette stores, candy stores, haberdasheries, picture story tellers, peddlers, brokers, pedicabmen, pawnshops, barbershops, carpenters, scaffold workers, shoe blacks, gardeners, etc.
			Private administrators	Includes managerial staff of unincorporated manufacturing, wholesale, retail or services firms which employ five or more employees.	Private hospital managers, private school managers, etc.
		Others	Corporae administrators	Includes managerial staff of incorporated manufacturing, wholesale, retail or services firms which employ five or more employees.	Presidents, directors, inspectors, trustees, ministers, governors, prefectural governors, parliamentary vice-ministers, mayors, etc.
			Professional services	Includes those who apply special skill or knowledge to their jobs.	Advocates, accountants, tax attorneys, medical practitioners, midwives, priests, painters, writers, fortune-tellers, composers.
			Others	Includes those who cannot be classified in any other groups mentioned above.	Models, professional athletes, actors and actresses, assemblymen, etc.
			With absent head for a long time	Includes households whose head is away from his home for a long period.	
			No occupation		Unemployed, pensioners, etc.
			Without earner[1]	No earner, among household members.	
			Aged not working[2]	Aged persons of 60 years or more.	
Regrouped			Farmers' households[1]	Households with cultivated land of o.1 ha (0.3 ha in case of Hokkaido) or more, excluding those whose head is solely or mainly engaged in agriculture, forestry or fishery.	

nomic characteristics to classify households, the meaning of socio-economic classes is not always so luminous as it allows us to use it as a guiding principle for the grouping of households. Additional experiments to determine effective characteristics, both social and economic, that exert decisive influences on the formation of such socio-economic classes should be necessary, no matter how the terminology of the socio-economic classes may be conveniently defined. The application of the statistical theory of the multi-variate analysis could be a powerful apparatus for the experiments.

The factor income distributed among its recipients through the process of the primary distribution of factor income is, moreover, redistributed between the recipients and spending units of income. The redistribution of factor income is essentially characterized as a transfer of purchasing power from the recipients to the spending units of income. Thus, various types of transfer of factor income take a leading part in the process of the redistribution of factor income. Two concepts are closely associated with the redistribution of factor income. They are (i) the transfer of factor income and (ii) the disposable income. The transfer of factor income is defined here as a unilateral transfer of purchasing power in the form of factor income from the recipients to the spending units of factor income and is often called the income (or current) transfer. The transfer of factor income is distinguished from the capital transfer which is characterized as a unilateral transfer of purchasing power that is directly related to acquisition of assets and liabilities. Taking into account the transfer of factor income between the recipients and spending units of factor income, the disposable income is derived from the factor income. Supposing that the row (and column) 6 is further subdivided according to the government agencies as recipients of factor income, the transfers of factor income between the market sector at large and the public soctor

Table 5. The sub-matrices of income transfers between the market sector and the public gsector

$[g_{rt}^{II}]$

row no. \ column no.	sector	6
		government agencies as recipients of income
4	recipients of income	$g_{11}^{II} \cdots g_{1t}^{II}$ $\vdots \quad \vdots$ $g_{r1}^{II} \cdots g_{rt}^{II}$

$[g_{tr}^{I}]$

row no. \ column no.	sector	4
		recipients of income
6	government agencies as recipients of income	$g_{11}^{I} \cdots g_{1r}^{I}$ $\vdots \quad \vdots$ $g_{t1}^{I} \cdots g_{tr}^{I}$

(G^{II} and G^{I}) are expressed in matrices as indicated in Table 5. A sub-matrix which expresses the disposable income of the market sector at large is easily derived from the matrices $[p_{rp}^{I}]$, $[g_{rt}^{II}]$ and $[g_{tr}^{I}]$. It clearly indicates that the redistribution of primary income is made between the recipients and the spending units of income, because the row and column of this matrix stand for the spending units and the recipients of income respectively. The matrix is shown, in detail, by Table 6.

Attention is particularly drawn to the matrices which represent the transfer of factor income between the market sector at large and the public sector, i.e. $[g_{rt}^{II}]$ and $[g_{tr}^{I}]$. As the structure of these matrices clearly displays, the concept of income transfer is characterized by a unilateral transfer of purchasing power from the recipients to the spending units of factor income. It is true that the additional classification of the concept of income transfer may complicate the structure of an extended system of national accounts. But, considerable interest is attached to the additional classification of income transfer for the reason that it unfolds the nature

Table 6. The sub-matrix of the disposable income of the market sector $[y_{sr}^{I}]$

row no. \ column no.		4
row no.	sector	recipients of income
7	spending units of income	$y_{11}^{I} \cdots y_{1r}^{I}$ $\vdots \quad \vdots$ $y_{s1}^{I} \cdots y_{sr}^{I}$

of income transfer. Taking note of the fact that the concept of income transfer is considered as the link between the recipients and the spending units of factor income, it may be of taxonomic use that the types of income transfer are classified into the following three categories:

(i) voluntary transfer
(ii) contractual transfer
(iii) compulsory transfer

The classification is based on the nature of initiative displayed by the person concerned. The voluntary transfer is termed as it is solely determined by the voluntary will of either the recipients or the spending units of factor income. If the income transfer is initiated by legal or other kinds of enforcement effected by either the recipients or the spending units of factor income, the income transfer is termed the compulsory transfer. The contractual transfer is termed as it is made by the mutual agreement between the recipients and the spending units of factor income. Broadly speaking, the tripartite classification of the concept of income transfer is comparable to its classification given in SNA, in which the concept of income (current) transfer is itemized into four categories:

(i)′ transactions arising from the ownership of corporate and quasi-corporate enterprises and other property,

(ii)′ other requited (contractual) payments and receipts,

Table 7. A numerical illustration of $[g_{tr}{}^{\mathrm{I}}]$: A case for the Recipients of the Government Managed Health Insurance

Male 25–29 years (unit: 10,000 yen)

	I	II	III	IV	V	VI	VII	VIII	IX	X
(i)	0.17	0.82	1.72	2.81	4.08	6.79	8.78	11.11	14.87	19.04
(ii)	5.86	6.81	7.62	8.79	10.61	12.50	14.06	15.62	17.96	20.01
(iii)	2.52	2.77	3.28	3.78	4.37	5.38	6.05	6.72	7.73	8.74
(iv)	2.23	2.46	2.90	3.35	3.87	4.76	5.36	5.95	6.84	7.44

Male 30–34 years

	I	II	III	IV	V	VI	VII	VIII	IX	X
(i)	0.05	0.05	0.15	0.84	2.06	4.39	6.27	8.38	11.93	15.75
(ii)	5.86	6.81	7.62	8.79	10.16	12.50	14.06	15.62	17.96	20.01
(iii)	2.52	2.77	3.28	3.78	4.37	5.38	6.05	6.72	7.73	8.74
(iv)	2.23	2.46	2.90	3.35	3.87	4.76	5.36	5.95	6.84	7.44

Male 35–39 years

	I	II	III	IV	V	VI	VII	VIII	IX	X
(i)	0.05	0.05	0.05	0.23	1.12	3.46	5.15	7.18	11.56	14.35
(ii)	5.86	6.81	7.62	8.79	10.16	12.50	14.06	15.62	17.96	20.01
(iii)	2.52	2.77	3.28	3.78	4.37	5.38	6.05	6.72	7.73	8.74
(iv)	2.23	2.46	2.90	3.35	3.87	4.76	5.36	5.95	6.84	7.44

Male 40–44 years

	I	II	III	IV	V	VI	VII	VIII	IX	X
(i)	0.05	0.05	0.05	0.21	1.09	3.39	5.09	7.17	10.48	14.26
(ii)	5.86	6.81	7.62	8.79	10.16	12.50	14.06	15.62	17.96	20.01
(iii)	2.52	2.77	3.28	3.78	4.37	5.38	6.05	6.72	7.73	8.74
(iv)	2.23	2.46	2.90	3.35	3.87	4.76	5.36	5.95	6.84	7.44

Table 8. A Numerical illustration of $[g_{tr}{}^{I}]$: A Case for the Recipients of the Society Managed Health Insurance

Male 25–29–years (unit: 10,000 yen)

	I	II	III	IV	V	VI	VII	VIII	IX	X
(i)	0.36	0.87	1.96	3.11	4.45	7.33	9.53	12.00	16.06	20.43
(ii)	5.88	6.87	7.65	8.83	10.20	12.56	14.13	15.69	18.05	20.11
(iii)	2.50	2.76	3.26	3.76	4.34	5.34	6.01	6.68	7.68	8.68
(iv)	2.23	2.46	2.90	3.35	3.87	4.76	5.36	5.95	6.84	7.44

Male 30–34–years

	I	II	III	IV	V	VI	VII	VIII	IX	X
(i)	0.05	0.05	0.73	1.78	3.09	5.74	7.87	10.16	14.10	18.28
(ii)	5.88	6.87	7.65	8.83	10.20	12.56	14.13	15.69	18.05	20.11
(iii)	2.50	2.76	3.26	3.76	4.34	5.34	6.01	6.68	7.68	8.68
(iv)	2.23	2.46	2.90	3.35	3.87	4.76	5.36	5.95	6.84	7.44

Male 25–39–years

	I	II	III	IV	V	VI	VII	VIII	IX	X
(i)	0.05	0.05	0.05	0.29	1.05	3.46	5.21	7.51	11.08	15.06
(ii)	5.88	6.87	7.65	8.83	10.20	12.56	14.13	15.69	18.05	20.11
(iii)	2.50	2.76	3.26	3.76	4.34	5.34	6.01	6.68	7.68	8.68
(iv)	2.23	2.46	2.90	3.35	3.87	4.76	5.36	5.95	6.84	7.44

Male 40–44 years

	I	II	III	IV	V	VI	VII	VIII	IX	X
(i)	0.05	0.05	0.05	0.23	0.88	3.28	5.45	7.28	10.76	14.73
(ii)	5.88	6.87	7.65	8.83	10.20	12.56	14.13	15.69	18.05	20.11
(iii)	2.50	2.76	3.26	3.76	4.34	5.34	6.01	6.68	7.68	8.68
(iv)	2.23	2.46	2.90	3.35	3.87	4.76	5.36	5.95	6.84	7.44

Note: The row of the tables distinguishes the categories of government agencies as recipients of income which are stated in page 143. The column distinguishes income classes, which are broken down according to the recipients' monthly earnings and grouped into classes as indicated below:

(unit: 10,000 yen)

	I	II	III	IV	V
monthly earnings	below 3.0	3.0–3.299	3.3–3.899	3.9–4.449	4.5–5.199

	IV	VII	VIII	IX	X
monthly earnings	5.2–6.399	6.4–7.199	7.2–7.999	8.0–9.199	over 9.2

(iii)′ obligations to, and commitments of, government organs, all of which are unrequited (non-contractual) transfers, and

(iv)′ other unrequited but voluntary grants.

It is seen that (i)′ and (ii)′ of the United Nations classification of SNA corresponds with the contractual transfer of our tripartite classification [(ii)] and that remaining items in both classifications are directly comparable each other. The category of the income transfer construction of (iii) or (iii)′ in the classifications has particular relevance to the matrix of either $[g_{rt}^{II}]$ or $[g_{tr}^{I}]$ that represent the transfer of primary income made between the public sector and the market sector at large.

A numerical illustration to show the structure of $[g_{tr}^{I}]$ is given in tables given before (Table 7–Table 8). The tables are produced on the basis of a comprehensive study made by Ichikawa and Sengoku concerning the size distribution of income and social insurance and adapted to the structure of the matrix. In the tables, the recipients of income are grouped by the size of their earned income into 10 income classes, whereas the government agencies as recipients of income are broken down according to institutions, whose classification follows, by and large, the way given above in relation to the breakdown of the general government. The institutional breakdown of government agencies is made by the following categories: (i) central and local government, (ii) social insurance, (iii) health insurance and (iv) welfare pension funds. Being the basic information of Ichikawa and Sengoku's study obtained from 1970 *Sample Survey of the Recipients of Health Insurance*, it should be further noted that the basic statistical unit in their study does not refer to the household but to the individual recipient of health insurance.[10)]

10) See Ichikawa and Sengoku [1972]. Brief accounts of the *Sample Survey of the Recipients of Health Insurance* will be given in the last essay of this volume, where the basic statistical materials are essentially supplied from the *1972 Sample Survey of the Recipients of Health Insurance*.

The concept of income in their study also differs from the primary income with which the matrix of $[g_{tr}{}^{\mathrm{I}}]$ is associated in that the former concept of income only refers to the earned income of the recipients. A variety of categories of income transfer from the public sector to the market sector at large which are not directed to the recipients of income in question is excluded from the scope of their study. Hence, such categories of income transfer as social assistance grants including relief payments, widow's, guardians' allowances, war bonuses, pensions and service grants and scholarships, fellowships and maintainance allowances for educational, training and similar purposes, and those which fall into the sundry categories of income transfer made by government agencies are predominantly excluded from the scope of income transfer in our numerical example.

The derivation of the disposable income deserves a few words in connection with the sub-matrix of $[y_{sr}{}^{\mathrm{I}}]$. In the construction of the matrix the spending units of income, which specify the sector breakdown of row 7, are distinguished from the recipients of income that appear in column 4. As we have noted before, the distinction between the spending units and the recipients of income would not be necessary, if the household was chosen as the basic statistical unit in the classification of the recipients of income. Then, a couple of possibilities of the construction of $[y_{sr}{}^{\mathrm{I}}]$ is conceivable. First, the same principle of sector breakdown is applied to row 7 and column 4 in Table identifying a set the spending units of income with that of the recipients of income. Suppose the recipients of income are appropriately subdivided into income classes. Then, the sub-matrix $[y_{sr}{}^{\mathrm{I}}]$, being a square matrix, represents the formation of disposable income between income classes in the course of the redistribution of primary income. The redistribution of income originating from the recipients of income that are arrayed in income classes of column 4 is channelled through the recipients of income, settling into the disposable of income the recipients of income similarly arrayed in income classes of row 7. In this case, the structure of the redistribution of primary income would provide invaluable information for the quantitative studies of the redistribution of primary income, whose theoretical basis will be discussed in the appendix of this essay. Second, different principles of sector breakdown may be applicable to row 7 and column 4, though a set of the spending units is identified with that of the recipients of income. In the case, the sub-matrix $[y_{sr}^{\mathrm{I}}]$ constitutes a rectangular matrix. Suppose a set of the recipients of income for column 4 is broken down according to suitably formulated income classes but they are displayed in row 7 according to the grouping by appropriate age groups. Then, the process of the redistribution of primary income that is portrayed in the sub-matrix of $[y_{sr}^{\mathrm{I}}]$ is looked upon as the redistribution of (primary) income between different age groups. It should be noted that a deep and subtle meaning is attached to the information incorporated in the derived sub-matrix of $[y_{sr}^{\mathrm{I}}]$. As the so-called 'old-aged society' is in progress in Japan, it is foreseen that the conflict in the interests between generations could be at the centre of the issues concerning the redistribution of primary income. The information incorporated in the matrix would be indispensable for the decision making of economic and social policies.

One more word deserves to be noted about the structure of the sub-matrix of $[y_{sr}^{\mathrm{I}}]$. The structure of sub-matrix is interdependent with the whole system framework of national accounts as Table 1 clearly stresses the point. In particular, the structure of $[y_{sr}^{\mathrm{I}}]$ is essentially conditioned by the construction of the matrices which represent the transfer of income between the private recipients of income and government agencies, i.e. $[g_{tr}^{\mathrm{I}}]$ and $[g_{rt}^{\mathrm{II}}]$. If the structure of $[g_{tr}^{\mathrm{I}}]$ were constructed as the numerical illustration displayed in Tables 7 and 8 could show, it would be necessary that adjustments be made for the breakdown of the corresponding column of $[y_{sr}^{\mathrm{I}}]$.

The disposable income of the public sector may be derived in the same way as that of the market sector at large. Let us suppose that the row (and column) 2 is further subdivided according to a number of government agencies which constitute the public sector and that the row (and column) 5 is also subdivided by a number of types of factor income. Then, Q^{II}, which stands for the net domestic product originated from the public sector, is expressed as a sub-matrix. The row of this matrix exhibits a type of factor income, and its column represents the classification of government agencies. Through the process of the primary distribution of factor income, the net domestic product originated from the public sector is distributed into the government agencies as

Table 9. The sub-matrix of the factor income received by the public secctor $[p_{tp}^{\mathrm{II}}]$

row no.	column no. / sector	5 / types of factor income
6	government agencies as recipients of income	$p_{11}^{\mathrm{II}} \cdots p_{1p}^{\mathrm{II}}$ $\vdots \quad \vdots$ $p_{t1}^{\mathrm{II}} \cdots p_{tp}^{\mathrm{II}}$

recipients of factor income. As the row (and column) 6 is subdivided according to the government agencies as the recipients of factor income, P^{II}, which stands for the net national product received by the public sector, is transformed into a sub-matrix, whose row indicates a classification of the government agencies as the recipients of factor income and column the types of factor income. In detail, the structure of the sub-matrix is shown in Table 9.

After the same manner as the derivation of the disposable income of the market sector at large, a sub-matrix which represents the disposable income of the public sector is derived from the matrix of factor income received by the public sector, $[p_{tp}^{\text{II}}]$, and those which stand for the transfer of factor income between the market sector at large and the public sector, $[g_{rt}^{\text{II}}]$ and $[g_{tr}^{\text{I}}]$. The matrix of the disposable income of the public sector is written as Table 10. In the derivation of this matrix, an assumption is made that the

Table 10. The sub-matrix of the disposable income of the public sector $[y_{ut}^{\text{II}}]$

row no.	column no. / sector	6 government agencies as recipients of income
8	government agencies as spending units of income	$y_{11}^{\text{II}} \cdots y_{1t}^{\text{II}}$ $\vdots \quad \vdots$ $y_{u1}^{\text{II}} \cdots y_{ut}^{\text{II}}$

row (and column) 8 is sub-divided according to the government agencies as spending units. Thus, the row in this matrix stands for a classification of the government agencies as spending units, and its column stands for a classification of government agencies as the recipients of factor income.

Appendix The Transfer of Income and Measures of Income Inequality

1. In section 3 of this article, I have noted that the structure of income redistribution could be portrayed by the sub-matrices eventually leading to the derivation of the disposable income by sectors and that the structure of income redistribution would provide invaluable information for quantitative studies of income inequality. I shall outline, in this appendix, the theoretical structure of income transfer and its association with measures of income inequality.[11]

In the beginning, a measure of income inequality in a society is formulated and is assumed to be comparable. Suppose a society constituted of n members. A state of the distribution of income in the society is given by a vector of members' income, which is expressed by y

$$y = (y_i),\ i = 1, 2, \ldots\ldots, n; \qquad (1.1)$$

where y_i, stands for the income of i-th member of the society. A measure of income inequality is a function of y and is expressed by $I[y]$. It is assumed that the measure of income inequality is

11) Further details on the discussion of the theoretical structure of income transfer and its association with measures of income inequality are dealt with in Kurabayashi and Yatsuka [1976] and Kurabayashi and Yatsuka [forthcoming].

comparable in the sense that for any pair of income distribution $(y, y',)$ one of the following alternatives is conceivable:

$$\begin{aligned} &\text{(i)} && I[y] < I[y'] \\ &\text{(ii)} && I[y] = I[y'] \\ &\text{(iii)} && I[y] > I[y'] \end{aligned} \tag{1.2}$$

In the alternatives of (1.2), y is called greater in equality than y' for (i), equal to y, (ii) and less than y' for (iii) respectively. Then, the structure of income transfer between members of a society can be asociated with a measure of income inequality by the following postulates.

Postulate 1. Suppose the transfer of income from i-th member to j-th member preserving the order of income size by members in a given distribution of income y. Let $y^T\ (i, j)$ stand for the state of income distribution after the transfer of income. Then, the following relation is fulfilled.

$$I[y^T(i, j)] < I[y] \text{ for any } y, \tag{1.3}$$

where

$$\begin{aligned} &y^T(i, j) = (y_{i'}^T),\ y = (y_{i'}),\ y_i > y_j, \\ &y_i^T = y_i - d, \\ &y_j^T = y_j + d,\ d \in \left[0,\ \frac{y_i - y_j}{2}\right]; \\ &y_{i'}^T = y_{i'} \text{ any } i' \neq i, j. \end{aligned}$$

Postulate 1 is termed the *Daltonian principle of income transfer.*[12]

Postulate 1′, Under the situation of income transfer in postulate 1, the following relation is fullfilled.

$$I[y^T(i, j)] \leqq I[y]. \tag{1.4}$$

Postulate 1′, is called the *weak Daltonian pı inciple of income transfer.*

12) Dalton, [1920], p. 351.

Postulate 2 Suppose the income of all members changes proportionately. Then, the measure of income inequality is left unchanged, *i.e.*

$$I[\lambda y] = I[y] \text{ for any } \lambda > 0 \text{ and } y > 0. \tag{1.5}$$

Postulate 2′ Under the situation of proportionate change in income of members in Postulate 2, the following relations are maintained for any $y>0$.

$$\begin{aligned} I[\lambda y] &< I[y] \text{ for any } \lambda > 1, \\ I[\lambda y] &> I[y] \text{ for any } \lambda < 1. \end{aligned} \tag{1.6}$$

Postulate 2′, is called the *Daltonian principle of proportionate additions to incomes.*[13] It is also noted that Postulate 2 states that $I[y]$ is homogeneous function of 0-th degree with respect to y.

Postulate 3 Suppose the income of all members is changed by equal amounts. Then, the measure of income inequality decreases (or increases) according to the increase (or decrease) of income by equal amounts. Hence, the following relations are maintained.

$$\begin{aligned} I[y+te] &< I[y] \text{ for any } t > 0, \\ I[y+te] &> I[y] \text{ for any } t < 0, \end{aligned} \tag{1.7}$$

where

$$y+te > 0,\ e = (1,\ 1,\ \ldots\ldots,\ 1).$$

Postulate 3 is termed the *Daltonian principle of equal additions to incomes.*[14]

Postulate 4 No special importance is attached to whom in particular the income is distributed in the formulation of income inequality. Putting it in other words, a state of income distribu-

13) Dalton, [1920], p. 355.
14) Dalton, [1920], p. 356.

tion is anonymous in the sense that $I[y]$ is symmetric with respect to y. Accordingly, the following relation is satisfied.

$$I[Py] = I[y] \text{ for any } y > 0, \tag{1.8}$$

where P stands for any permutation matrix.

Postulate 5 The measure of income inequality assumes zero if and only if the income of all members is equaly distributed. Hence,

$$\begin{aligned} &\text{(i)} \quad I[y] \geqq 0 \text{ for any } y > 0, \\ &\text{(ii)} \quad I[y] = 0 \text{ if and only if } y = \mu e, \end{aligned} \tag{1.9}$$

where

$$\mu = (1/n) \sum_{i=1}^{n} y_i .$$

It is implied by the Daltonian principle of income transfer that the improvement of income inequality becomes greater the larger is the amount of income transfer from a higher income earner i to a lower income earner j and that the improvement of income inequality becomes greater the smaller is the income of a lower income earner j who receives the same amount of income transfer from a higher income earner i, provided that an initial state of income distribution does not satisfy (ii) of (1.9). It is also noted that the Daltonian principle of income transfer ensures the improvement of income inequality resulting from the transfer of income from a higher income earner i to a lower income earner j, unless the order of income size by members is disrupted. The structure of income transfer which accepts the Daltonian principle of income transfer may be simply termed the D-structure of income transfer.

The D-structure of income transfer is compared with a structure of income transfer generated from a sequence of income transfer. Suppose a state of income distribution y' is generated from a finite sequence of the income transfer for any pairs of members. Let y stand for the initial state of income distribution in the sequence of income transfer. The relation between the generated state of income distribution by the sequence of income transfer and the initial state is expressed by

$$y' \geq_{DT} y. \tag{1.10}$$

A set of the states of income distribution with a given level of total income of a society is defined by S_Y as indicated below:

$$S_Y = \{y|\Sigma y_i = Y, y \in R^n_+\}, \quad Y \in (0, +\infty).$$

Following properties are readily seen as for the relation generated by the sequence of income transfer.

(i) $\mu e \geq_{DT} y$, for any $y \in S_Y$, where $\mu = (1/n) Y$.

(ii) $\alpha y + (1-\alpha)\mu e \geq_{DT} y$, for any $y \in S_Y$ and $\alpha \in [0, 1]$.

(iii) If an arbitrary permutation is made possible by the sequence of income transfer, then (1.10) is equivalent to saying that there exists a bistochastic matrix such that

$$y' = Qy\text{[15)]}.$$

Property (i) states that the state of equal distribution of income is generated by a finite sequence of income transfer, whereas Property (ii) claims that a linear combination of the initial state and the state of equal distribution is also generated by the sequence of income transfer, which is expressed in terms of a bistochastic matrix Q by Property (iii). The property (iii) is further spelled out by considering an instance of income transfer fulfilling the following conditions:

15) A bitochastic matrix is a square matrix, whose elements are non-negative and the sum of each rows and columns is cqual to unity. For the properties of bistochastic matrix, see, in particular, C. Berge [1963], p. 180 et seq. (iii) owes to a Theorem by Hardy, Littlewood and Polya which is referred by P. Dasgupta, A. Sen and D. Starrett [1973] in their Lemma 2.

$$y = (y_k),\ y_i \geqq y_j\,,$$
$$y(i,\ j) = (y_k(i,\ j))\,,\ y_k(i,\ j) = y_k\ \ k \neq i,\ j\,,$$
$$y_i(i,\ j) = y_i - t,\ y_j(i,\ j) = y_i + t\ \ \ t \in [0,\ y_i - y_j]\,,$$

where $y(i, j)$ denotes the transfer of income from a higher income earner i to a lower income earner j. The structure of income transfer that satisfies these conditions is called the B-structure of income transfer. It follows from the B-structure of income transfer that there exists a bistochastic matrix B such that

$$y(i,\ j) = By \qquad (1.10)'$$

It is easily seen that a state of income distribution y' generated from y by a finite sequence of income transfer on the basis of the B-structure of income transfer can be obtainable from a sequence of income transfer on the basis of the D-structure of income transfer, if y' is not identical with y. On the contrary, a state of income distribution y' generated from y by a finite sequence of income transfer on the D-structure of income transfer can be attainable by a sequence of income transfer on the basis of the B-structure of income transfer.

The specification of a measure of income inequality in relation to the postulates set forth before is given by the following theorem.[16)]
(Theorem 1) (i) A function $I[y]$ satisfies Postulates, 1, 2, 3, 4 and 5 if and only if (a), (b) and (c) are satisfied[17)]:

---

16) The proof of Theorem 1 is given in Kurabayashi and Yatsuka [forthcoming].

17) $I[y]$ is called a strictly S-convex function on D, if

(i) for all y in D and all bistochastic matrices B

$$I[By] \leqq I[y], \text{ and}$$

(ii) whenever By is not a permutation of y

$$I[By] < I[y].$$

It is noted that $I[y]$ is strictly S-convex if $I[y]$ is strictly quasi-convex and symmetric with respect to y.

For the definition of S-convexity, see C. Berge [1963], p. 219.

(a) $I[y]$ is strictly S-convex in $R^n_+ - \{0\}$,

(b) $I[y]$ is homegeneous of degree zero with respect to y,

(c) $I[\mu y] = 0$, for any $\mu \in (0, +\infty)$.

(ii) $I[y]$ satisfies Postulates 1, 2′, 3, 4 and 5 if and only if (a) (c) and (b′) in place of (b) are fullfilled:

(b') For any $y > 0$,

$$I[\lambda y] < I[y], \text{ for any } \lambda > 1,$$
$$I[\lambda y] > I[y], \text{ for any } \lambda \in (0, 1).$$

(iii) (b′) is satisfied if $I[y]$ is a negatively super-homogeneous function of y or its strictly increasing transformation. A function $H(y)$ is called negatively super-homogeneous with respect to y if for any $\lambda \in [1, +\infty)$

$$H(\lambda y) \leqq (1/\lambda)H(y) \text{ and } H[(1/\lambda))y] \geqq \lambda H(y).$$

So far we have assumed that the size of the members in the society is fixed in n. It is conceivable to relax the assumption by establishing the Postulate 6 as below:

Postulate 6 For any state of income distribution $y=(y_i)$, $i=1, 2, \ldots, n$, the level of the measure of income inequality is left unchanged, if the size of members that receive the amounts of income y_i, $i=1, \ldots n$, is changed proportionatly. The postulate is termed the *principle of proportionate addition to persons* by Dalton.[18] The postulate is restated in the following manner. Let Z stand for a $n\lambda$ dimensional vector defined by

$$Z = (Z_{ir}), \text{ where } Z_{ir} = y_i,\ i = 1, 2, \ldots, n;\ r = 1, 2, \ldots, \lambda.$$

Measures of income inequality corresponding to y and Z are ex-

18) Dalton [1920], p. 357.

pressed by $I_n[y]$ and $I_{n\lambda}[Z]$ respectively. Postulate 6 states that

$$I_{n\lambda}[Z] = I_n[Z], \text{ for any } n, \lambda \in N \text{ such that } n > \bar{n} \in N. \quad (1.11)$$

2. Following measures of income inequality have been conveniently used in the literature of income inequality and its distribution.[19] They are:

(i) $E = [\text{Max}(y_i) - \text{Min}(y_i)]/\mu$ (2.1)

(ii) $M = \sum_i |\mu - y_i| / n\mu$ (2.2)

(iii) $V = \sum_i (\mu - y_i)^2 / n$ (2.3)

(iv) $C = (V)^{1/2}/\mu$ (2.4)

(v) $H = [\sum_i (\log \mu - \log y_i)^2 / n]^{1/2}$ (2.5)

(vi) $G = (1/2n^2 \mu) \sum_i \sum_j |y_i - y_j|$ (2.6)

(vii) $T = \sum_i (y_i / Y) \log n(y_i / Y)$ (2.7)

E, M, V, C, H, G and T are respectively the range, the relative mean deviation, the variance, the coefficient of variation, the standard deviation of longarithms, Gini coefficient and Theil's entropy measure. It is interesting to see how the conventional measures of income inequality are associated with the postulates set forth in section 1. The association serves to grasp the hidden economic meaning for the distributional judgment that underlies in these statistical measures. Theorem 2 below indicates the association.[20]

(Theorem 2) (i) C, G and T satisfy the Postulates 1, 2, 3, 4, 5 and 6.

(ii) E and M satisfy the Postulates 1′, 2, 3, 4, 5 and 6.

---

19) Further accounts of these measures of income inequality are given in A. Sen [1973], ch. 2. For the convenience of reference, the same notations as he used there are employed.

20) The proof of Therems 2 and 3 below is given in Kurabayashi and Yatsuka [forthcoming].

(iii) H does not satisfy the Postulates 1 and 3, whereas V does not satisfy the Postulates 2 and 3.
In place of the Postulates 2 and 3, the following properties are satisfied by V.

$$V[\lambda y] = \lambda^2 V[y]\,,\ \text{for any } \lambda>0; \tag{2.8}$$

$$V[y+te] = V[y]\,,\ \text{for any } t \in R \text{ and } y+te \geqq 0\,. \tag{2.9}$$

Suppose a strictly S-convex (or S-concave) function of y, which is denoted by $H[y]$. It is noted that a strictly increasing (or decreasing) transformation of H[y], say $F(H[y])$, such that

$$\phi(y) = F(H[y/\mu]) - F(H[e])$$

$$(\text{or } \phi(y) = F(H[e]) - F(H[y/\mu])\,, \tag{2.10}$$

yields a measure of income inequality.
Alternative measures of income inequality are derived from the specification of $H[y]$ such that (1) the distance function, (2) the type of Cobb-Douglas function, (3) the type of CES function, (4) the type of factor limitational Leontief function and (5) the type of the additive long-linear function. Theorem 3 illuminates the derived measures of income inequality by such specification without giving the proof for the saving of space.
(Theorem 3) (i) Measures of income inequality $I_1[y]$, $I_2[y]$, $I_3[y]$ and $I_5[y]$ are derived from the specification of $H[y]$ that corresponds to (1) the distance function, (2) the Cobb-Douglas type function, (3) the CES type function and (5) the additive log-linear function applying the transformation of (2.10). They satisfy the Postulates 1, 2, 3, 4, 5 and 6.
(ii) The measure of income inequality $I_4[y]$ is derived from the specification of $H[y]$ by (4) the Leontief type of factor limitational function. It satisfies the Postulates 1, 2, 3, 4, 5 and 6.

These measures of income inequality are expressed below:[21]

$$I_1[y] = (1/\mu)(\sum y_i^2)^{1/2} - n^{1/2} \quad (2.11)$$
$$I_2[y] = 1-(1/\mu)\prod y_i^{1/n} \quad (2.12)$$
$$I_3[y] = n^{1/\alpha}-(1/\mu)(\sum y_i^{\alpha})^{1/\alpha}, \ \alpha \in (0, 1) \quad (2.13)$$
$$I_4[y] = 1-(1/\mu) \text{ Min } (y_i) \quad (2.14)$$
$$I_5[y] = \sum (\log \mu - \log y_i)^{1/n} \quad (2.15)$$

The Daltonian principle of income transfer postulated in section 1 incorporates some relative evaluation of income transfer to different income classes. The point may be more explicitly spelled out by the following consideration. Suppose a couple of pairs or members of the society whose differences in income level are same between the pairs in such a way that for a couple of pairs (i, j) and (i', j'),

$$y_i > y_j,\ y_{i'} > y_{j'},\ y_{i'} > y_i \text{ and } y_i - y_j = y_{i'} - y_{j'} > 0. \quad (2.16)$$

Let us consider a couple of the states of income distribution, $y^T(i, j)$ and $y^T(i', j')$, resulting from the same amounts of income transfer for (i, j) and (i', j') that satisfies Postulate 1. It is said that a measure of income inequality is evaluated with greater weights to the members of lower incomes if the following condition (a) is always maintained.

(a) $$I[y]-I[y^T(i, j)] > I[y]-I[y^T(i', j')], \text{ for } y_{i'} > y_i. \quad (2.17)$$

21) (2.11) is derived as a special case from a more generalized form,

$$I[y] = (1/\mu)(\sum y_i^{\alpha})^{1/\alpha} - n^{1/\alpha}, \ \alpha > 1,$$

by putting $\alpha = 2$.
It is conceivable to use Max $| y_i |$ as a distance function in R^n.
A function formulated by the distance function such that

$$I[y] = (1/\mu) \text{ Max } | y_i | - 1, \ y \in R_+^n - \{0\},$$

is also a measure of income inequality satisfying Postulates 1′, 2, 3, 4, 5 and 6.
It is readily seen that for this $I[y]$

$$E = I_4[y] + I[y]$$

In parallel with the condition (a), it is said that a measure of income inequality is evaluated with greater weights to the members of upper incomes if the following condition (b) is always satisfied.

$$\text{(b)} \qquad I[y]-I[y^T(i, j)] < I[y]-I[y^T(i', j')], \text{ for } y_{i'} > y_i. \qquad (2.18)$$

It is also said that a measure of income inequality is evaluated with equal weights to the members of all incomes if the condition (c) is held.

$$\text{(c)} \qquad I[y]-I[y^T(i, j)] = I[y]-I[y^T(i', j')], \text{ for } y_{i'} > y_i. \qquad (2.19)$$

Suppose $I[y]$ is generated from a real valued function $G(y)$, applying a strictly increasing transformation F mapping R^+ into R^+ such that

$$I[y] = F((\sum_i G(y_i)), \text{ for given } \mu.$$

Then, it is noted that the conditions (a) and (b) are satisfied if a function $V(X)$ defined by

$$V(X) = G(X+t)-G(X), \ t > 0,$$

is strictly concave (for (a)) or strictly convex (for (b)) and that the condition (c) is held if $V(X)$ is linear. The conditions (a), (b) and (c) cited above are associated with alternative measures of income inequality by Theorem 4 below.[22]

(Theorem 4) (i) Measures of income inequality, T, I_2, I_3 and I_5 satisfy the condition (a).

(ii) Measures of income inequality, C and I_1, satisfy the condition (c).

(iii) A measure of income inequality G does not necessarily satisfy the conditions (a), (b) and (c).[23]

---

22) The proof of Theorem 4 is given in Kurabayashi and Yatsuka [forthcoming].

23) (ii) and (iii) of Theorem 4 have already been noted by Atkinson [1970] and Sen [1973] referring to the measures of C and G.

(iv) A measure of income inequality that is defined by

$$I[y]=(1/\mu)(\sum y_i^{\alpha})^{1/\alpha}-n^{1/\alpha}$$

satifies the condition (a) if $1<\alpha<2$, condition (b) if $\alpha>2$ and condition (c) if $\alpha=2$.

REFERENCES

Anthony B. Atkinson, " On the Measurement of Inequality ", *Journal of Economic Theory*, 2, 1970.

Anthony B. Atkinson, " How Progressive Should Income-tax Be? ", M. Perkin, ed., *Essays on Modern Economics*, London 1973.

Claude Berge, *Topological Spaces*, London 1963.

Bureau of Statistics, the Prime Minister's Office, 1974 *Nationa l Survey of Family Income and Expenditure*, Tokyo 1976 (in Japanese with English summary).

Hugh Dalton, " The Measurement of the Inequality of Incomes ", *Economic Journal*, 30, 1920.

Partha Dasgupta, Amatya Sen and David Starrett, " Notes on the Measurement of Inequality ", *Journal of Economic Theory*, **6**, 1973.

H. Ichikawa and T. Sengoku, " Social Insurance and Size Distribution of Incomes ", *Keizai Bunseki*, No. 41, 1972 (in Japanese).

International Monetary Fund, *Balance of Payments Manual*, 3rd ed., Washington D.C. 1961.

Leif Johansen, *Public Economics*, Amsterdam 1965.

Y. Kurabayashi and A. Yatsuka, " Economic Theory of Income Inequality ", *Gendai Keizai*, No, 23, 1976 (in Japanese).

Y. Kurabayashi and A. Yatsuka, " Redistribution of Income and Measures of Income Inequality ", R. Sato and T. Fujii, ed., *Resource Allocation and Spatial Dispersion*, Heidelberg (forthcoming).

Edmund S. Phelps, " Taxation of Wage Income for Economic Justice ", *Quarterly Journal of Economics*, 1973.

Nancy Ruggles and Richard Ruggles, The *Design of Economic Accounts*, Princeton 1970.

Michael Rothschild and Joseph E. Stiglitz, " Some Further Remarks on the Mesurement of Inequality ", *Journal of Economic Theory*, 6, 1973.

Amartya Sen, *On Economic Inequality*, Oxford 1973.

United Nations, *A System of National Accounts*, New York 1968.

United Nations, A Draft System of Statistics of the Distribution of Income Consumption and Accumulation, E/CN. C/425, 1972.

5

USE OF NATIONAL ACCOUNTS AS A BASIS OF ECONOMIC DATA SYSTEM

1. The Structure of an Economic Data System

1.1. The Scope of Economic Data

The economic data system, EDS for short, is termed here as a set of systems by which the economic data are classified, collected and processed according to a coherent and systematic method. In the determination of the scope of the economic data it must be kept in mind that the economic data are subject to the following considerations. First, the scope of the economic data is conditioned by a present state of economics. The scope of the economic data may enlarge as the scope and the formulation of economic theory may change. The theory of consumer's choice, for example, is currently formulated on the presumption that the strong covexity and the insatiatility of the preference relation hold. In order to verify the hypotheses postulated in the theory of consumer's choice, then a large amount of statistical information is collected for empirical testing. To collect the statistical information which is inconsistent with the formulation of the theory of consumer's shoice, particularly with the basic axioms of the preference relation, is not of great interest for taking the information in the scope of the economic data for consumer's choice. But, it is quite possible that the scope of the economic data for consumer's choice may be modified, if the formulation of the theory of the consumer's choice allows the existence of those goods to which the law of decreasing marginal rates of substitution may no longer be applied. It is supposed in this case that the preference relation of certain commodities representing public disamenities such as environmental disruptions, may fall into the case. The reformulation of the theory of consumer's choice taking into account of such public disamenitied may necessarily change the scope of economic data for consumer's choice.

Second, the scope of the economic data is conditioned by the availability of statistical information. The availability differs according to times and countries. Though it may not be difficult to give a general rule for distinguishing the economic data from other

Table 1. Broad categories of economic data in Japan

1.	labour	8.	balance of payments and foreign exchange
2.	agriculture, forestry and fishery	9.	wages and prices
3.	mining, manufacturing, electricity and gas	10.	households surveys
4.	construction	11.	business surveys
5.	transportation and communication	12.	finance
6.	retail and wholesale trades	13.	public finance
7.	international trades	14.	national income

Note: The categories listed in the table follows the classification given in Administrative Management Agency of Prime Minister's Office, *Supplement to the Monthly Statistics of Japan: Explanatory Notes*, 1970 edition.

statistical information it is not altogether practical to set the rule to all circumstances regardless of spatial differences or differences over time. It is easily understood that the scope of the economic data is, in practice, offered in relation to the availability of the statistical information with respect to a particular country and the time with which we are concerned.

Taking note of these conditions, the economic data in Japan are conveniently itemized under the broad headings indicated in Table 1.

1.2. Micro-economic Data and Macro-economic Data

For the collection and processing of economic data two sources of data are distinguished. They are (1) the primary data and (2) the adjusted data respectively. The primary data are again classified according to the purposes of data collection. A group of data is collected and used for the purely limited purposes of administration by government agencies or of management by business enterprises. The collection and storage of such data are not primarily intended for public uses. The data which fall into the second group of classification are collected and used for public use in the sense that they are not restricted by any particular economic agents and are not specified by any particular purposes. The data which fall into the first group of classification may be conveniently called *the data for particular purposes*, whereas those which fall into the second group of classification may be called *the data for general purposes*. An important example of the data for particular purposes, which is generally used for the administration of local government agencies, is regional register records of residents. There is no need to say that a great amount of information is usually collected and stored by business enterprises purely for their own uses, being often stored in electronic computers.

Table 2. The information collected from Nattional Population Census in Japan

(Mark ○…Collected, Mark ×…Not collected)

Type of data	1920	1925	1930	1935	1940	1947	1950	1955	1960	1965	1970
Name	○	○	○	○	○	○	○	○	○	○	○
Relation with head of household	○	×	○	×	○	×	○	○	○	○	○
Sex	○	○	○	○	○	○	○	○	○	○	○
Date of birth	○	○	○	○	○	○	○	○	○	○	○
Nationality	○	×	○	×	○	○	○	○	○	○	○
Place of birth	○	×	○	×	○	×	○	×	×	×	×
Marital status	○	○	○	○	○	○	○	○	○	○	○
Duration of marriage	×	×	×	×	×	×	○	×	○	×	○
Number of children	×	×	×	×	×	×	○	×	○	×	○
Level of education	×	×	×	×	×	×	○	×	○	×	○
Economic activity status[1]	○	×	○	×	○	○	○	○	○	○	○
Industry[1]	×	×	○	×	○	○	○	○	○	○	○
Occupation[1]	○	×	○	×	○	○	○	○	○	○	○
Status or class of worker	○	×	○	×	○	○	○	○	○	○	○
Place of work, location of school	×	×	○	×	×	×	×	○[2]	○	○	○
Type of household	○	○	○	○	○	○	○	○	○	○	○
Type of dwelling[3]	×	×	○	×	×	×	×	○	○	○	○
Additional information	Secondary occupation		Secondary occupation	Usual place of residence	Craft specified	Physical disabilities	Temporary residence		Usual place of residence a year ago	Previous address Source of income Means of transportation to work or to attend school	

Notes: 1) Prior to 1941 refer to gainful worker approach and beginning 1947, labour force approach.
2) The seat of establishment only. 3) Tenure and number of rooms and *tatami* etc.

The data for general purposes consist of, by and large, the data obtained from various statistical surveys. It should be noted, however, that all the data obtained from statistical surveys is not necessarily published in tabulated form so as to be readily accessible for public uses. A lot of valuable information which is stored by statistical organizations but left unpublished, may effectively be utilized for filling the gap between the data for particular purposes and the data for general purposes. An example of the information of this kind is those economic data which are collected and stored by National Population Census, whose inquiry is conducted, in principle, every five years. The information obtained from Japanese National Population Census is listed in Table 2. Among the information obtained from the National Population Census, information on economic activity status, industrial and occupational classification of the population and dwelling condition may be utilized to supplement the corresponding published data for general purposes.

The data for general purposes may be further subdivided into two categories The first category of data is those for which the objectives of the statistical inquiry are concerned with particular economic agents, like households, business enterprises and the government, both central and local, institutions. The data which fall into the second category are those whose objectives focus on particular objects, like various kinds of commodities and different types of financial claims (and liabilities).

Major data for general purposes available in Japan are categorized and listed in Table 3.

In some cases, it proves useful to subdivide economic data into micro-economic data and macro-economic data. The economic data which describe the economic activities of an individual economic agent or a set of particular economic agents may be

Table 3. The structure of the economic data for general purposes available in Japan

1. labour
   1. 1. labour force (Labour Force Survey, Basic Survey of Employment Structure)
   1. 2. employment (Monthly Labour Survey, Employment Indices, Labour Turnover Survey, Demand for and Supply of Skilled Labour)
   1. 3. labour productivity survey
2. agriculture, forestry and fishery
   2. 1. census of agriculture, forestry and fishery (World Census of Agriculture and Forestry, Census of Fisheries, Sample Survey of Agriculture)
   2. 2. production survey (Crop Survey, Livestock Products Survey, Sericulture and Cocoon Production Survey, Lumber Statistics Survey, Survey on Catches of Domestic Marine Fisheries, Survey of Production Cost of Agricultural Products)
   2. 3. economic survey of agriculture, forestry and fisheries (Farm Household Economy Survey, Forestry Economy Survey, Fisheries Economy Survey)
   2. 4. distribution survey of agricultural products
   2. 5. processed statistics (Production Indices of Agriculture, Forestry and Fisheries, Food Balance Sheet)
3. mining, manufacturing, electricity and gas
   3. 1. basic census of mining and manufacturing (Survey of Mining Trend in Japan, Census of Manufactures, Basic Surveys of Smaller Enterprises)
   3. 2. curent production statistics
   3. 3. survey of machines and equipments
   3. 4. orders received for machinery
   3. 5. indices relating to mining and manufacturing (Index of Production, Index of Producer's Shipment, Index of Producer's Inventory of Finished Goods, Index of Raw Materials, Index of Sales Trader's Stocks, Index of Production Capacity)
4. Construction
   4. 1. construction and civil engineering work (Statistical Survey of Construction, Survey of Construction Work Orders Received, Statistical Survey on Building Construction Started, Statistical Survey on Building Losses)
   4. 2. dwelling houses (Housing Survey, Survey of Housing Demands)

5. transportation and communication
   5. 1. transportation (National Railway Statistics, Local Railways and Streetcar Statistics, Mortorcar Transportation Statistics, Ships and Seamen Statistics, Vessel Transportation Statistics along Coast, Civil Airway Transportation Statistics)
   5. 2. communication
   5. 3. ports, harbour and warehouse service
   5. 4. comprehensive transportation activity index
6. retail and wholesale trade
   6. 1. basic surveys (Census of Commerce, Basic Survey of Commercial Enterprises)
   6. 2. statistics of current activity (Current Survey of Commerce, Department Stores Sales Statistics, Current Survey of Demand and Supply of Certain Commodities)
   6. 3. indices relating to retail and wholesale trades (Indices for Sales and Merchandise in Stock of Wholesale and Retail Trades, Index of Wholesale Trader's Stocks)
7. international trade
   7. 1. actual exports and imports (The Foreign Trade Statistics of Japan)
   7. 2. exports and imports reported from the acceptance of letters of credit
   7. 3. exports confirmed and imports approved
   7. 4. indices relating to exports and imports (External Trade Unit Value Index, External Trade Quantum Index, Export and Import Price Index)
8. balance of payments and foreign exchange
   8. 1. balance of payments
   8. 2. foreign exchange statistics
9. wages and prices
   9. 1. wages (Basic Survey of Wages Structure, Outdoor Workers' Wages Survey by Occupation, Occupational Wages Survey of Forestry Workers, Survey of Wages and Salaries at Private Firms, Survey of Wages and Salaries by Occupation at Private Firms, Seamen's Labour Survey, Fisheries Worker's Wages Survey, Survey of Wages and Salaries at Central Government Institutions, Survey of Wages and Salaries at Local Government Agencies)
   9. 2. wholesale prices (Wholesale Price Index, Producers' Price Index of Industrial Products, Survey of Prices and Wages in Agricultural Community, Price Index of Commodities in Agricultural Community)

9. 3. retail prices (National Survey of Retail Price, Retail Price Survey, Retail Price Index at Tokyo, Consumer's Price Index, Consumer's Price Index for Farms, Index of Service Charges, Survey of Rents)

10. household surveys
 10 1. non-agricultural and non-fishery householdes economy (Family Income and Expenditure Survey, National Survey of Family Income and Expenditure, Saving Behaviour Survey)
 10. 2. agricultural and fishery households economy (Farm Households Economy Survey, Fisheries Economy Survey)
 10. 3. other surveys (Consumer Behaviour Survey, Survey on Cost of Living for Recipients of Assistance under the Daily Life Security Law, Level of Consumption Expenditure)

11. business surveys
 11. 1. census of establishments
 11. 2. business administration (Statistical Survey of Incorporated Enterprises, Survey of Companies, Unit Corporated Enterprise Survey, Analysis of Financial Statements of Main Industrial Corporations, Analysis of Financial Statements of Small Businesses, Survey of Trading Corporations)
 11.3. corporate investment (Corporate Enterprises Investment Survey, Investment Forecasting Survey of Incorporated Enterprises, Planning and Realization of Investment for Equipments)
 11. 4. anticipation statistics of enterprises (Prospective Survey by Enterprise Managers, Short-term Forecasting of Main Industrial Corporations, Short-term Forcastings of Small Enterprises)

12. finance
 12. 1. statistics on finance at large
 12.2. financial statements of financial institutions
 12. 3. deposits, loans and discounts
 12. 4. clearing of bills
 12. 5. interest rates
 12. 6. securities

13. public finance
 13. 1. central government (Revenue and Expenditure of Budgets and their Settlement, Treasury Account Statistics, Debt Statistics, Tax Statistics, Statistics on Property)
 13. 2. local government (Revenue and Expenditure of Budgets and their Settlement, Tax Statistics, Debt Statistics, Statistics on Property)

14. national income
    - 14. 1. national income statistics
    - 14. 2. input-output tables
    - 14. 3. flow of funds accounts
    - 14. 4. national wealth survey

Notes: 1. Different forms of statistical information that belongs to the same classification are indicated in brackets.
2. Necessary information for preparing this table is obtained from Prime Minister's Office, *Supplement to the Monthly Statistics of Japan: Explanatory Notes*, 1970 edition.

termed here *the micro-economic data.* It is essential for the classification that the characteristics which specify each category of economic agent be clearly defined. Following the convention prevailing in national accounts, it is convenient to distinguish three major categories of economic agents. They are (1) business enterprises, (2) the general government and (3) households and non-profit private institutions. Although it is generally recognized that the characteristics of these major categories of economic agents are clearly defined by internationally standard manuals of national accounts, a few comments may still be worthwhile in this connection. The essential characteristics of business enterprises are, as they are accustomed to say, that they consist of organizations the activities of which purpose to produce goods and services for sale in the market at a price that is normally designed to cover, at least, the costs of production. But it must be borne in mind that the activities with which business enterprises are concerned are not necessarily limited to the production activity. Those activities which are related to the appropriation of incomes, the accumulation or real capital stocks and the financing for the accumulation of capital are equally important for business enterprises. The entire complex of economic activities undertaken by them has a great effect on their organization character. Business enterprises may be regarded as the organization which is made up of establishments equipped with various means of production if the emphasis is chiefly laid on their production activity. This organization character of business enterprises should be distuiguished from the enterprises as legal entity.

The idea of the enterprises as legal entity is often useful, in particular, for the analysis of those activities which are concerned with the appropriation of income and the financing of the accumulation of capital, for those activities have a direct effect on the ownership of real capital stocks and financial claims (and liabilities) of the enterprises.

The scope and function of government activities have attracted considerable attention in the fields of national accounting as well as public economics. Taking note of the recent exploration made in these fields, the authentic functions of government activities are reduced to the two basic activities: (1) the supply of public goods and (2) the redistribution of income. The scope of government activities, consequently the classification of government institutions, is basically conditioned by these basic activities. A salient feature that the supply of and demand for public goods may be governed by the outside forces of the market mechanism reveals itself one of the genuine characteristics of public goods. It should be noted that the generally accepted definition of the general government directly follows from the characteristic of public goods stating that the general government furnishes, but normally does not sell, to the community those common services which cannot otherwise be conveniently and economically provided. In view of this characteristics of public goods, the role of the general government as the supplier of public goods cannot be ignored. The genuine character of government activities is also exhibited in the redistribution of incomes. The redistribution of incomes takes the form of the transfer of purchasing power initiated or enforced by the government institutions. The transfer of purchasing power initiated by the government institutions largely consists of income transfer, but some of it may assume the form of capital transfer. Typical forms of income transfer of the government institutions received from the households or business enterprises are different kinds of taxes, dues and contributions to social insurances.

Before we go into the discussion of the macro-economic data, a few remarks on another source of economic data, the adjusted data, which may be seen as distinguished from the primary data must be made. In this place, the primary data means those which are taken directly from statistical censuses and surveys without making further adjustments. The adjusted data are termed here those economic data which are processed and derived from the primary data. Different sorts of indexes, such as price and quantity indexes, represent an example of the adjusted data. Also, it is readily seen that the economic data related to the national accounting in the broadest sense, including its major components such as the input-output tables, the flow of funds accounts, the national balance sheet and the balance of payments together with the national accounts in the proper sense, fall into this category of economic data. It has often been argued by Japanese statisticians that the adjusted data be produced for serving particular purposes, largely for administration, on the grounds that the design of the flow of funds, for example, must be strictly coordinated with the necessity of the monetary analysis for the monetary authorities no matter how it may ignore the interdependence of the flow of funds with the other components of national accounts (in the broadest sense). But the argument is wrong because the lack of coordination in Japanese economic data which is often discovered results in yeilding mutually inconsistent figures. It follows from this shortcoming that the accurate information will not be accumulated unless we grasp the full meaning of the complex conceptual framework underlying the real and financial transactions on which the focus of the national accounting (in the broadest sense) in recent years has been placed.

In this article *the macro-economic data* may be termed a set of economic data to which the components of national accounts on the broadest sense are related. It should be noted in this terminology that the scope of the macro-economic data is not necessarily limited to aggregate data, with which the macro-economic theories are directly concerned, e.g. gross national product, consumers' expenditure on goods and services, gross domestic capital formation and so forth. Because the data of input-output tables should be necessarily disaggregated in a great number of industries and commodities. Indeed, it is not altogether possible to see the crystul clear line of division between the micro-economic data and the macro-economic data in disaggregated level, as the case of the input-output tables clearly indicates. It is conceivable, on the contrary, that the gaps between the macro-economic data and the micro-economic data which would be found unsurmountable might be filled in if an effective method of linking the two kinds of data together could be invented. In this connection it may be instructive to note that the utilization of the data for particular purposes for the data linkage might get the problem out of the way.

Table 4. Classification of the Economic Data

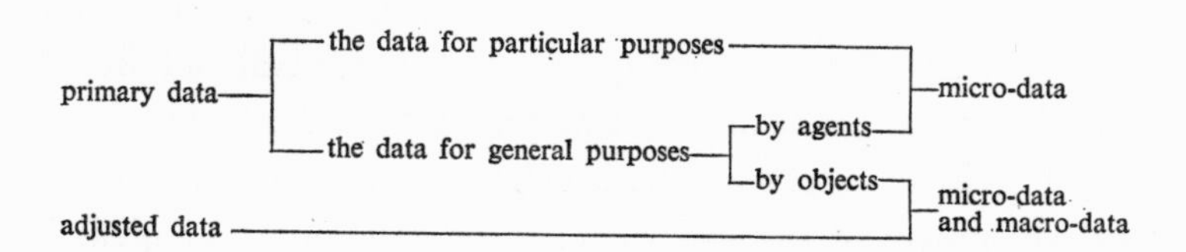

Summing up the discussion in the foregoing sections, the classification of the economic data is given in Table 4.

1.3. Economic Data and Social Data

In connection with the classification of economic data, a few comments on the relation between economic data and social data may be useful for clarifying the nature of economic data as well as the design of EDS. Similar to economic data, a line of demarcation that distinguishes social data from economic data is not obviously clear-cut. One may argue that social data should be defined as a collection of those data which are closely associated with the standard of living of the people. Yet, the definition leaves ambiguity, because some data which are concerned with the standard of living of the people, e.g. those of wages and of the costs of living index are often classified as economic data. Keeping in mind the ambiguity which is involved in distinguishing social data from economic data, the social data may be conveniently grouped as a collection of those data which are concerned with population, health and medical care, social security, housing, education, and community services. A growing importance is attached to the role on these social data which plays not only in the studies of social problems but also in the development of economies. What is especially significant, in the author's view, is the recent development of the social data, in which a system of social data has been called on a growing importance. In spite of the arresting importance attached to the system approach for social data, it appears that the approach has not attracted much attention in Japan. It becomes apparent to us that the necessity of social data, invaluable for the studies of social problems such as public hazards, is acutely felt in Japan. In parallel with the development of EDS, the research and development of the social data system should be of great interest not only for developing the social data but also for establishing a global system which integrates the economic and social data. One may say that it is still too premature to argue for the structure of such a global system. But the considerable significance

Table 5. List of social data in Japan

1. population
    1. 1. population census (National Population Census)
    1. 2. changes in population (Vital Statistics, Vital Statistics according to Social and Economic Characteristics, Statistics on Legal Migrants, Survey on Movement of Registered population)
2. social welfare, health and sanity
    2. 1. general survey (Basic Survey for the Health and Welfare Administration)
    2. 2. social insurance (Survey of Medical Cares Supported by Social Insurances, Monthly Report on Health Insurance for Daily Workers, Welfare Annuity Insurance and Seamen's Insurance)
    2. 3. social welfare (Social Welfare Statistics based on the Administrative Reports Instruction Order, Survey on Social Welfare Institutions)
    2. 4. national sanity (Survey of Medical Institutions, Survey on Economy of Medical Cares, Hospital Report, Survey of Physicians, Dentists and Pharmacists, National Health Survey, Patient Survey, Survey on Communicable Diseases and Food Poisoning, Survey on Tuberculosis, National Nutrition Survey)
3. criminality (Monthly Bulletin of Statistics on Criminal Offences)
4. damages by fire, traffic accidents and sea casualities (Fire Monthly, Statistics on Traffic Accidents, Statistics on Train Operation Accidents, Sea Casualities Statistics)
5. education (Scholl Basic Survey, Survey on School Teachers, Survey on Social Education, School Health Survey, Survey of Local Health Educational Administration and Finance)
6. science (Survey on Research and Development for Science and Technology)
7. religion (Survey of Religious Bodies, Religious Teachers and Believers)

Note: The list is based on the information obtainable from Prime Minister's Office, *Supplemet to the Monthly Statistics of Japan: Explanatory Notes*, 1970 edition.

attached to a global system should not be underrated merely because the development of such global system will belong to the remote future. A list of major social data now available in Japan is given in Table 5.

1.4. The Structure of the Economic Data System

EDS, which is set out and discussed in this paper, is composed of three major component systems that are mutually interrelated. The component systems are called (i) the major system, (ii) the supporting system and (iii) the sub-system. The structural interdependence of the systems may be conveniently displayed in a form of a chain diagram, as indicated below:

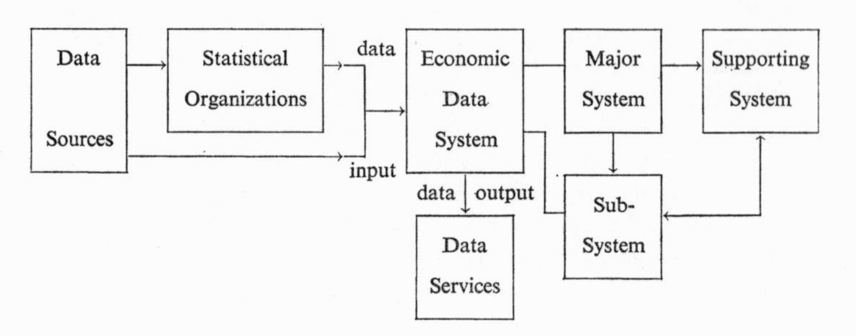

The major system is chiefly concerned with the macro-economic data, whose scope, accordingly, embraces the national accounts in proper sense, the input-output tables, the flow of funds accounts, the national and sector balance sheets and the balance of the payment table. The information of the major system is supplemented by additional and detailed data supplied by the *supporting system*; the structure of the supporting system has therefore to be be closely coordinated with the structure of the major system. Two major roles are fulfilled by *the sub-system*. First, the details of information concerning individual economic agents or groups of particular agents, like households, government agencies and business enterprises, are mapped out within the framework of the sub-system. Puting it in other words, the sub-system is basically concerned with the collection, processing and storage of micro-economic data. Second, it should not be overlooked that the feed-back effects of the sub-system to the major system greatly influence the structure of the major system. The feed-back may be manifested both in the direct form and in the indirect from. In the direct case, on the one hand, the sub-system directly affects the major system, in the indirect case, on the other hand, the feedback goes through the supporting system.

The construction of EDS is of special relevance to work out a system of economic data in Japan. The necessity of such system chiefly originates from the present organization of Japanese statistical agencies. Generally speaking, the organization of statistical agencies may be grouped into the two broad categories, which are termed the centralized statistical organization and the decentralized statistical organization. *The centralized statistical organization* means that the collection, tabulation and storage of statistical information are centralized in a single statistical agency and its ancillary offices. In contrast with this institution, *the decentralized statistical organization* means that the statistical information is collected, tabulated and stored by many decentralized and departmental statistical agencies. According to the classification, the present organization of Japanese statistical agencies seemingly falls into the category of the decentralized statistical organization. The main feature of Japanese statistical organization is well portrayed in the government statistical organization, whose activities are widely diversified, each department having its own statistical agencies by departments, as shown in Table 6.

It mast be admitted that both types of organization have their own advantages and disadvantages. But, it must be remembered that a real shortcoming of the decentralized statistical organization is rooted in the fact that the mutual coordination between various statistical surveys undertaken by different statistical agencies is not necessarily secured, owing to the differences in scopes and methods of statistical surveys. In the case of Japanese statistical organization, it is safe to say that the disadvantages arising from her statistical organization far outweigh the advantage which it entails. Because the duplication of survey items resulting from similar statistical surveys, undertaken by different departmental agencies, often imposes no small amount of burden on the statistics units of local government agencies, responsible for the field works of the surveys. It is expected that the by thə construction of EDS an opportunity to review the contents of statistical surveys in systematic perspective and to remove the unnecessary and redundant information from these statistical surveys may be given especially for the decentralized statistical organization like Japan.

Table 6. Japanese Statistical Organization

Central Government			Local Government	
Administrative Management Agency	Administrative Management Bureau	Statistical Planning Section	Prefectural Government Section in Charge of Statistics	Municipal Governmnet Statistical Unit
		Statistical Clearance Office		
		International Training Co-operation Officer		
	Statistics Council			
		Director of Statistical Standards		
Office of Prime Minister-Brueau of Statistics	Survey Department	General Affairs Section		
		Census Statistics Section		
		Labour Force Statistics Section		
		Economic Statistics Section		
		Consumer's Statistics Section		
	Tabulation Department	Entrusted Tabulation Section		
		Population Tabulation Section		
		Economic Tabulation Section		
		Electronic Data Processing Section		
	Training Institute of Statisticians			
Police Agency	Criminal Investigation Bureau	Research and Statistical Officer		
Economic Planning Agency	Research Bureau	Statistics Section		
	Economic Research Institute	Senior Research Officers		
		National Income Statistics Department		
Scientific and Technical Administration Agency	Planning Bureau	Research Section		

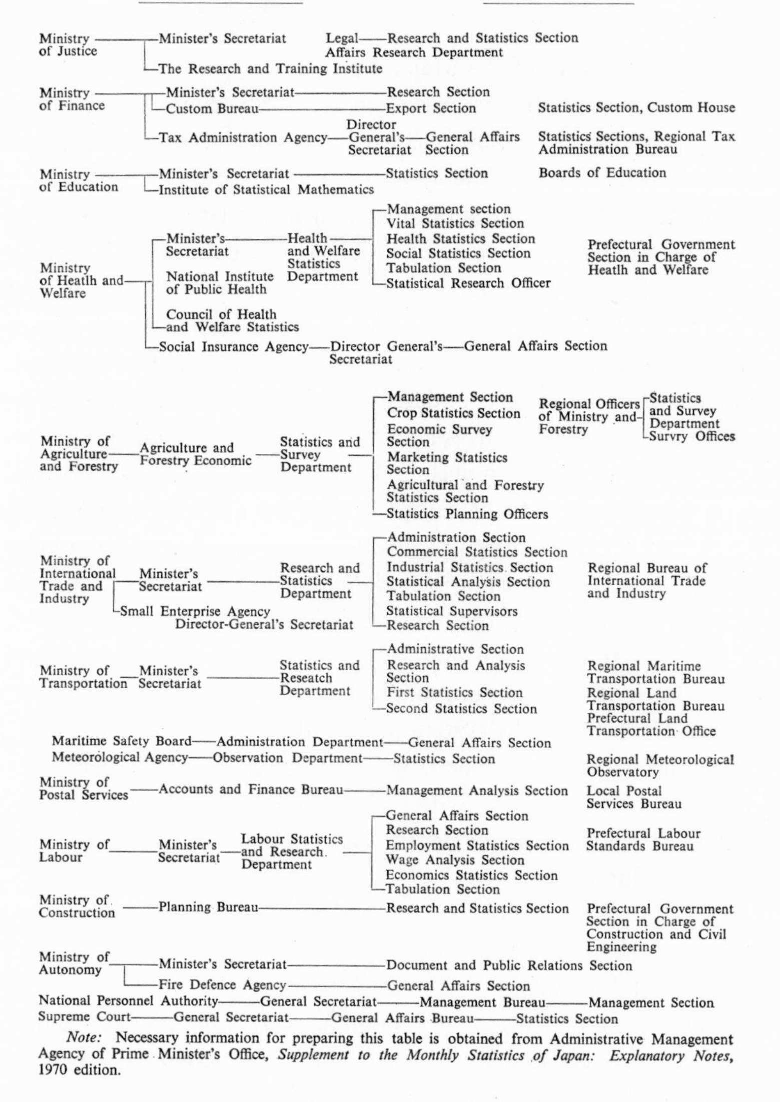

Note: Necessary information for preparing this table is obtained from Administrative Management Agency of Prime Minister's Office, *Supplement to the Monthly Statistics of Japan: Explanatory Notes,* 1970 edition.

2. National Accounts as a Basis of the Major System

2.1. The Structure of the Major System

The structure of the major system of EDS is constructed on the basis of a system of relations. Two arpects of the term of relations may be distinguished in the system. The first may be termed *the form of the relation.* On ccount of the form of relation the system is so constituted that each element which compose the system may be represented by a binary relation. As we readily see that a binary relation may be regarded as a subset of the Cartesian set, the form of relation is unequivocally determined if the Cartesian set is clearly defined. For the system under discussion, the Cartesian set may be defined as a set of Cartesian product whose elements are taken from a set of economic objects. It is assumed that a set of economic objects consists of either goods and services or financial claims, to which non-negative values are assigned. The second may be termed *the content of the relation.* The content of relation is necessary for specifying the characteristic of a binary pair, indicating that it represents the flow of economic object from one economic activity to another economic activity. It is essential for the content of relation in the system to formulate a set of basic economic activities in an unambiguous way. It is reasonable to classify a set of basic economic activities according to the following four categories, which are conveniently listed below:

(1) production
(2) capital formation
(3) income and consumption
(4) capital financing

Generally speaking, a set of economic activities may be termed here a set of operations by which a particular economic object is transformed from one economic state into the other. Thus, the production activity, for instance, may be characterized by the transformation of a particular good or service from a state of input into a state of output. It should be noted that the first two activities among the classification are basically associated with the transformation of goods and services, whereas it should also be noticed that the last two are closely associated with the transformation of financial claims. A question may arise as to the treatment of the income and consumption activity, as it might be argued that the activity be considered as the transformation of goods and services. The reason that the income and consumption activity is associated with the transformation of financial claims is found in the fact that the income flow is most conveniently embodied in the flow of purchasing power that faithfully reflects the transformation of financial claims. The unique role of saving by which the flow of purchasing power is stored for the accumulation of wealth can be fully recognized by the procedure according to which the income and consumption activity is put into the category of economic activities which are associated with the transformation of financial claims. The classification immediately implies the dichotomy of real and financial activities. The *dichotomy of real and financial activities* refers to the fact that a set of those economic activities which are associated with the transformation of goods and services has no common element with a set of economic activities associated with the transformation of financial claims.

A system of relations which is characterized by the form of relation and the content of relation is most appropriately set out in a matrix form. From a formal point of view, it is readily seen that a matrix form is particularly appropriate for expressing any binary relations. Indeed, it is readily shown by the graph theory that a matrix may be defined as a form of graph that is characterized by a set of indexes. Recalling that the structural interdependence of a matrix is exhibited in the specification made by a set of indexes, it is argued that the major system of EDS be explicitly set forth by a matrix, which will be often called *the major system matrix* in the subsequent discussion, being indicated in Table 7.

In the major system matrix, the row and column is divided into two regions, which represent the domestic economy and the rest of the world respectively. The row and column that refer to the

Table 7. The major system matrix

		DE						*RW*
		1	2	Σ_0	3	4	Σ_1	
DE	1	(U)	V	·	C	·	·	X
	2	D	(J)	·	·	I	·	·
	Σ_0	·	·	·	·	A_0	·	·
	3	P	·	·	(G)	·	·	P^+
	4	·	·	L_0	S	(F)	L_1	K^+
	Σ_1	·	·	·	·	A_1	·	·
RW		M	·	·	G^+	F^+	·	·

Notations

U, intermediate products
C, purchases of goods and services for consumption
X, sales of goods and services to RW
D, capital consumption
J, transfer of real capital stocks
V, gross capital formation
I, net capital formation
A, assets ; L, liabilities
P, factor income (or net domestic products)
G, transfer of income
S, saving ; K, capital transfer
F, changes in financial claims
M, purchases of goods and services from RW
(+ mark stands for a net amount)

domestic economy are further subdivided into the groups of economic activities, one of which is concerned with the transformation of the *flow* of goods and services or of financial claims. Another group of economic activities, on the other hand, is related to the transformation of the outstanding *stock* of goods and services or of financial claims. The first group of economic activities consists of four basic economic activities explained before and is indicated by the code number of classification given previously. The second group of economic activities is constituted by the initial and closing stock of assets and liabilities and is expressed by the Σ_0 and Σ_1 respectively. Elements of the major system matrix stand for the important categories of economic transactions which are characterized by the indexes derived from the axiom of relation. Based on this axiom, the indexes clearly indicate the transformation of goods and services and of financial claims which is specified by their originating and terminating activities. Gross capital formation, for example, is indicated by a pair of 1st row and 2nd column, which amounts to saying that gross capital formation is characterized by the transformation of goods and services from the production activity to the capital formation activity. Saying it in other words, gross capital formation is called the inflow of goods and services into the capital formation activity originating from the production activity. Those elements which are located on the principal diagonal are often termed the *internal booking entries*, which are indicated in parenthesis, because the transformation of goods and services or financial claims is limited within the same activity.

In consideration of the noticeable feature that national accounts have provided a basic framework for the collection of economic statistics, it is not really surprising that the structure of the major system matrix closely resembles the structure of national accounts. In fact, it is easily seen that the major system matrix is a variant presentation, in a matrix form, that may be analogous with the revised SNA. Looking at the question from a different angle, the striking resemblance of the major system matrix to a system of national accounts naturally gives us to understand that a system of national accounts performs an important part in working out a system of economic data.

2.2. The Supporting System that Supplements the Major System

The details of information attached to the major system are enlarged and supplemented by devising the supporting system. Such divice gives the major system maximum flexibility in putting the collection of data and their storage in better order. Paralled to the design of the major system which makes most use of the knowledge of national accounts that has been expounded in the last decades, the elaboration of the constituent systems of national accounts furnishes the basis for considering the supporting system. In line with the classification of basic economic activities in the major system, it is the logical order that the elaboration of the input-output table, the national accounts and other constituents be considered one after another. In view of the fact that the national and sector balance sheets constitute an important component of an extended system of national accounts, we can not fail to discount the function of the national and sector balance sheets as a substantial constituent for the supporting system. But the consideration of the supporting system in this article is limited to the elaboration of the selective elements of national accounts (in broad sense). The national and sector balance sheets are omitted from the scope of the present consideration merely because the data that are available from the Japanese National Wealth Survey, which is carried out by Economic Planning Agency every five years, are far from what is desired for the material of the supporting system.

Table 8. The major system matrix and the input-output table

		DE						*RW*
		1	2	Σ_0	3	4	Σ_1	
DE	1			·		·	·	
	2		(J)	·	·	I	·	·
	Σ_0	·	·	·	·	A_0	·	·
	3		·	·	(G)	·	·	P^+
	4	·	·	L_0	S	(F)	L_1	K^+
	Σ_1	·	·	·	·	A_1	·	·
RW			·	·	G^+	F^+	·	·

		1		*R*1
		OOM	*ACT*	
1	*COM*	·	U	$C+V+X$
	ACT	Z	·	·
*R*1		$D+M$	P	·

(*R*1 stands for the all row and columns of the rest of the first row and column.)

(i) the input-output table as a component of the supporting system

The elements which are pertinent to the input-output table are to be found in the shaded elements of the major system matrix, as indicated in Table 8. A system of sub-matrices which correspond to the shaded elements in the major system matrix of Table 8 immediately follows from the break down of those rows and columns

Table 9. The input sub-matrix and output sub-matrix

input (*U*)

		ACT CODE			
		1	2	3	....
COM CODE	1				
	2				
	3				
	⋮				

output (*Z*)

		COM CODE			
		1	2	3	....
ACT CODE	1				
	2				
	3				
	⋮				

which refer to the shaded elements in the major system matrix. The sub-matrices proposed for the supporting system has the structure spelled out below.

1. The production activity which is represented by 1st row and column may be subdivided according to (1) the categories of products, which is often termed commodities, and (2) the production agents, which is commonly termed activities. It follows from this break down that the structure of inputs and outputs is exhibited separately in the input sub-matrix and output sub-matrix as given in Table 9.

Noting the fact that the production agents are conveniently categorized according to establishments, the sub-matrices are of great use for sorting out the data which are concerned with the production activity. Particularly, it is important to keep in mind that the Current Production Survey of the Ministry of International Trade and Industry (MITI in abbreviation), which constitutes the basic information of the Japanese input-output table, supplies the data of inputs and outputs by commodities on the establishments basis. It should be also noted that the organization of production statistics according to the input sub-matrix and output sub-matrix carries no immediate implication that the input-output table constructed from the production data retains the structure of input and output matrices as indicated in Table 9.

It is essential for the elaboration of the input sub-matrix and the output sub-matrix that the codes of commodities and activities be clearly formulated. In Japan two types of code system are in current use for the classification of commodities. They are (i) the Standard Commodity Classification for Japan (SCCJ for short) and (ii) the commodity classification specially designed for Japanese input-output table. The commodity classification specially designed for the Japanese input-output table contains about 3,000 commodities which are coded with 9 digits. Not only the classification exactly represents the characteristics of products resulting from various production activities, but also it is of particular importance to note that the classification is so designed that it may be regrouped to follow the 6 digits categories of the United Nations' International Standard Industrial Classification of All Economic Activities (ISIC for short). As for the classification of industries, it must be noted that the classification portrays the character of production agents, which is delineated by a complex of physical production capacities whose function is to become an agent for a production activity. Neither the ownership of capital assets nor the legal entities of business organizations are distinguished by the classification. In Japan it has been requested by a government ordinance that the industrial classification of statistical data be made on the basis of the Standard Industrial Classification for Japan (SICJ for short). In spite of the existence of the official classification, ISIC has been employed for the construction of Japanese input-output tables, because ISIC is better for the classification of economic activities.

2. Suppose the 2nd row and column of the major system matrix

Table 10. Sub-matrices for capital formation

		ACT CODE			
		1	2	3	....
COM CODE	1				
	2				
	3				
	⋮				

		TYPE CODE			
		1	2	3	....
ACT CODE	1				
	2				
	3				
	⋮				

Table 11. Groups of real capital stocks according to types

(i)	Residential buildings
(ii)	Non-residential buildings
(iii)	Other construction
(iv)	Machinery and equipment
(v)	Transportation equipment
	(v. i) ships
	(v. ii) other transportation equipment
(vi)	Tools and instruments
(vii)	Breeding stock, dairy cattle and plantation etc.
(viii)	Land improvement

are subdivided by activities and functional uses of real capital stocks. It follows by the subdivision that those elements which are related to 2nd row and 2nd column of the major system matrix form sub-matrices whose structure is shown in Table 10 and Table 12. It is indicated by Table 10 that the statistical information for gross capital formation is clearly sorted out by (a) a sub-matrix with the commodity row and activity column and (b) a sub-matrix with the activity row and the types of capital stocks column. The types of real capital stocks may be grouped according to the categories of real capital stocks as is shown in Table 11.

It should be noted that the grouping of real capital stocks according to types is particularly well fitted into the classification of assets and liabilities which are pertinent to Σ_0 row and column (their initial stocks) as well as Σ_1 row and column (their closing stocks). Indeed, Japanese National Wealth Survey, which is undertaken every five years since 1955, compiles the data of real capital stocks cross-classified by the categories of production activities and the type of real capital stocks. The classification for the types of real capital stocks in Japanese National Wealth Survey is virtually identical with what is indicated in Table 11.

Owing to the subdivision of 2nd row into the row that represents the categories of production activity and the row that represents the types of real capital stocks, the elements which appear in the 2nd row of the major system matrix can be easily transformed into sub-matrices, whose structure is spelled out in Table 12. It is interesting to see that the function of J matrix may be interpreted as a converter in which V matrix in Table 10 is transformed into J matrix of Table 12 with no need for further adjustments. The structure of I matrix deserves to be mentioned on account of its relation to the subdivision of row and column 4. Supposing that row and column 4 are subdivided by a set of economic agents that are classified according to the ownership of assets and liabilities, which are often called institutional sectors, it is readily seen

Table 12. The interrelationship between D, J and I matrices

		1	
		COM	*ACT*
2	*ACT*	·	·
	TYPE	*D*	·

		2	
		ACT	*TYPE*
2	*ACT*	·	*J*
	TYPE	·	·

		4
2	*ACT*	·
	TYPE	*I*

that I matrix is composed of the row which represents the types of real capital stocks and the column which represents the institutional sectors.

3. Similar to the sub-matrices for capital formation, it is possible to consider the submatrices for consumers' expenditure. Remembering that consumers' expenditure is mapped out as an element of 1st row and 3rd column of the major system matrix, the structure of sub-matrices for consumers' expenditure is subject to the subdivision of the row and the column. In accordance with the subdivision of 1st row and 1st column according to commodities and activities, the structure of consumers' expenditure takes the form indicated in Table 13. In the table, the structure of factor incomes, which is located on the symmetrical position with consumers' expenditure in the major system matrix, is also shown.

Suppose 3rd column of the major system matrix is further subdivided according to income earning groups as indicated in Table 13. It is readily seen that C element in the right of the table (consumers' expenditure) forms a sub-matrix, whose structure is shown in the left of Table 14. The classification of consumers' expenditure according to purposes often turns out useful not only for the collection of statistical information but also for analytical purposes.

Table 13. Structures of Consumers' expenditure and factor incomes

		1	
		COM	*ACT*
3	*SECTOR*	·	*P*

		3
		SECTOR
1	*COM*	*C*
	ACT	

Table 14. Sub-matrices for consumers' expenditure

		SECTOR CODE			
		1	2	3	....
COM CODE	1				
	2				
	3				
	⋮				

		SECTOR CODE			
		1	2	3	....
PURPOSE CODE	1				
	2				
	3				
	⋮				

A sub-matrix of consumers' expenditure which has purpose rows and income group columns as indicated in the right of Table 14 is derived from the sub-matrix that is shown in the left of Table 14 without much difficulties. Indeed, the form of the derived matrix for consumers' expenditure such as the right of Table 14 is appropriate for the collection and storage of data which are obtained from Family Budgets Data in Japan.

Family Budgets Data in Japan are broadly itemized into two categories: (i) those for non-agricultural and non-fishery households and (ii) those for agricultural, forestry and fishery households. The data of the first category are available from *the Family Income and Expenditure Survey* on monthly basis and from *the National Sureyv of Family Income and Expenditure* on every five years basis. The data which are particularly concerned with lower income classes are supplemented with the data obtained from *the Survey on Cost of Living for Recipients of Assistance under the Daily Life Security Law*, which is annually undertaken by Ministry of Health. The data which fall under the second category are obtained from three major sources. They are (i) *the Farm Household Economy Survey*, (ii) *the Fisheries Economy Survey* and (iii) *the Forestry*

Economy Survey. These surveys are undertaken by the Ministry of Agriculture, Forestry and Fisheries on monthly basis. All family budgets data in Japan give full account of receipts and expenditure items which are classified according to major expenditure purposes. Major expenditure purposes are generally constituted of five categories: (i) food, (ii) housing, (iii) fuel and light, (iv) clothing and (v) miscellaneous. It is also possible to obtain information that is further subdivided according to detailed categories of expenditure purposes. Family Budgets Data in Japan are well fitted into the form of the derived sub-matrix as indicated in the right of Table 14.

4. The most comprehensive and elaborate work for producing annual series of input-matrix and output-matrix as mentioned before beginning with 1951 both in current and constant 1970 prices is currently carried out by the Center for Econometric Data Development and Research, a private non-profit research organization in Tokyo. In the work, considerable efforts have been exerted to collect much detailed information concerning the time series of both inputs and outputs which is compiled both from hitherto published tables and from other scattered sources on the basis of an unified code system. Basically, the system is formulated according to the classification of approximately 3,000 commodities coded with 9 digits, so that it is readily adapted to th ecommodity classification used for the published input-output tables in Japan. Using the notations shown in Table 8, the collected series of data may be distinguished under the following headings: (i) U and Z series, (ii) X and M series, (iii) V series and (iv) C series. Hence, the input and output sub-matrices of Table 9 may serve for the reference framework of collection of data for U and Z series. Similar idea is applied to the collection of data concerning X and M series. CEDDR intends to construct a matrix of fixed capital

formation, but the exercise is simply the application of some type of capital formation sub-matrix, as appeared in the right of Table 11. In connection with the data collection for C series, a project which explores the possibility of combining the information collected from family budgets data with what is obtained from the input-output tables is established. The orientation of the project may be brought into clear understanding by reference to the consumers' expenditure sub-matrices which have been set out in Table 14. Thus, it is possible to give strong support to the idea that the proposed EDS is especially useful for the elaborate work CEDDR undertakes.

(ii) the place of national accounts as a component of the supporting system

Elements related to the national accounts proper in the major system matrix appear in the shaded elements in Table 15. It is readily seen by the presentation that special emphasis should be placed on the activities which are concerned with the formation and consumption of incomes if we would consider the place of national accounts as a component of the supporting system. In

Table 15. The major system matrix and the national accounts

		DE						RW
		1	2	Σ_0	3	4	Σ_1	
DE	1	(U)		•		•	•	
	2		(J)	•	•		•	•
	Σ_0	•	•	•	•	A_0	•	•
	3		•	•	(G)	•	•	
	4	•	•	L_0		(F)	L_1	
	Σ_1	•	•	•	•	A_1	•	•
RW			•	•			•	•

		DE				RW
		1	2	3	4	
DE	1	·	V	C	·	X
	2	D	·	·	I	·
	3	P	·	(G)	·	P^+
	4	·	·	S	·	K^+
RW		M	·	G^+	F^+	·

Table 16. Sub-matrices for factor incomes

			ACT CODE			
			1	2	3	…………
SECTOR CODE	1	*W*				
		O				
	2	*W*				
		O				
	3	*W*				
		O				
	⋮					

		SECTOR CODE			
		1	2	3	……………
FORM CODE	1				
	2				
	3				
	⋮				

this connection, two elements in the national accounts are taken up for consideration. They are (i) factor incomes and (ii) the transfer of incomes. The structure of the supporting systems which are used for the collection and storage of the data that are related to those elements is conditioned by the break down of rows and columns with which they are associated. The break down of the first row and column has been examined in detail when we considered the supporting systems concerning the input-output table. Recalling that the third row and column may be subdivided according to the income earning groups, the supporting system concerning the factor incomes are indicated in detail by the matrix in the left of Table 16.

The information classified by the sub-matrix shown in the left of Table 16 is further supplemented by a sub-matrix that is shown in the right of Table 16. In the sub-matrix that appears in the right of Table 16, the income earning groups are transposed to columns, and the rows are again broken down according to the forms of factor incomes. The forms of factor incomes may be classified according to their function. An example of the classification of factor incomes that is employed in Japanese national accounts is given below. Japanese national accounts distinguish seven forms of factor incomes. They are (i) compensation for employee, (ii) proprietors incomes, (iii) rents of persons, (iv) property incomes of persons, (v) corporate incomes, (vi) incomes from entrepreneurship by the government and (vii) property incomes of the government. It is also noted that the sub-matrix in the left of Table 16 may be derived from the data stored in the input-output table as we have already hinted in Table 13. The co-existence of the two forms of sub-matrices for factor incomes is by no means an accident: two methods are often made use of at the same time for collecting the estimates of factor incomes. They are usually termed (i) the production approach and (ii) the income approach. The statistical information that follows the production approach is collected by and stored in the sub-matrix in the left of Table 16, whereas the information that follows the income approach is conveniently collected by and stored in the sub-matrix in the right of Table 16.

Transfer of incomes is especially pertinent to the redistribution of income. Essentially, the redistribution of income is effected by the public sector. It is convenient, for the formulation of the income redistribution structure, to consider the income earning groups which constitute a subdivision of the 3rd row and column of the major system matrix are consolidated into two major groupings. They may be termed *the public sector* and *the market sector at large* respectively. The redistribution of income takes place between the public sector and the market sector at large. Two points are raised when we proceed to the formulation of the sub-matrices of transfer of incomes. First, it is important that the statistical information be organized well. Particularly, the classification of expenditure according to purposes, the functional classification as it used to be called, is essential for the formulation. In Japan the expenditure statistics of budgets and their settlement, for central and local governments, are categorized under three headings. They are called (i) the major item, which is said *kan* in Japanese, (ii) the sub-item, called *kho*, and (iii) the detailed item, which *moku*. According to the regulations, the detailed items may not be used as a payment for other purposes than those indicated in the budgets. It follows from the nature of the detailed item that the functional classification is generally possible if we go down to the detailed item. In this connection it is noted that a code system has been introduced to the records of Japanese budgets since 1969. The introduction of a code system into the budgets makes a great step forward the functional classification. Unfortunately, the introduction of code system is limited to the budgets and is not applied to the records of their settlement. It must be stressed that the introduction of a code system remains only half way in the direction of effecting the economic data system unless it is universally adopted in government statistics.

Second, it should be recognized that the transfer of incomes by the public sector is got backed with a large number of administrative institutions. Available statistical information for the transfer of incomes is, by and large, collected and classified according to this institutional basis. It would extremely useful to conceive a converter system which translates the statistical information on the institutional basis into the elements of the sub-matrices for the transfer of incomes. Following this line of thought, the design of the sub-matrices for the transfer of incomes was given in greater detail in the essay preceding to this article.

3. Acknowlgements and Additional Remarks

This article is a reproduction of my paper under the same title, presented to 12th General Conference of the International Association for Research in Income and Wealth held at Ronneby, Sweden in August 30—September 4, 1971; no substantial alterations were made. I express deep appreciation for the comments raised by Mr. Per Sevaldson, who accepted the discussant of my paper, and by other participants.

In particular, I am in full agreement with the point made by him at the IARIW conference, to the effect that a consistent system of statistical concepts and a closely coordinated statistical organization are essential for the efficient collection, processing and storage of economic data. Originally, this article grew out of the works made in a research project, financially supported by the Center for Econometric Date Development and Research of Tokyo, for the development of an economic data system. The project was intended to establish an effective link between decentralized and scattered economic data, within the framework of a consistent and comprehensive statistical system for the coordination of the economic data. Economic data of general use in Japan, as I have noted, were collected and processed by decentralized statistical organizations without any consideration for their mutual coordination. Then, it was considered of great help for the research of the CEDDR that a consistent and comprehensive statistical system for the coordination of economic data be invented so as to form a conceptual basis of the statistical works in the CEDDR. I wish to extend my hearty thanks to Professor Iwao Ozaki of Keio University, the former Director of Research of the CEDDR, for his unaltered interest and encouragements for developing such a consistent system. My thanks are also due to Mr. Naoki Kitayama, then Senior Research Associate of the CEDDR and now is the Chief of Population Census Section of the Bureau of Statistics, for his valuable comments.

After this article was written, the Economic Planning Agency has embarked on a project undertaking a radical revision of the official Japanese system of national accounts and their estimates. It is aimed by the revision that Japanese system of national accounts be completely updated taking fully into account the recent progress of SNA. It is interesting to note that the scope of the EPA's project for the revision of national accounts is easily translated into the framework of our EDS. Indeed, the focal point of the revision is the construction of sector production accounts and their integration with the official system of national accounts. The design of the sector production accounts may be explained in terms of the input and output sub-matrices (Table 9) and the sub-matrices for factor incomes (Table 16) of the supporting system. In our framework, the EPA's project first constructs a Z matrix, then the Z matrix is transformed into a U matrix applying the assumption of commodity technology. As we have noted in the first essay of this book, the use of the assumption of commodity technology provides a close approximation to the result from the assumption of F technology. A sub-matrix of factor incomes cross-classified by activity and sector (the left of Table 16) immediately follows from the information of Z and U matrices.

As we have explained in this article, the introduction of Z and U matrices into a system of national accounts necessarily affects the other constituent elements of our major system matrix. Therefore, it is natural to consider sub-matrices for capital formation (Table 10) and for consumers' expenditure (Table 14) in this connection. In the EPA's project, sub-matrices for capital formation and consumers' expenditure both cross-classified by commodity and activity (or sector) are designed as a consequence of the commodity flow estimates of Z and U matrices.

The derivation of the value added in constant princes by production sector naturally follows from the design of sector production accounts. In fact, the derivation of the sector value added in constant prices by the double deflation method occupies a top priority in the programme of the EPA's project. The discussion raised in the third essay of this book about the effect of changes in terms of trade between intermediate input prices and output prices may stand as a warning against a straightfoward application of the double deflation method for the derivation of the sector value added in constant prices. It deserves to be empirically tested whether the derived series of the value added by production sector in constant prices appreciably contain the effect of changes in terms of trade between the intermediate inputs and output as available from the derived series.

It must be stressed for the construction of sector production accounts that the computational work for it makes enormous progress with the help of computers, limiting the manual works for computation to the minimum. In the EPA's project, the computational framework for the construction of sector production accounts is so designed, from the outset of the work, that it may be carried out on the basis of an extensive use of computers. Thus, starting with the formation of an appropriate data base, processing of data, listing of computation and the storage of the result are consecutively executed following the computer programmes. The manual works still remain in the project but they are kept within limited amounts. It should be recognized here that the application of the potential of computers to the construction of sector production accounts is a natural consequence of the idea of the EDS that places special emphasis on the systems approach of collection, processing and storage of economic data.

I have discussed in this article about the necessity of the statistical system for social data with certain reservation. When I wrote this article, it was generally considered, at least in Japan, that the systems approach to social statistics is too premature. The situation has been greatly changed since then. In particular, the development of the System of Social and Demographic Statistics (SSDS) by the United Nations and the initiation of the Basic Survey of Social and Community Life by the Bureau of Statistics of the Prime Minister's Office of the Japanese Covernment have given a fresh impetus to the systems approach to social statistics. Further thoughts on the topic will be developed in the seventh essay of this book.

6

PROBLEMS OF NATIONAL ACCOUNTS DATA ADJUSTMENTS FOR DEVELOPING COUNTRIES

1. The Scope and Method of the Present Work

The scope of national accounts data adjustments for developing countries that have been carried out by the author is basically limited by several conditions. They are the availability of data, sources of information, constraints of observation and purposes of data adjustments. Among these conditions, the purpose of data adjustments assumes an essential part. The purpose of the author's work for national accounts data adjustments is to supply a series of data for national accounts aggregates on a consistent basis in the most comprehensive coverage of developing countries, so that the series may be used as the basic material for the quantitative analysis of the economic development in developing countries, in an international perspective. For this purpose, it is considered to be useful that the potential of computers be extensively utilized, not only for the compilation and adjustments of data but also for their the storage and retrieval. It is true that the scale of data that are processed within a computer is necessarily limited by its capacity, but I shall not discuss in full details the optimum use of computers for national accounts data adjustments in relation to their capacities. The topic is seemingly outside of the scope of the present work. The use of computers for national accounts data adjustments and compilation has once been taken up as a subject for the one of the sessions of the 9th General Conference of the International Association for Research in Income and Wealth, and the principle and the methods of the use of computers for national accounts data compilation have been discussed there. It is only noted here that the present work by the author is carried out by the use of a moderately small-scale computer.[1)]

The availability of data and sources of information invites the second consideration for the national accounts data adjustment. The points will be discussed in further detail in the subsequent section. Before the discussion, a few words may deserve to be noted here. In the present work, most of national accounts aggregates for the adjustments are taken from the United Nations', *Yearbook of National Accounts Statistics*, which will subsequently be written by YBNAS for short; yet the consultation of national sources is made when necessary. The reason why the basic statistical sources of the present study are obtained from YBNAS is that YBNAS collects the data for national accounts aggregates at the most comprehensive coverage of countries with a uniform basis of presentation. The uniform form of presentation is based on *National Accounts Questionnaire*. The questionnaire form, in essence, follows the presentation of the supporting tables of SNA,

---

1) The point has been discussed by Mayer and Schioetz. See, J. Mayer, [1966] and T. Schioetz [1966].

which is an abbreviation of United Nations, *A System of National Accounts*. The applicability and usefulness of SNA for the development of a system of national accounts in developing countries have again been put into question since the publication of the revised SNA. Even if the point may be of indirect concern, it should be kept in mind that the results of the present work by the author are necessarily associated with the question. The code number of developing countries with which our national accounts data compilation is concerned is given in Table 1.

Table 1. Basic country code for GDP data compilation

(° indicates no independent estimates are available. Such countries are included in the " n.e.c." classification of relevant regions.)

2000	*Developing market economies*
2100	*Latin America (excluding Cuba)*
2110	*Central American and Carribean*
2111	Costa Rica
2112	Dominican Republic
2113	El Salvador
2114	Guatemala
2115	Haiti
2116	Honduras
2117	Nicaragua
2118	Panama
2120	*Semi-industrialized countries*
2121	Argentina
2122	Brazil
2123	Chile
2124	Colombia
2125	Mexico
2126	Peru
2127	Uruguay
2128	Venezuela
2130	*Other Latin American countries*
2131	Bolivia
2132	Ecuador
2133	Paraguay

2200	*Africa (excluding South Africa)*
2210	*North Africa*
2211	Algeria
2212	Libya
2213	Morocco
2214	Sudan
2215	Tunisia
2216	United Arab Republic
2220	*West Africa, English-speaking*
°2221	Gambia
2222	Ghana
2223	Liberia
2224	Nigeria
2225	Sierra Leone
2230	*West Africa, French-speaking*
°2231	Dahomey
°2232	Guinea
2233	Ivory Coast
°2234	Mali
°2235	Mauritania
°2236	Niger
°2237	Senegal
2238	Togo
2239	Upper Volta
°2265	Former French Equatorial Africa
°2266	Former French West Africa
2240	*Central Africa*
2241	Cameroon
°2242	Central African Republic
°2243	Chad
°2244	Congo (Brazaville)
2245	Congo (Democratic Republic)
2246	Gabon
2247	Angola
2248	Mozambique
2250	*East Africa*
2251	Ethiopia
2252	Kenya
2253	Madagascar
2254	Malawi, Rhodesia and Zambia combined

°2255 Burundi and Ruanda combined
°2256 Somalia (former Italian part)
2257 Tanzania
2258 Uganda
2260 *African dependencies*
2261 Mauritius
°2264 African n.e.c.

(Notes)
1. The coverage of 2265 is indicated as below: Central African Republic, Chad, Congo (Brazzaville) and Gabon.
2. The coverage of 2266 is indicated as below: Dahomey, Guinea, Ivory Coast, Mali, Mauritania, Niger, Senegal and Upper Volta.
3. The following countries are included in 2264: Cape Verde Islands, Gambia, Portuguese Guinea Reunion, French Somaliland, Somalia, Seychelles, Zanzibar and Pemba, Rwanda and Brundi, Comoro Islands, Ifni, Spanish Equatorial Region, Spanish North Africa, Spanish Sahara and St. Helena.

2300 *Far East (excluding Japan)*
2310 *India*
2320 *Other semi-industrialized countries*
2321 Taiwan (China)
2322 Pakistan
2323 Philippines
°2324 Hong Kong
2330 *Rice-exporting countries*
2331 Burma
2332 Cambodia
°2333 Laos
2334 Thailand
2335 Viet-Nam
2340 *Raw material-exporting countries*
2341 Ceylon
2342 Indonesia
2343 Malaysia (excluding Sabah and Sarawak)
2350 *Other Far Eastern countries*
°2351 Afghanistan
°2352 Nepal
2353 Republic of Korea

°2355	Far East n.e.c.
(Note)	2355 includes the following countries: Cambodia, Viet-Nam, Laos, Singapore, Afghanistan, Brunei, Hong Kong, Sabah and Sarawak.
2400	*West Asia*
2410	*Selected countries other than Israel*
2411	Iran
2412	Iraq
2413	Jordan
2414	Kuwait
2415	Lebanon
°2416	Saudi Arabia
2417	Syria
°2418	Yemen
°2420	West Asia n.e.c.
(Note)	The following countries are included in 2420: Aden (including Protectorate), Qatar and Bahrain, Gaza Strip, Trucial Oman, Muscat and Oman, and Yemen.
2500	*Other developing market economies*
2511	Barbados
2512	Guyana
2513	Jamaica
2514	Trinidad and Tobago
°2515	Other developing market economies n.e.c.
(Note)	The following territories are included in 2515: Bahama, Bermuda, British Honduras, Leeward Islands, Windward Islands, Virgin Islands (U.K.), Virgin Islands (U.S.), Fiji Islands, Cayman Islands, Turks and Caicos Islands, Guadeloope, Martinique, New Hebrides, New Caledonia, French Polynesia, French Guiana, St. Pierre and Miquelon, Falkland Islands, Greenlands, Panama Canal Zone, British Solomon Islands, Western Samoa, New Guinea, Papua, Guam, Gilbert and Ellice Islands, Tonga, Netherlands Antilles and Surinam.

As the third consideration for the present work the length of the period of observation and the subject items of which data are compiled may be noted. In the absence of adequate information for the early nineteen-fifties, the numerical series of national accounts aggregates which are referred to in this article are largely those of the period between 1958 and 1967 that corresponds broadly with the first Development Decade. In spite of the limitation of the period of observation in this article, the utmost efforts are exerted for processing the longer series of data so that the period of observation may be extended to the begining of nineteen fifties. It is generally recognized that a close correlation exists between the specification of the period of observation and the availability of the details of national accounts aggregates. The longer the period of observation we may need, the smaller the amount of information for national accounts aggregates we may have. Thus, the selection of subject items that are processed for data storage is partially dependent on the specification of the period of observation. After the careful consideration of this close correlation, the subject items that are processed for national accounts data adjustments are limited to the series of GDP by expenditure components and by industry origin. These series of data are expressed not only in current values but also in constant values uniformly expressed at 1960 prices.

Furthermore, the GDP series in constant values are converted into U.S. dollars, so that the regional or sub-regional total may be readily calculated. An additional difficulty often arises from the conversion, because the official exchange rate does not necessarily represent a real conversion factor of national accounts aggregates. The point will be further examined in the subsequent section taking a concrete example from national accounts aggregates of selected Latin American countries.

The availability of the processed GDP series both by expenditure components and by industry origin is indicated in Table 2. It is readily seen from Table 2 that the author's efforts to derive

Table 2. Summary table of processed GDP series

	By Expenditure		*By Industry Origin*	
	Data in Current Prices	Data in 1960 Prices	Data in Current Prices	Data in 1960 Prices
Latin America				
Costa Rica	1958–1967	1958–1967	1958–1967	1958–1967
Dominican Rep.	1958–1967	1958–1967	1958–1967	1958–1967
El Salvador	1958–1967	1958–1967	1958–1967	1958–1967
Guatemala	1958–1967	1958–1967	1958–1967	1958–1966
Haiti	1958–1967	1958–1967	1958–1962	n.a.
Honduras	1958–1967	1958–1967	1958–1967	1958–1967
Nicaragua	1958–1967	1958–1967	1960–1967	1960–1967
Panama	1958–1967	1958–1967	1958–1967	1958–1967
Argentina	1958–1967	1958–1967	1958–1967	1958–1967
Brazil	1958–1967	1958–1967	1958–1967	1958–1967
Chile	1958–1967	1958–1967	1958–1967	1958–1967
Colombia	1958–1967	1958–1967	1958–1967	1958–1967
Mexico	1958–1967	1958–1967	n.a.	1958–1967
Peru	1958–1967	1958–1967	1958–1967	1958–1967
Uruguay	1958–1967	1958–1967	1958–1967	1958–1967
Venezuela	1958–1967	1958–1967	1958–1967	1958–1967
Bolivia	1958–1967	1958–1967	1958–1967	1958–1967
Ecuador	1958–1967	1958–1967	1958–1967	1958–1967
Paraguay	1958–1967	1958–1967	1958–1967	1958–1967
Africa				
Algeria	1958–1967	1958–1967	1958–1967	1958–1967
Libya	1958–1967	1958–1967	1958–1967	1958–1967
Morocco	1958–1967	1958–1967	1958–1967	1958–1967
Sudan	1958–1967	1958–1967	1958–1967	1958–1967
Tunisia	1958–1967	1958–1967	1960–1967	1960–1967
U.A.R.	1958–1967	1958–1967	1962–1965	1958–1965
Ghana	1958–1967	1958–1967	n.a.	1958–1967
Liberia	1958–1967	1958–1967	n.a.	n.a.
Nigeria	1958–1967	1958–1967	1958–1965	1958–1965
Sierra Leone	1958–1967	1958–1967	1963–1967	1963–1967
Ivory Coast	1958–1967	1958–1967	1960–1966	1960–1966
Togo	1958–1967	1958–1967	1963–1966	n.a.

	By Expenditure		*By Industry Origin*	
	Data in Current Prices	Data in 1960 Prices	Data in Current Prices	Data in 1960 Prices
Cameroun	1958–1967	1958–1967	1964–1967	n.a.
Congo (D.R.)	1958–1967	1958–1967	1958, 1959 1964–1967	1958, 1959 1964–1967
Angola	n.a.	1958–1967	n.a.	n.a.
Mozambique	n.a.	1958–1967	n.a.	n.a.
Ethiopia	1958–1967	1958–1967	1961–1967	1961–1967
Kenya	1958–1967	1958–1967	1958–1967	1958–1967
Madagascar	1958–1967	1958–1967	n.a.	n.a.
Malawi, Rhodesia and Zambia	1958–1967	1958–1967	1958–1967	1958–1967
Tanzania	1958–1967	1958–1967	1958–1967	1958–1967
Uganda	1958–1967	1958–1967	1958–1967	1958–1967
Mauritius	1958–1967	1958–1967	1958–1967	1958–1967
Africa n.e.c.	n.a.	1958–1967	n.a.	n.a.
Former French Equatorial Africa	n.a.	1958–1967	n.a.	n.a.
Former French West Africa	n.a.	1958–1967	n.a.	n.a.
Far East				
India	1958–1967	1958–1967	1958–1967	1958–1967
Taiwan (China)	1958–1967	1958–1967	1958–1967	1958–1967
Pakistan	1958–1967	1958–1967	1958–1967	1958–1967
Philippines	1958–1967	1958–1967	1958–1967	1958–1967
Burma	1958–1967	1958–1967	1958–1967	1958–1967
Cambodia	1962–1966	1962–1966	1960–1966	1960–1966
Thailand	1958–1967	1958–1967	1958–1967	1958–1967
Viet-Nam	1960–1966	1960–1967	1960–1967	1960–1965
Ceylon	1958–1967	1958–1967	1958–1967	1958–1967
Indonesia	1958–1967	1958–1967	1958–1967	1958–1967
Malaysia	1958–1967	1958–1967	1958–1967	1958–1967
Korea	1958–1967	1958–1967	1958–1967	1958–1967
Far East n.e.c.	n.a.	1958–1967	n.a.	n.a.
West Asia				
Iran	1958–1967	1958–1967	1959–1967	1959–1967
Iraq	1958–1967	1958–1967	1958–1967	1958–1967

	By Expenditure		*By Industry Origin*	
	Data in Current Prices	Data in 1960 Prices	Data in Current Prices	Data in 1960 Prices
Jordan	1958–1967	1958–1967	1958–1967	1958–1967
Kuwait	1958–1967	1958–1967	n.a.	n.a.
Lebanon	1958–1967	1958–1967	1964–1967	1964–1967
Saudi Arabia	1958–1967	1958–1967	1962–1966	n.a.
Syria	1958–1967	1958–1967	1958–1965	1958–1965
West Asia n.e.c.	n.a.	1958–1967	n.a.	n.a.
Other Developing Countries				
Barbados	1958–1967	1958–1967	1958–1967	1958–1967
Guyana	1958–1967	1958–1967	1958–1967	1958–1967
Jamaica	1958–1967	1958–1967	1958–1967	1958–1967
Trinidad and Tobago	1958–1967	1958–1967	1958–1967	1958–1967
Netherlands Antilles	1958–1967	1958–1967	1958–1967	1958–1967
Other Developing Countries n.e.c.	n.a.	1958–1967	n.a.	n.a.

Notes: 1. The time period and years indicated in the table refer to the availability of processed GDP series.
2. n.a. indicates that data are not available.

the estimates in constant values at 1960 prices are concentrated on GDP by expenditure components. For some countries of developing market economies, the estimates of GDP by expenditure in current values are not necessarily available. This is particularly true for those countries which belong to the regions of Africa and West Asia. Estimates of GDP by expenditure in constant values for those countries to which no adequate information is available are largely obtained from scattered and fragmentary sources. As a natural consequence it is often the case that the estimates have no more qualities than filling the gaps in observations so that the regional or sub-regional total may be constructed. Careful examination of the qualities of the estimates is still needed for a number countries. The quantitative analysis of the economic development of developing countries by major regions using the estimates is, therefore, outside of the interest of the present article. In the next section, I shall give a summarized account of major problems that I have encountered in processing GDP series of developing countries.[2]

2. Problems of Data Adjustments

The types of national accounts data adjustments that I have encountered in this project are broadly itemized under the following headings: (1) the adjustments due to changes in estimates, (2) those due to changes in base years, (3) conceptual adjustments and (4) the adjustements in the case of missing observations. I shall take up the problems one after another and give a short account of them.

The national accounts statistics are under a continuous process of revision and improvement both in the form of presentation and in the methods of estimation. This is the case not only for developing countries but also for developed countries. The revision of national accounts estimates usually go back a number of years. Accordingly, the necessity of adjustments due to change in estimates arises regarding GDP series both by expenditure components and by industry origin. This is also the case for the series of data both in current and in constant prices. The nature of the adjustments due to changes in estimates is essentially reduced to establishing an effective link between the revised series of data and the old series. The adjustments become necessary if the revised series do not go back to a sufficient number of years. After a

2) As noted in Statistical Appendix appended below, further details for deriving the processed GDP series are explained in Y. Kurabayashi, [1974].

careful examination of the gap that arises between the revised series and the old series for the overlapping years, an effective way to establish a link between the two series of data must be found. If these revisions are frequent, the entire process of adjustments is repeatedly undertaken, almost every year. This creates an additional problem when the data are stored on tapes by computers, because the obsolete series of data must be discarded and replaced by the revised series. The work is often too basic to be disregarded as an unimportant detail.

The adjustments of data arising from the changes in base years are characteristic of the series of data in constant prices. The nature of this kind of adjustements is a combination of establishing a link between the revised series and the old series, on the one hand, and of shifting the base years on the other. Similar to the adjustments due to changes in estimates, the gap that appears between the revised series and the old series, both in constant values, must be carefully examined so that a workable method to establish a link between the two series of data may be discovered. But, the shift of base years demands a different set of considerations. In the absence of adequate information for filling the gap that arises between the revised series of data and the old series, it is often the case, particularly for developing countries, that the link between the two series is simply formed by the backward extrapolation after the base year is shifted. In this case, the balance that was maintained in the old series between GDP in constant values and each GDP components by expenditure in constant values is, as a general rule, destroyed by the shift of the base year. Consequently, additional ajustments for absorbing the discrepancy that may be produced by the shift of base year between GDP in constant values and the sum of each expenditure components in constant values, both of which are values at the new base year, must be attempted. Two possibilites may be considered for this adjustments. First, an additional term for adjustments may be introduced for restoring the GDP balance. Second, the discrepancy may be absorbed by a GDP component or be distributed to GDP components. Because the shift of base year is often caused merely by the revision of statistical data, the first alternative is not considered as meaningful. Indeed, it is almost hard to attach a definite meaning to an additional term thus introduced. The case reminds the author of the introduction of the adjustment term for establishing "the rest of the world" account in constant values. But, it should be recognized that a remarkable difference exists between the cases.[3] It has been discussed by authors that the introduction of an additional term for restoring the balance of the rest of the world account in constant values is not only necessary but also meaningful, because the additional term can represent changes in terms of trade after appropriate selection of deflators. No particular meaning should thus be attached to the additional term introduced by the adjustment. In the second alternative, the distribution of the dicrepancy into GDP components is not practical and remains arbitrary. It is not practical because hazardous results may be produced by this method. Arbitrariness may not be completely ruled out, from this alternative, in the determination of the share of the discrepancy for GDP components. Thus the only practical solution is that the discrepancy may be absorbed by one of GDP components. In view of the relative weights in GDP components, it seems preferable that the discrepancy be absorbed by private consumption.

As is widely recognized by national accounts statistician, the

3) For those who are interested in major literature concerning this topics reference should be made to that is indicated in the essay 2.

item of inventory changes is subject to volatile changes, in every country. It is not unusual that the item records a violent change in sign from positive to negative values. The change in sign of the item poses another difficulty, because a straightforward application of the shift of base year to the series of this item not infrequently produces awkard results, such that inventory changes in constant values for a particular year happen to show a negative value despite the corresponding figure in current values shows a positive sign. Data adjustments for this item demand much more sophisticated solutions, which require more detailed information such as the data for inventory valuation adjstuments. It is extremely difficult for developing countries to collect such detailed information. My suggestion is that this item should be excluded from the work of data adjustments until the adequate information becomes available, and that, as for this item, a top priority of collection of data should be put on detailed data in current values so that the composition of inventories according to the diffrent commodity groups and different sectors may be structured.

The shift of base year in the series of data in constant values naturally exercises a great influence on the quantity and price indices of national accounts aggregates which underlie those in current and constant values. Such an influence is especially decisive on the quantity indices of national accounts aggregates, whereas the influence on their price indices is indirect. By nature and construction, the quantity indices of national accounts aggregates that are derived from data in current and constant values are expressed in Laspeyres form. Against the quantity indices, the corresponding price indices of national accounts aggregates assume a Paasche form. As the Laspeyres form of quantity indices has fixed weights, the shift of the base year necessarily has an influence on the structure of weights. The influence of the shift of the base year on the price indices becomes indirect insomuch as the weights in the price indices are flexible. The effect of a shift of the base year on the structure of weights in quantity indices in national accounts aggregates deserves much attention particularly for the developing countries which are under the strong pressure of structural changes in their economies.

Conceptual adjustments for GDP by expenditure and by industry origin impose another exacting task. The following cases which require the conceptual adjustments are frequently observed:

(1) In a good number of developing countries exports and imports are indicated as net without showing individual items.

(2) Factor incomes are included in both exports and imports for some countries.

(3) Even private consumption and gross domestic capital formation are not indicated as independent items and are reported together for a few countries.

The adjustments that are required by changes in territorial coverage may fall into the category of conceptual adjustments. This is the case of Rhodesia, Nyasaland (with Southern Rhodesia, Malawi and Zambia) and Malaysia (with Singapore). The adjustments for differences in industrial breakdown of GDP are also the one of the aspect in conceptual adjustments. In principle, the industrial breakdown of GDP in YBNAS exactly follows the standard classification that appears in Table 2 of old SNA. In view of the fact that such detailed breakdown as old SNA is not applicable for developing countries in the absence of adequate data, the straightforward application of the industry classification is not of great advantage for GDP data adjustments by industry as regards developing countries. In this respect, it is much preferable that the broader industry classification be applied for developing countries. A number of such classification may be conceived. The subdivision of industries into the primary, secondary and tertiary industries have long earned the celebrated popularity with economists. Those economic historians who follw Kuznets' theory may cast grave doubt on this classification and insist that another tripartie grouping of industries is more tenable. The tripartite grouping, according to Kuznets, consists of (i) agriculture together with such related industries as fisheries, forestry and trapping, (ii) industry proper—mining, manufacturing, construction, power and light utilities, transportation and communication and (iii) services—trade, finance, business, domestic, professional and government. Still, a simpler classification may be proposed: industries would be classified into a dual structure, which is constituted by the directly productive sector and the others. The directly productive sector in the dual structure consists of agriculture, mining, manufacturing, construction and power and light utilities. Furthermore, the dual structue of industries according to so-called modern and traditional categories may be another choice, although the dividing line of the modern and traditional sectors is not necessarily crystal-clear.

National accounts statistics are not necessarily available for all years of the period under examination. This is particularly the case of developing countries for the early nineteen-fifties. Broadly speaking, the missing observation produces two types of discontinuity in national accounts statistics:

---

4) The tripartite grouping of industries by (i) agriculture and related industries, (ii) industry-proper and (iii) services is suggested by S. Kuznets [1966]. The importance of distinguishing the directly productive sector from the rest of industries is hinted in United Nations, *Economic Survey of Africa* [1968]. The dichotomy of modern and traditional sectors is strongly recommended for the sector breakdown of the national accounts that are adapted for developing countries in the revised SNA. (United Nations, [1968])

(i) The discontinuity arises when the data are entirely missing during a certain period. This is the case of, for example, the Republic of Korea for 1950–1953.

(ii) The discontinuity is also discovered when two series of data in constant values with different base years, as regards the same item, are presented without supplying any clue to link the relevant series. This is true of, for example, Ceylon's GDP in constant values.

The discontinuity throws formidable obstacles in the way of processing regional or subregional aggregates throughout the entire period. All possible efforts to make most of national sources and supplementary information must be exerted so that the obstacles may be removed. But, it is also noted that the limited and scattered information for supplementing the discontinuity is only available for developing countries, particularly in the early nineteen-fifties.

3. The Reconcilation of Foreign Trade Stastistics with National Accounts Aggregates: A Case for Selected Latin American Countries

As I have noted in section 2, Latin America belongs to one of the most leading area among developing countries so far as compilation and use of national accounts statistics are concerned. Enormous amounts of work and experience have been accumulated in developing the methodology and measurement of national accounts by national agencies; further, an international organization like ECLA has contributed to the development of international studies of national accountes aggregates. ECLA studies have received wide recognition by those who are seriously concerned with national accounts statsitics; it has developed a unique application of the purchasing power equivalent of GDP and its components to the group of developing countries. At the bottom of the development continuous efforts to improve the quality and reliability of national accounts statistics have been exerted not only by ECLA but also by national agencies of member countries. Having in mind this development, I shall discuss two interesting topics for national accounts data adjustments and make experiments on selected Latin American countries. The topics that will be discussed in what follows are: (1) the reconciliation of foreign trade statistics with national accounts and (2) problems of inter-country comparison of GDP.

Suppose a fully articulated system of national accounts. It is readily seen that the rest of the world account is derived from the system by the consolidation of those accounts which are associated with domestic economic activities. It is discovered by this derivation that foreign trade statistics provide basic materials for constructing national accounts aggregates. Apart from this relation, a question is often raised about the comparability of foreign trade statistics with national accounts statistics. At the outset of the comparison, the conceptual difference that exists between two sorts of statistics should be clearly distinguished. Generally speaking, the foreign trade statistics refer to exports and imports of merchandise, whereas exports and imports in national accounts statistics include those of goods and services. If the two sources of data are perfectly consistent, the conceptual difference is reduced to exports and imports of services.

Before going into the detail in comparison, it is useful to give an approximate idea of the importance of services in exports and imports of goods and services. The ratio of imports of goods and services (excluding investment income) to imports of merchandise (including freight and insurance on merchandise) is calculated from the data in IMF, *Balance of Payment Yearbook*. The result of computation is shown in Table 3, which refers to 1965.

Table 3. The ratio of imports of goods and services to imports of merchandise, 1965

Ratio	Number of countries
1.050–1.099	15
1.100–1.149	26
1.150–1.199	16
1.200–1.249	12
1.250–1.299	7
1.300–1.399	4
1.400–1.499	2
1.500–	2
Total	84

The simple arithmetic mean of the ratio is 1.183 amounting to saying that imports of services are on the average 15–20 per cent of merchandise imports (c.i.f.). For a number of countries, the ratio indicates remarkably high values. Those countries which have the ratio over 1.250 are listed below.

Colombia	1.429	Nicaragua	1.252
Haiti	1.306	Tunisia	1.266
Indonesia	1.272	France	1.259
Iran	1.302	Iceland	1.417
Iraq	1.278	Israel	1.504
Libya	1.720	United Kingdom	1.297
Ivory Coast	1.390	United States	1.344
Mexico	1.297		

In the case of Libya, imports of services by foreign-owned oil companies are included in the ratio. It is also noted that the distribution of the number of countries according to the size of the ratio appears to follow the type of a log-normal distribution.

The statistical sources of the comparison in what follows is strictly limited to those which are published by international organizations. Forein trade statistics that are compared with national accounts data are available in IMF, *International Financial Statistics;* UN, *Yearbook of International Trade Statistics;* ECLA, *Statistical Bulletin for Latin America.* The series of data taken from the IMF source, in most cases, are given both in US dollars and in local currency units, whereas the ECLA data are only given in US dollars. Yet, closer inspection reveals the fact that all of them are derived from the same sources except minor discrepancies that happen to arise on some occasions. Therefore, it is resonable and meaningful to compare imports in current values taken from national accounts that are compiled and processed by the author of the present article and those from trade statistics, both in national currency units. Let:

M^a=imports of goods and services taken from national accounts (in national currency units),

M_g^a=imports of goods (c.i.f.) taken from national accounts (in national currency units),

$M_g^t(n)$=imports of goods (c.i.f.) taken from IMF, *IFS* (in national currency units).

Table 4 shows the ratio $M_g^a/M_g^t(n)$ for a selection of five Latin American countries, 1958–1967. The gap between M_g^a and $M_g^t(n)$ becomes less than 10 per cent of $M_g^t(n)$ with the exception of a few cases. They are Ecuador for 1958–1962 and Dominica and Panama for 1965. Although the samples are not sufficiently large to draw a definite conclusion, the general impression created from Table 4 is that national accounts statistics in current values are in general consistent with foreign trade statistics. Table 5 pre-

Table 4. The ratio of M_g^a to $M_g^t(n)$ for five selected countries

	1958	1959	1960	1961	1962	1963	1964	1965	1966	1967
Costa Rica	0.9847	0.9857	0.9965	0.9788	0.9909	0.9860	0.9914	0.9840	0.9948	1.0269
Dominican Re.	0.0000	0.0000	0.0000	0.0000	0.0000	1.0268	1.0520	1.3162	0.9981	0.9971
Guatemala	0.0000	0.0000	0.0000	0.0000	0.0000	0.0000	0.0000	0.0000	0.0000	0.0000
Honduras	1.0297	1.0234	0.9122	0.9208	0.9254	0.9280	0.9816	0.9282	0.9259	0.9250
Nicaragua	0.0000	0.0000	0.0000	0.0000	0.0000	0.0000	0.0000	0.0000	0.0000	0.0000
Panama	1.0042	1.0037	1.0041	0.9984	0.9965	1.0076	1.0267	1.1596	1.0801	1.0514
Argentina	0.0000	0.0000	0.0000	0.0000	0.0000	0.0000	0.0000	0.0010	0.0010	0.0010
Brazil	0.0000	0.0000	0.0000	0.0000	0.0000	0.0000	0.0000	0.0000	0.0000	0.0000
Chile	0.0000	0.0000	0.0000	0.0000	0.0000	0.0000	0.0000	0.0000	0.0000	0.0000
Colombia	0.0000	0.0000	0.0000	0.0000	0.0000	0.0000	0.0000	0.0000	0.0000	0.0000
Mexico	0.0000	0.0000	0.0000	0.0000	0.0000	0.0000	0.0000	0.0000	0.0000	0.0000
Peru	0.0000	0.0000	0.0000	0.0000	0.0000	0.0000	0.0000	0.0000	0.0000	0.0000
Uruguay	0.0000	0.0000	0.0000	0.0000	0.0000	0.0000	0.0000	0.0000	0.0000	0.0000
Venezuela	0.0000	0.0000	0.0000	0.0000	0.0000	0.0000	0.0000	0.0000	0.0000	0.0000
Bolivia	0.0000	0.0000	0.0000	0.0000	0.0000	0.0000	0.0000	0.0000	0.0000	0.0000
Ecuador	1.1391	1.1799	1.1618	1.2325	1.4132	1.0813	0.9594	0.0000	0.0000	0.0000
Paraguay	0.0000	0.0000	0.0000	0.0000	0.0000	0.0000	0.0000	0.0000	0.0000	0.0000

Note: Zero in the table indicates that necessary information is not available.

Table 5. The ratio of M^a to $M_g{}^t(n)$ for selected Latin American countries

	1958	1959	1960	1961	1962	1963	1964	1965	1966	1967
Costa Rica	1.0911	1.0938	1.0989	1.0837	1.1100	1.1296	1.1240	1.1086	1.1195	1.1563
Dominican Re.	1.2525	1.1881	1.3437	1.4216	1.4268	1.4092	1.3810	1.8146	1.3308	1.3125
Guatemala	1.1029	1.1052	1.1037	1.0943	1.1096	1.1794	1.1603	1.1352	1.2707	1.1557
Honduras	1.2064	1.1989	1.0648	1.0611	1.0583	1.0557	1.0728	1.1070	1.0990	1.0977
Nicaragua	0.0000	0.0000	1.1775	1.1643	1.1455	1.1686	1.1124	1.1361	1.1355	1.1372
Panama	1.3834	1.4134	1.3723	1.3282	1.3174	1.3202	1.3350	1.3026	1.1917	1.2039
Arsentina	1.1777	1.1721	1.1042	1.0944	1.1527	1.2179	1.3010	1.1452	1.1679	1.2062
Brazil	0.9679	0.0000	0.9939	1.0021	0.8795	1.5470	1.1908	1.1919	1.1119	1.1347
Chile	1.1625	1.2823	1.2641	1.2319	1.2318	1.4374	1.2466	1.2294	1.2224	0.0000
Colombia	1.1636	1.1945	1.2167	1.1881	1.1965	1.2442	1.3585	1.4211	1.2689	1.3629
Mexico	1.2192	1.2954	1.2609	1.3138	1.3298	1.3487	1.3021	1.3132	1.3211	1.3655
Peru	1.1334	0.0000	1.1801	1.1633	1.1380	1.1438	1.3327	1.2550	1.3373	1.4380
Uruguay	0.0000	0.0000	0.0000	0.0000	0.0000	0.0000	0.0000	0.0000	0.0000	0.0000
Venezuela	1.4106	1.3407	1.3744	1.4245	1.4629	1.4643	1.4576	1.5124	1.5021	1.4469
Bolivia	0.0000	0.0000	0.0000	0.0000	0.0000	0.0000	0.0000	0.0000	0.0000	0.0000
Ecuador	1.5121	1.6532	1.6289	1.6858	1.9119	1.4490	1.2524	0.0000	0.0000	0.0000
Paraguay	1.5839	1.5835	1.5852	1.8907	1.5667	1.5522	1.7342	1.5997	1.5112	1.2758

Note: See the note of Table 4.

sents the ratio $M^a/M_g^t(n)$ for 1958–1967. The broad impression that can be formed from this table is that a fair degree of stability of the ratio over time is maintained for most Latin American countries.

4. The Inter-country Comparison of GDP by expenditure for Selected Latin American Countries by Means of Official Exchange Rates

The inadequacy of official exchange rates for inter-country comparisons of GDP and related aggregates has long been recognized, because the conventional rates are only relevant to actual recordings of international transactions and do not reflect the real purchasing parities of GDP and related aggregates. Unfortunately, owing to paucity of available information for determining the purchasing power of GDP and related aggregates, it is often the case, for developing countries, that we are forced to use the conventional rates for the conversion of GDP and related aggregates into a common currency unit, usually U.S. dollars. The present work of compiling and processing of GDP data by expenditure components and by industry origin also follows the use of conventional rates. A caution is needed against the idea that the resulting GDP aggregates in a common currency unit be hastily applied to further quantitative analysis, in particular to sophisticated econometric studies, without careful examination of the nature and quality of the converted figures. Although the attempt to formulate the purchasing power parities of GDP and related aggregates for developing countries has been scarce, ECLA has cultivated a way of inter-country comparison of GDP aggregates that is meaningful for developing their international comparison. Following the well-known method of formulating the purchasing power parities of

GDP components by expenditure that was presented by Kravis and Gilbert in their OEEC publication, ECLA has computed the purchasing power equivalents of GDP components by expenditure using both Latin American weights and U.S. weights, deriving the geometric mean of the two types of purchasing power equivalents. Applying the purchasing power equivalents for the conversion of GDP components in local currency units into U.S. dollars, Braithwaite has carefully examined the quality of the converted figures of GDP aggregates. Especially, he has compared the converted figures of GDP aggregates using the geometric mean of the above mentioned purchasing power equivalents with those which are converted by the conventional rates drawing several interesting and striking conclusions from the comparison. One of the most striking conclusion, as he has put it, is that changes in the relative importance of fixed capital formation are effected where the price level of producer's equipment was very much higher than that applicable to other goods and services. On the other hand, as he has also shown, the values of consumption in dollars in terms of constant prices are likely to be overstated, because of the relatively low price level for consumer goods and services. This is particularly true of the item of government consumption. Yet, this comparison only refers to the figures of 1960 leaving the over time comparison of these characteristics untouched for further examination. The comparison over time attracts considerable attention in the perspective of a wide variety of character of economic development for Latin American countries. In what follows I shall present the results of the comparison over time so as to supplement the striking conclusions that are drawn from his article.

I have compared per-capita GDP components in 1960 prices converted into U.S. dollars using the official exchange rates with

Table 6. Relative variation of GDP components by countries

	Mean				Standard deviation			
	(8)	(9)	(10)	(11)	(8)	(9)	(10)	(11)
Dominican Re.	1.0669	0.9541	1.7814	1.0949	0.0081	0.0229	0.0106	0.0336
Guatemala	1.0715	0.9946	1.7057	1.2242	0.0060	0.0228	0.0098	0.0095
Honduras	1.0651	0.9462	1.9319	1.2810	0.0131	0.0161	0.0813	0.0362
Nicaragua	1.9021	0.9228	1.3375	0.9411	0.0699	0.0429	0.1415	0.0662
Panama	1.1601	1.0653	1.8349	1.0428	0.0151	0.0125	0.0083	0.0239
Argentina	1.5645	1.5696	3.0691	0.7909	0.0404	0.0087	0.0398	0.0454
Brazil	0.9188	0.8845	1.5105	0.6408	0.0190	0.0381	0.0351	0.0232
Colombia	1.2344	1.1191	2.3176	1.3537	0.0102	0.0269	0.1142	0.0549
Peru	1.6438	1.5614	3.3627	1.1732	0.0319	0.0124	0.0466	0.0671
Uruguay	1.6801	1.5476	3.4157	1.1131	0.0310	0.0422	0.0633	0.0916
Bolivia	1.6237	1.4415	3.5419	1.1691	0.0169	0.0263	0.0289	0.0598
Ecuador	1.4125	1.2183	2.5391	1.4108	0.0203	0.0566	0.0170	0.1072
Paraguay	1.6194	1.5001	3.1426	1.3404	0.0355	0.0835	0.0380	0.2259

Note: The column numbers stand for the following items: (8)=per-capita GDP, (9)=per-capita private consumption, (10)=per-capita government consumption, (11)=per-capita gross fixed capital formation.

the corresponding components computed by Braithwaite. These GDP components include private consumption, government consumption, gross fixed capital formation and GDP itself. For each individual components the ratio of Braithwaite estimates to my estimates is computed. As it is easily confirmed by inspection that both series of estimates are derived from almost the same statistical sources, the deviation of the ratio from unity is largely caused by the difference in the use of conversion factors. The results of computation are attached in the Statistical Appendix in the end of this article together with statistical materials that are basic for the computation. The comparison is confined to the 1958–1964 period, during which both series of data are coincidentally available. The results of computation are summarised in the following two tables: Table 6 and Table 7. Table 6 indicates the simple arithmetic mean of the ratio for each individual GDP components and the standard deviation of corresponding components over time, whereas Table 7 shows the simple arithmetic mean and the standard deviation of relevant components among countries. The former table characterizes the over-time effect of difference in conversion factors relative to the official exchange rates on each individual GDP components by different countries. On the other hand, the latter table furnishes the inter-country effect of difference in conversion factor relative to the official exchange rates on each individual components for different years.[5)]

5) The works by ECLA and Braithwaite are particularly remarkable for the intercountry comparison of national accounts aggregates between Latin American countries. See, ECLA, [1968], and S. N. Braithwaite, [1968]. In parallel with the international comparison of real income levels, some notable works for international price comparisons in Latin American attract our attention. They are, among others, R. Ruggles, [1967], and S. N. Braithwaite, [1970]. The recent works by Jorge Salazar-Carrillo came to attract the author's attention after the earlier draft of this paper had been completed. It appears that major

Some notable findings that are drawn from careful examination of Table 6 are put forth below:

(1) The Braithwaite estimates of per-capita GDP in U.S. dollars exceed the corresponding estimates by the author of the present article for most Latin American countries with the only exception of Brazil. The observation suggests that the official exchange rates for most Latin American countries are undervalued in relation to the purchasing power equivalent of GDP. In the exceptional case of Brazil, it appears that the overstatement of the official exchange rate relative to the purchasing power equivalents of private consumption and gross fixed capital formation has substantially contributed to the case. About one half of those countries whose official exchange rates are undervalued, the degree of undervaluation falls within the range of less than 50 per cent. Among the remaining half of those countries the degree of undervaluation is within the range of less than 100 per cent.[6]

(2) The comparison of the purchasing power equivalent of private consumption with the official exchange rate for each individual countries does not seem to lead to the result as definite as is the case of GDP. For the one third of Latin American countries the overstatement of the official exchange rate relative to the purchasing power equivalent of private consumption is the case, although the degree of overstatement does not seem to be significantly large.

---

conclusions drawn from the discussion in the subsequent sections of this paper are not substantially influenced by his works. See, Jorge Salazar-Carrillo, [1973] and D. Daly, [1972].

6) An official exchange rate of a certain country is said to be overstated in relation to the purchasing power equivalent of individual GDP components if the amounts of dollars that are obtained in exchange for one unit of national currency applying the official rate is greater than those obtained from the application of the purchasing power equivalent. If the opposite is the case, a official exchange rate of a certain country is said to be undervalued.

The degree of undervaluation is within the range of less than 50 per cent for another one third of the countries. In the remaining one third of the countries the degree of undervaluation is within the range of less than 100 per cent.

(3) The striking feature of the comparison of the purchasing power equivalent of government consumption with the official exchange rate is that remarkable undervaluations of official rates are observed. The degree of undervaluation exceeds 200 per cent range for one half of Latin American countries. The feature seems to stem from the relatively low level of prices for services in Latin America. This observation accurately corresponds with what has been noted by Braithwaite.

(4) The official exchange rate shows an overstatement relative to the purchasing power equivalent of gross fixed capital formation for one third of Latin American countries. The degree of the overstatement is within the range of less than 50 per cent. But, a fairly wide margin of overstatement for Argentina and Brazil may be noted. On the contrary, the official rates of the remaining two thirds of the countries turn out to be undervalued in relation to the purchasing power equivalent of gross fixed capital formation.

Table 7. Relative variation of GDP components over time

	Mean				Standard deviation			
	(8)	(9)	(10)	(11)	(8)	(9)	(10)	(11)
1958	1.4039	1.2412	2.4916	1.1186	0.2961	0.2655	0.7695	0.1954
1959	1.4282	1.2337	2.5129	1.1711	0.2842	0.2477	0.7192	0.1857
1960	1.3972	1.2275	2.4173	1.1122	0.3183	0.2734	0.7783	0.2043
1961	1.3823	1.2108	2.4240	1.1076	0.3092	0.2736	0.7834	0.2087
1962	1.3831	1.2016	2.4216	1.1252	0.2917	0.2605	0.7757	0.2465
1963	1.3696	1.1944	2.4164	1.1388	0.2896	0.2604	0.7699	0.2530
1964	1.3700	1.1863	2.3870	1.1314	0.2984	0.2747	0.7527	0.2867

Note: For the explanation of the column numbers, see the note of Table 6.

The degree of undervaluation indicates a margin of variation that falls into the range of less than 50 per cent.

The inter-country effect of the relative variation between the Braithwaite estimates and the author's estimates for GDP components is summarized in Table 7. The following features may be noted from the table:[7]

(1) The ratios that indicate the relative variation over time for GDP components are kept within a narrow margin of variation suggesting that the over-time stability of the relative variation is prevalent over the inter-country averages for every components of GDP.

(2) The official exchange rates are, on the average, undervalued relative to the purchasing power equivalents for each individual components of GDP. Notably, a significant amount of undervaluation is observed for the item of government consumption. The degree of undervaluation is much less significant for the item of gross fixed capital formation. It is also noted that the degree of undervaluation for private consumption is not significantly different from that of gross fixed capital formation.

7) The replacement of the figures of simple arithmetic mean by those of weighted averages for Table 7 does not seem to change the general feature of the table. The figures of weighted average are indicated below;

	(8)	(9)	(10)	(11)
1958	1.3531	1.2003	2.4505	0.9966
1959	1.1886	1.0210	2.1057	0.8818
1960	1.4718	1.3137	2.6016	1.0940
1961	1.4511	1.3015	2.6136	1.0666
1962	1.4561	1.2867	2.5992	1.0862
1963	1.4231	1.2683	2.5872	1.1045
1964	1.4295	1.2652	2.5369	1.1094

It is quite reasonable to suppose that individual countries affect the over-time changes in the relative variation for GDP components with equal weights as Table 7 assumes.

In order to separate the effect of the different uses of conversion factors relative to the official exchange rates between countries from the effect of those between different years, the analysis of variance is applied. Let the relative variation between the Braithwaite estimates and the author's estimates for each individual components of GDP be decomposed according to the following equation:

$$Y_{ij} = m+c_i+t_{i_j}+e_{i_j}$$

where Y_{ij} stands for the ratio of the relative variation for i-th country of j-th year, and c_i and t_j represent the i-th country and j-th year effects respectively. m is constant and e_{ij} is an error term. Then, the analysis of variance tables for individual GDP components are computed as indicated in Table 8.

Table 8. Analysis of variance

(8) Sources of variation	D.F.	Sum of squares	Mean square	(9) Sources of variation	D.F.	Sum of squares	Mean square
Between country	12	1.1595	0.0966	Between country	12	0.9038	0.0753
Between time	6	0.0026	0.0004	Between time	6	0.0026	0.0004
Error	72	0.0881	0.0012	Error	72	0.1077	0.0015

(10) Sources of variation	D.F.	Sum of squares	Mean square	(11) Sources of variation	D.F.	Sum of squares	Mean square
Between country	12	7.6067	0.6339	Between country	12	0.6069	0.0506
Between time	6	0.0125	0.0021	Between time	6	0.0028	0.0005
Error	72	0.3680	0.0051	Error	72	0.6506	0.0090

Note: The following abbreviations are used in the table: (8)=per-capita GDP, (9)=per-capita private consumption, (10)=per-capita government consumption, (11)=per-capita gross fixed capital formation.

It is readily seen by the results indicated in Table 8 that the differential effect between countries is significantly different from zero at 1 per cent probability level for all cases of GDP components. On the contrary, the hypothesis of $t_j=0$ against the alternative that some t_j are different from zero can not be rejected at 1 per cent probability level for the cases of GDP and government consumption, whereas the alternative is the case at the same probability level for private consumption and gross domestic capital formation. It appears that the differential effect between years does not necessarily produce homogeneous results as regards GDP components for the stated period of observation. On the basis of the conclusions drawn from the analysis of variance, the following points can be made:

(1) It is likely that the use of the purchasing power equivalent for the conversion of GDP components into U.S. dollars produces significant deviation from what is converted by the use of the official exchange rate. This is true for each individual countries in Latin America and for each individual components of GDP.

(2) On the average of Latin America as a whole, it appears that the use of the purchasing power equivalent for the conversion of GDP and government consumption into U.S. dollars produces significant deviation from what is converted by the use of the official exchange rate. But, this is not necessarily the case for private consumption and gross fixed capital formation. The divergent results suggest that much detailed examination and elaboration of the construction of the purchasing power equivalent for the analysis of GDP components at regional or sub-regional level are accordingly required.

5. The Inter-country Comparison of GDP by Expenditure for Selected Latin American Countries by Means of Free Exchange Rates

It is interesting to compare the differences in the inter-country comparison of GDP by expenditure components that may arise according to the use of different conversion factors.[8] In this regard, the inter-country comparison of GDP by expenditure components converted into a common currency unit by the application of free exchange rates is of our special interest, for it is often argued that the free rates of exchange are more closely associated with the real purchasing power parity of GDP components than the official rates. The results of the exercise of comparison are reported below. Before we start with the presentation of the results, a few remarks deserves to be given here.

In the first place, it should be noted that the results of inter-country comparison of GDP obtained from the application of the free exchange rates would not be directly comparable with those obtained from the results of computation made in the preceding section, because a set of countries which adopt the free exchange rates is narrowed to a limited number of countries. Consequently, the exercise must be restricted to a number of selected Latin American countries repeating the same procedure as the preceding section. The question raised in the exercise is whether the conclusions drawn from the analysis in the preceding section remain unchanged by the application of the free exchange rates. If they are not influenced by the application of free exchange rates, we

8) The point taken up here has originally suggested by the comments given at 13th General Conference of International Association for Research in Income and Wealth by Dr. B. Feran when the earlier version of this article was presented to the Conference.

are allowed to generalize the conclusions drawn from the results of computation made in the preceding section.

A limited number of Latin American countries for which the data for free exchange rates are available consists of Nicaragua, Agentina, Brazil, Colombia, Urguay, Ecuador and Paraguay during the period between 1958 and 1964. They are selected simply on the ground that the results of the exercise in this section are comparable with those in the preceding section. Neither any theoretical nor institutional considerations are taken into the selection of those countries. The availability of data is the only determinant factor of the selection. The question whether this procedure of limiting the set of sample countries for our exercise may influence

Table 9. Relative variation of GDP components by countries

	Mean				Standard deviation			
	(8)	(9)	(10)	(11)	(8)	(9)	(10)	(11)
Nicaragua	1.9021	0.9228	1.3375	0.9411	0.0699	0.0429	0.1415	0.0662
Argentina	1.5645	1.5696	3.0691	0.7909	0.0404	0.0087	0.0398	0.0454
Brazil	0.9188	0.8845	1.5105	0.6408	0.0190	0.0381	0.0351	0.0232
Colombia	1.2344	1.1191	2.3176	1.3537	0.0102	0.0269	0.1142	0.0549
Uruguay	1.6801	1.5476	3.4157	1.1131	0.0310	0.0422	0.0633	0.0916
Ecuador	1.4125	1.2183	2.5391	1.4108	0.0203	0.0566	0.0170	0.1072
Paraguay	1.6194	1.5001	3.1426	1.3404	0.0355	0.0835	0.0380	0.2259

Table 10. Relative variation or GDP components over time

	Mean				Standard deviation			
	(8)	(9)	(10)	(11)	(8)	(9)	(10)	(11)
1958	1.4860	1.2775	2.4971	1.0933	0.2917	0.2627	0.7275	0.2442
1959	1.5775	1.3334	2.6777	1.1468	0.2083	0.2289	0.6243	0.2229
1960	1.5064	1.2916	2.4658	1.0465	0.3281	0.2772	0.7792	0.2502
1961	1.4820	1.2630	2.4649	1.0433	0.3171	0.2882	0.7858	0.2537
1962	1.4751	1.2360	2.4746	1.0987	0.2917	0.2688	0.7809	0.3216
1963	1.4518	1.2246	2.4654	1.1248	0.2857	0.2678	0.7638	0.3381
1964	1.4471	1.2000	2.4534	1.1098	0.2851	0.2811	0.7264	0.3816

the results of computation is left open for further studies.

Table 9 and Table 10 illustrate the comparison of relative variation of GDP components over time in 1958–1964 period by countries and they are comparable with Tables 6 and 7 respectively. Observation of the tables immediately reveals the fact that Table 9 is merely the reproduction of Table 6 for the limited number of Latin American countries mentioned and that the development over time of GDP components is apparently different from what is displayed in Table 7. By the comparison of Table 10 with Table 7 the following features can be sketched.

(1) The mean of relative variation of GDP components shows a light increase in the computation for a limited number of countries. Putting aside the exception of 1959, the dispersion of the magnitude of the relative variation also indicates a parallel increase with the movement of the mean variation.

(2) In comparison with the case of Latin American countries as a whole, the order of magnitude in the relative variation for GDP components in this limited number of countries is kept relatively stable. Thus, we may conclude that the significant amount of undervaluation caused by the application of the official rate relative to the purchasing power equivalent is also the case for the item of government consumption and that the degree of undervaluation is much less significant for such items as gross fixed capital formation and private consumption.

The features described above provide fairly reasonable grounds to believe that an experiment similar to what has been carried out in the foregoing section is also applicable to the case of a limited number of countries. Applying the same model as that is rendered in section 4, the table of the analysis of variance is easily computed and is shown in Table 11. The points made by the observation of Table 11 are as follows:

Table 11. Analysis of variance

(8)

Sources of variation	D.F.	Sum of squares	Mean square
Between country	6	0.6254	0.1042
Between time	6	0.0115	0.0019
Error	36	0.0944	0.0026

(9)

Sources of variation	D.F.	Sum of squares	Mean square
Between country	6	0.5124	0.0854
Between time	6	0.0121	0.0020
Error	36	0.0858	0.0024

(10)

Sources of variation	D.F.	Sum of squares	Mean square
Between country	6	3.9395	0.6566
Between time	6	0.0381	0.0063
Error	36	0.4071	0.0113

(11)

Sources of variation	D.F.	Sum of squares	Mean square
Between country	6	0.5494	0.0916
Between time	6	0.0088	0.0015
Error	36	0.5539	0.0154

(i) Except for the case of (per capita) gross fixed capital formation, the differential effect between countries is significantly different from zero at 1 per cent probability level for all other GDP components. In the exceptional case of gross fixed capital formation, the hypothesis that $c_i=0$ is not necessarily rejected at 1 per cent probability level.

(ii) On the other hand, the differential effect over time is significantly different from zero for (per-capita) gross fixed capital formation at 1 percent probability level, whereas for other GDP components the alternative hypothesis holds at the same level of probability.

The reasoning advanced on the basis of Table 11 for the set of a limited number of Latin American countries does not give the entirely different picture obtained from the experiment applied to the set of overall Latin American countries with some exception for the component of gross fixed capital formation. Hence, the following points are naturally made by a reasoning similar to the preceding section.

(1) It easily turns out that GDP conversion by the application of free exchange rates generally undervalues it in relation to the application of the purchasing power equivalent of GDP. The degree of undervaluation is generally amplified by the application of free exchange rates comparing with the application of official rates.

(2) The conversion of private consumption and government consumption revealed itself the fact that they are generally undervalued by the application of free exchange rates relative to the application of purchasing power equivalents of corresponding components and that the degree of the undervaluation is comparatively amplified by taking free exchange rates for conversion instead of official rates. A general impression following from the observation is that free exchange rates should not be used as a substitute for the purchasing power equivalents of relevant GDP components.

(3) In the over time comparison of the relative variation of GDP components, it is observed that the magnitude of the relative variation of the components, though it is not appreciably high, is rising. This implies that the degree of undervaluation caused by the application of free exchange rates as conversion factors becomes conspicuous in the early sixties.

6. Acknowledgements

This article is a revised version of my paper under the same title which has been presented to 13th General Conference of the International Association for Research in Income and Wealth, held at Balatonfured, Hungary in August 31–September 5, 1973. The author expresses his hearty thanks for the comments, both pro and con, raised by Professor R. Goldsmith and Drs. B. Feran and W. Novak and others. He also thanks for the encouragement given by Professor M. Mukherjee of presenting the paper to the session he organized at the Conference. Needless to say, any errors and shortcomings that may be contained in this article are author's own.

Statistical Appendix

1. Table 12 to Table 15 refer to the computation of the relative deviation between the Braithwaite estimates and the author's estimates for GDP components, in U.S. dollars at 1960 prices on per-capita basis. Table 12 indicates the relative deviation for GDP. Table 13 refers to the relative deviation for private consumption, whereas Table 14 shows the relative deviation for government consumption. Finally, Table 15 refers to the relative deviation for gross fixed capital formation.

2. Table 16 is indicated as an example of the author's estimates. The table refers to the estimates of GDP expressed in U.S. dollars at 1960 prices. The following steps are taken to reach the estimates. First, the estimates of GDP at 1960 prices in local currency units are derived from *YBNAS* and various national sources. Further details in the derivation and data adjustments are explained in the author's memorandum.[9] Second, GDP in 1960 values of local currency units is converted into U.S. dollars using the official exchange rates at 1960. For those contries which adopt the multiple exchange rates, considerable efforts are made to make our figures of the official exchange rates consistent with those

9) See, Y. Kurabayashi, [1974]. Succeeding to the work, an attempt to constuct a data base and programme package for the effective control of compiling, processing and storage of national accounts data is making way in operation of large scale computer systems.

Table 12. Relative deviation for GDP

(8)	1958	1959	1960	1961	1962	1963	1964
Dominican Republic	1.07833	1.06502	1.06030	1.06059	1.07447	1.07406	1.05540
Guatemala	1.07817	1.07939	1.07360	1.07422	1.06659	1.06339	1.06481
Honduras	1.06854	1.06893	1.07332	1.07427	1.07236	1.06392	1.03405
Nicaragua	1.88401	1.91021	2.03731	1.96004	1.81928	1.86259	1.84112
Panama	0.00000	0.00000	1.16390	1.13896	1.18527	1.15310	1.15911
Argentina	1.57635	1.57029	1.54256	1.56493	1.64872	1.50946	1.53921
Brazil	0.94460	0.00000	0.94045	0.88908	0.90939	0.91794	0.91111
Colombia	1.24486	1.25146	1.23298	1.22976	1.23593	1.22754	1.21839
Peru	1.61265	0.00000	1.62868	1.62951	1.63427	1.64638	1.71156
Uruguay	1.67735	1.66492	1.73532	1.66304	1.71782	1.65761	1.64489
Bolivia	1.60700	1.60404	1.61895	1.61807	1.62190	1.64133	1.65486
Ecuador	1.40367	1.40793	1.42350	1.44681	1.42724	1.39887	1.37953
Paraguay	1.67141	1.66020	1.63238	1.62045	1.56701	1.58854	1.59547

Notes: Zero in the tables 12–16 indicates that necessary information is not available.

Table 13. Relative deviation for private consumption

(9)	1958	1959	1960	1961	1962	1963	1964
Dominican Republic	0.93378	0.94256	0.92642	0.93993	0.99084	0.98029	0.96481
Guatemala	1.02692	1.03070	0.99417	0.98724	0.97377	0.97538	0.97372
Honduras	0.98080	0.94918	0.93155	0.94785	0.93500	0.95035	0.92912
Nicaragua	0.93122	0.97393	0.96090	0.92053	0.91503	0.92852	0.82974
Panama	0.00000	0.00000	1.07507	1.06262	1.07037	1.04216	1.07628
Argentina	1.57310	1.54855	1.57217	1.57262	1.57201	1.57387	1.57505
Brazil	0.95744	0.00000	0.91079	0.85012	0.86419	0.85422	0.87027
Colombia	1.09988	1.13205	1.16240	1.13235	1.13085	1.10249	1.07376
Peru	1.55688	0.00000	1.55211	1.55925	1.55563	1.55566	1.58858
Uruguay	1.53130	1.48768	1.60676	1.58440	1.58402	1.53995	1.49885
Bolivia	1.45367	1.41462	1.43651	1.40214	1.44282	1.45088	1.48972
Ecuador	1.29445	1.26106	1.24289	1.24123	1.21232	1.15745	1.11854
Paraguay	1.55533	1.59687	1.58549	1.54004	1.37382	1.41562	1.43372

Table 14. Relative deviation for government consumption

(10)	1958	1959	1960	1961	1962	1963	1964
Dominican Repubric	1.78537	1.77754	1.77458	1.79347	1.76611	1.77452	1.79822
Guatemala	1.68902	1.71296	1.69651	1.71057	1.71813	1.71274	1.69988
Honduras	1.97227	1.96701	1.97089	1.97857	1.95564	1.94467	1.73456
Nicaragua	1.54032	1.57560	1.25269	1.27235	1.19997	1.27030	1.25119
Panama	0.00000	0.00000	1.82874	1.83787	1.84979	1.83130	1.82673
Argentina	3.09045	3.08708	3.08789	3.08070	3.07614	3.08897	2.97222
Brazil	1.46252	0.00000	1.51038	1.48256	1.57341	1.52886	1.50529
Colombia	2.25655	2.28566	2.24812	2.25043	2.29968	2.28930	2.59348
Peru	3.42137	0.00000	3.37529	3.38809	3.35168	3.36967	3.27000
Uruguay	3.42860	3.43494	3.40997	3.47748	3.44742	3.44388	3.26770
Bolivia	3.55174	3.60515	3.51873	3.54938	3.51752	3.52234	3.52849
Ecuador	2.54127	2.54509	2.55659	2.53345	2.55363	2.54238	2.50131
Paraguay	3.16011	3.13757	3.19475	3.15742	3.17193	3.09428	3.08234

Table 15. Relative deviation for gross fixed capital formation

(11)	1958	1959	1960	1961	1962	1963	1964
Dominican Republic	1.12372	1.04548	1.08790	1.15335	1.10219	1.08992	1.06190
Guatemala	1.23389	1.22511	1.20394	1.22087	1.22900	1.23385	1.22306
Honduras	1.25196	1.30081	1.30434	1.32619	1.31363	1.24139	1.22873
Nicaragua	1.00782	0.86371	0.90833	0.98519	1.00254	0.98608	0.83418
Panama	0.00000	0.00000	1.08078	1.01023	1.02658	1.05126	1.04538
Argentina	0.87104	0.84838	0.77792	0.74977	0.74511	0.77496	0.76930
Brazil	0.66215	0.00000	0.65213	0.65185	0.63382	0.65250	0.59257
Colombia	1.40607	1.43852	1.29650	1.30568	1.35756	1.38516	1.28612
Peru	1.04505	0.00000	1.21422	1.20311	1.17771	1.14196	1.25712
Uruguay	1.23746	1.21414	1.19469	1.06798	0.99352	1.03820	1.04591
Bolivia	1.11626	1.25919	1.24221	1.18155	1.08793	1.17306	1.12383
Ecuador	1.32478	1.34320	1.36124	1.40245	1.42283	1.35930	1.66207
Paraguay	1.14349	1.17289	1.13493	1.14038	1.53527	1.67715	1.57854

which are indicated in Braithwate's article.

3. The comparison of the author's estimates with the Braithwaite estimates is made on per-capita basis because of the convenience of computation. It is readily seen that unreasonable figures due to incorrect computation are easily discovered by inspection if they are expressed in per-capita basis. Adjustments for the difference in the population figures that are used by the author and Braithwaite are also made. But, it appears that the difference is, on the average, of a negligible order, as Table 17 shows. The table indicates the ratio of population figures that are used by Braithwaite and by the author.

REFERENCES

S. N. Braithwaite, " Real Income Levels in Latin America ", *Review of Income and Wealth*, June 1968.

S. N. Braithwaite, " Price Statistics Required by Developing Countries for National Accounting Purposes: Availabilities, Limitations and Priorities ", *Review of Income and Wealth*, June 1970.

D. Daly, ed., *International Comparisons of Prices and Output*, New York, 1972.

ECLA, " The Measurement of Latin American Real Income in U.S. Dollars ", *Economic Bulletin for Latin America*, Vol. XII No. 2, 1968.

Y. Kurabayashi, *Series of GDP by Expenditure for Developing Countries, 1958–1967*, Computer Section, Institute of Economic Research, Hitotsubashi University, March 1974.

S. Kuznets, *Modern Economic Growth*, New Haven and London, 1966.

S. Kuznets, " Problems in Comparing Recent Growth Rates for Developed and Less Developed Countries ", *Economic Development and Cultural Change*, January 1972.

J. Mayer, " Quelques remarques sur l'utilisation des calculateurs électroniques en comptabilité nationale ", *Review of Income and Wealth*, March 1966.

R. Ruggles, " Price Indexes and International Price Comparisons ", in *Ten Economic Studies in the Tradition of Irving Fisher*, New York 1967.

Jorge Salazar-Carrillo, " Price, Purchasing Power and Real Product Comparisons in Latin America ", *Review of Income and Wealth*, March 1973.

T. Schioetz, " The Use of Computers in the National Accounts of Norway ", *Review of Income and Wealth*, December 1966.

United Nations, *A System of National Accounts*, New York 1968.

United Nationals, *Economic Survey of Africa*, Vol. II North African Subregion, New York 1968.

Table 16. GDP at 1960 prices (Million dollars)

	1958	1959	1960	1961	1962	1963	1964
Dominican Republic	687.40	691.25	723.00	691.03	780.77	820.31	876.85
Guatemala	947.19	991.33	1020.50	1058.63	1085.89	1217.17	1302.95
Honduras	357.55	370.71	377.90	392.42	416.69	426.55	449.97
Nicaragua	364.25	367.52	375.54	404.87	457.68	476.65	533.05
Panama	0.00	0.00	415.80	460.90	498.90	541.50	565.50
Argentina	11432.08	10769.00	11630.52	12446.06	12213.74	11781.77	12746.14
Brazil	18644.72	0.00	21606.00	24433.62	25250.49	25499.38	26615.96
Colombia	3771.70	4026.47	4215.17	4449.88	4685.84	4850.85	5167.80
Peru	1811.18	0.00	2080.50	2235.67	2439.58	2529.25	2633.78
Uruguay	1227.19	1196.33	1224.45	1275.87	1222.61	1238.69	1279.16
Bolivia	361.15	362.93	376.68	387.60	407.27	433.30	451.85
Ecuador	822.11	864.55	921.93	936.08	978.52	1016.92	1095.95
Paraguay	272.51	271.65	276.18	291.86	304.73	311.95	321.04

Table 17. Relative variation of population figures

	1958	1959	1960	1961	1962	1963	1964
Dominican Republic	1.00495	1.00205	0.99442	0.99555	0.99386	0.99230	0.99085
Guatemala	1.00000	1.00000	1.00000	0.99537	0.99079	0.98842	0.97956
Honduras	1.00274	1.00372	1.00515	1.00699	1.00967	1.01123	1.01268
Nicaragua	1.03609	1.03942	1.04678	1.05231	1.05816	1.06295	1.06137
Panama	0.95726	0.95934	0.96139	0.96161	0.96018	0.95887	0.95768
Argentina	0.99995	1.00000	1.00000	0.99995	0.99995	1.00000	1.00000
Brazil	1.00713	1.00792	1.00830	1.00837	1.00815	1.00772	1.00718
Colombia	1.01043	1.00696	1.00337	1.00000	0.99653	0.99292	0.98931
Peru	1.00000	1.00000	1.00000	1.00000	1.00000	1.00000	1.00000
Uruguay	0.98981	0.98360	0.98226	0.98019	0.97818	0.97622	0.97576
Bolivia	1.05327	1.06166	1.07037	1.07943	1.08848	1.09842	1.10831
Ecuador	0.98636	0.98889	0.99196	0.98978	0.98367	0.98172	0.97951
Paraguay	1.00000	1.00000	1.00971	1.00611	1.00216	0.99791	0.99339

IV.

EXTENSION OF NATIONAL ECONOMIC ACCOUNTING

7

A SOCIO-ECONOMIC STATISTICAL SYSTEM FOR MEASURING A SOCIETY'S SOCIAL AND ECONOMIC PERFORMANCE

1. Introduction

In recent years industrialized societies have been subject to great and radical changes. It is particularly the case in such industrialized country that has undergone drastic structural changes, both social and economic, in a past few decades like Japan. Having achieved a remarkable economic growth, more than doubling the GNP, in the sixties, she is acclaimed as one of industrial giants in the world. In the course of this development, her industrial structure has shifted from agriculture to manufacturing and services. It is also apparent to us that the composition of manufacturing industry has brought about parallel changes adding the weight of such heavy industries as metals, engineering works and petrochemicals. Sweeping transformations that are observed in the demographic and social structure have been caused by the changes in economic structure. Owing to a sharp drop of the birth-rate, decrease of death-rate and extending life-expectancy, she stands at the threshold of the so-called "old-aged society". The structure of man-power has been transformed in the decade from the labour surplus to the labour shortage. The participation of female workers in the labour force has been firmly instituted and has grown, particularly in the part-time employment of middle-aged female; it anticipates recycling of the flow of female man-power from the inactive part to the active part along the age-profile of female man-power.

In parallel with the structural changes in her economy and demography, her social structure has also experienced enormous transformations. The progress of urbanization caused by the changes in economic structure has widened the gap in the community life between the congested urban area and the isolated rural area. But, the quality of urban life has suffered from various kinds of disamenity such as air and water pollution and congestion of people and traffic arising out of the progress of urbanization and the changes in industrial structure. It is often pointed out by some social scientists that the importance of professional people and technocrats predominates over the social classes as the industrialized society makes progress towards the technological society. Looking ahead the future of the technological society, sociologists not infrequently worry about the danger of bureaucratization that the technological society may fall into unless an effective safeguard against it is put into operation. Neverthless, the progress of the technological society has a bright side which comes into sight with the technological progress resulting in the shortening of working hours together with the increase in leisure hours. It is interesting to study how the resulting increase of leisure hours is distributed among the people of different income and social classes. It is also a matter of great concern for social scientists whether opportunities to climb up the ladder of social success are equally and widely open to all those who desire to take them or not with the progress of the material affluence. It is true that the income distribution statistics of Japan in the past decade clearly indicate a remarkable decrease of the measures of income inequality.[1] But, it appears that nobody would be as innocently optimistic as he conclude from the measurement of income inequality that unequal opportunities could be entirely rooted out by such a decrease of income inequality. Hence, it is important from the view point of social justice to investigate what factors contribute to and determine unequal opportunities, which often plant the root of social discontent in the people.

All the issues raised here urgently requires sufficient amounts of statistics to meet the demand, the government statistical agencies and research institutions of industrialized societies are eager to collect, compile and analyze the necessary statistics for the issues. It is not difficult to discern a common characteristic underlying the attempts of collecting and compiling the statistical information by such agencies and institutions. The characteristic is that they collect and compile a coherent set of statistical information for the measurement of economic and social performance of their societies, not a hotch-potch of scattered and sporadic information. As the social and economic activities in an industrialized society are closely interwoven, it is necessary for the collection and compiling of such statistical information that their statistical design should be drawn

1) The Gini coefficients for the size distribution of the primary income by urban households in the past decade are computed by Mizoguchi [1976]. The summary of the results of computation is given below:

	1962	1963	1964	1965	1966
Gini Coefficient	0.2745	0.2563	0.2380	0.2276	0.2284
	1967	1968	1969	1970	1971
Gini Coefficient	0.2307	0.2104	0.2002	0.2043	0.2076

in a system such that its components prove to be mutually interconnected. A few examples deserves to be noted in this connection. First, the United Nations' proposal for a System of Social and Demographic Statistics, SSDS for short, exactly makes the point at issue, contending that the purpose of the proposed SSDS is to provide a connected information system for social and demographic statistics which will be useful for description, analysis and policy making in the different fields of social life.[2] Second, another approach that should be noted here is the project that has been undertaken by the National Bureau of Economic Research under the guidance of Professor Richard Ruggles of Yale University. In the methodology of the project, the emphasis is particularly placed on relating social indicators and social statistics directly to the national economic accounts, insisting that the hard core of the problem is the linkage between the economic and social information.[3]

In what follows of this article, it is intended to discuss an alternative and synthetic approach for the measurement of economic and social performance of an industrialized society. The approach is proposed as an alternative to aforementioned examples in that it is primarily designed to provide a system framework for the measurement of economic and social performance of an industrialized society that is subject to rapid social and economic transformations like Japan. Moreover, the approach claims to be synthetic in that it attempts to present a synthetic approach between the United Nations' system and the National Bureau of

2) See, in particular, United Nations [1975].

3) The research project has its origin in the 1971 Conference on the Measurement of Economic and Social Performance held at Princeton University under the joint sponsorship of the University's Department of Economics and NBER's Conference on Research in Income and Wealth. The scope and aims of 1971 conference are summarized by Milton Moss in Moss [1973].

Economic Research project. Our approach is common to the United Nations system in that a mutually interlocked system is designed for the collection and compilation of necessary statistics. It should be stressed that our approach has also something in common with the emphasis placed on the project of the National Bureau of Economic Research, because an initial attempt to build an appropriate data base for the linkage between social and economic data in our system framework is made in the subsequent section of this chapter. In the following section, the design of a mutually interlocked system framework for the measurement of economic and social performance of a society, which is termed a socio-economic statistical system in what follows, will be presented. In section 3, a fairly exhaustive account of the Basic Survey of Social and Community Life which is initiated by Statistics Bureau, of the Prime Minister's Office of Japanese government will be provided. The stress of the account will be placed on the point that the Survey should serve for building an effective data base linking social data with economic statistics. In the final section, the structure of man-power balance which constitutes a sub-system of a socio-economic statistical system will be discussed dealing with actual figures taken from Japanese statistics.

2. The Design of a Socio-economic Statistical System

The question of the organization of statistical information for the empirical studies in economics, particularly for econometric studies, has been one of the important centres of interest for economists in the past decades. It is essential for the empirical studies that the statistical data are systematically collected, classified and processed for use. The system of national accounts has been developed to work for meeting the statistical requirements. The distinct advantage of the system of national accounts that surpasses any other collection of economic statistics is embedded in the characteristic that the system provides a coherent and comprehensive economic structure that is interwoven with (i) economic activities, such as production, consumption and accumulation, (ii) different groupings of agents, such as business enterprises, general government and households, (iii) different objects of transaction, such as goods and services and types of financial claims. Putting it in other words, the system of national accounts presents an ingenious device of recording the economic performance of a society within a systematic framework.

It is important to bear in mind that the system of national accounts represents a structure not only in literal sense of the word but also in the sense of formal logic. The point has received through and detailed discussions in the preceding article. As has been noted there, the essence of a system of national accounts lies in its ' state of being related ' that is displayed by a related structure constituted by the flow of real and financial transactions. In an abstract sense, such a system may be considered as an entire integrity composed of and interwoven with components that form the totality but are open to the higher level of totality acting as part. Thus, a system of national accounts shows how the entire integrity of economic performance is composed of component transactions and what relations are established between the constituent components. It is this indisputable and outstanding property that the empirical knowledge on the working of the economic structure owes to a system of national accounts. It naturally follows from the characteristics of a system of national accounts that the system serves as a powerful instrument of the collection, classification and storage of statistical data for the comprehensive analysis of the economic structure. The so-called ' instrumental use of a system of national accounts ' to which SNA refers bears a special importance to the inherent character of a system of national accounts that has also been one of the subjects of discussions in the preceding chapter.

What has been discussed so far about economic data, in particular about the system of national accounts, is common in character to social statistics, although there exists more or less a difference in degree. The systematic collection, classification and processing of social data, however, had not the interest of social scientists until recent years. Only fragmentary and scattered information is collected for some specific empirical studies of social research. Moreover, it is noted that qualitative aspects generally supersede quantitative aspects in the methodology of social studies. Yet, in recent years, it appears that the centre of gravitation of social studies has been gradually changing. The awakened interest in measurement, in social studies, has created a vehement fashion of producing social indicators.[4] The invention of a new measure for social welfare that aims to either supplement or replace GNP is regared as a parallel of the prevailing fashion of the social indicators movement. Indeed, in Japan, the effort of seraching for a new measure of social welfare has been culminated in the measurement of NNW (Net National Welfare) by the Economic Planning Agency.[5] For these efforts, it is generally re-

4) As an example the joint research project for the measurement of social change by American economists and sociologists under the sponsorship of Russell Sage Foundation should be mentioned. The scope and methods of the research project are given by Eleanor B. Sheldon in Eleanor B. Sheldon and Wilbert E. Moore [1968].

5) See, in particular, Economic Planning Agency, [1973]. The work bears close resemblance with William D. Nordhaus and James Tobin [1972] in its scope of measurement. The related works for the measurement of social welfare in Japan are briefly reviewed in his recent work of Siegfried Lörcher [1976], with a detailed bibliography.

cognized that social indicators and new measures of social welfare are especially relevant tools for developing the measurement in social studies. In spite of these efforts, it is essential for promoting such trend in social studies to remember that these measures do not necessarily constitute the adequate basis for the quantitative analysis for two reasons. First, they barely indicate one-dimensional measures expressed in a simple scalar that share common shortcomings with GNP which can not bear the whole burden of recording the mutiplicity of economic performance in industrial societies. It is extremely difficult for industrial societies that their economic performance could be gauged by the help of such simplified scalar as GNP or national income. In this regard, it is instructive to recall that GNP has once been the target of caricature by one of prominent Japanese press under the malicious campaign to shout 'Kutabare GNP' (GNP in the dust). Certainly, it is not on the concept of GNP that the whole blame should be placed, but what should be squarely blamed and criticized is the single-minded adherence to the obsolete thinking by the press that the economic performance of any industrial societies be adequately expressed by a simple scalar. Second, these measures only represent a single facet of social activities disregarding entirely the mutiform complexity of industrial societies emerging from the diversification of value judgements by the members of industrial societies.[6)]

A social indicator is often defined as 'a statistic of direct normative interest which facilitates concise, comprehensive and balanced judgements about the condition of major aspects of a society'.[7)]

---

6) See, in particular, The Asahi Press, [1971]. It appears that the editors of the press and those who actively take part the arguments in the book are entirely ignorant of the recent developments of national economic accounting to cope with the multiform coplexity of industraialized societies.

7) U.S. Department of Health, Education and Welfare, [1969].

As noted before, the social activities that are represented by a set of social indicators are, in reality, inextricably associated with economic activities for which a system of national accounts provides a comprehensive and detailed account. Unfortunately, a set of social indicators can not necessarily meet the theoretical and statistical requirements that are imposed on it, the complexity arising out of contemporary issues of social and economic changes in industrialized societies can not be easily resolved into a mixed and disorganized array of one-dimensional magnitude. In the face of the urgent tasks for the contemporary issues faced by industrialized societies that must be addressed to social scientists and of the reality that social and economic systems are mutually and inseparably connected with, the time has come to design a system of collecting, classifying and processing social statistics within the comprehensive and coherent scope going in parallel with the development in a system of national accounts which gives an appropriate basis for the collection, classification and processing of economic data. Such a system of social statistics will constitute a new departure for the systematic collection, classification and processing of necessary information for analysing the contemporary issues in industrialized societies. In what follows of discussions in this article the system is termed a system of socio-economic statistics, SESS for short, taking into account the fact that such a system of social statistics is closely interrelated with relevant economic statistics.

The structure of SESS is designed for screening out the profile of social and community life in a society, which is constituted by major spectra of social and community life. The *major spectra of social and community life* are composed of basic activities in social and community life together with the structure and changes in population and the structure and changes in man-power. The basic activities consist of the primary, secondary and tertiary activities in social and community life. The primary activity in social and community life refers to those activities which are necessary to get the minimum necessity of keeping subsistence in the community life such as sleeping and eating. The secondary activity in social and community life, on the other hand, represents one of the most typical activities in social and community life encompassing it those which refer to learning and earning. The tertiary activity in social and community life is not as insignificant in its importance as other activities particularly in industrialized societies, because it is, in essence, constituted by those activities which arise out of the growing increase of leisure hours, including such activities as recreational, cultural and sporting activities. As Johan Huizinga has once put it in his argument of the play-concept in culture, it is in the form of liberal disposal of leisure hours that the culture of any society finds its completion and sophistication.[8)]

The spectra of social and community life are closely associated with the structure of and changes in population, on the one hand, and the structure of and changes in man-power on the other. It is readily seen that the structure of and changes in population are basically dependent on the primary activity in social and community life. The structure of and changes in man-power are directly influenced by the secondary activity of social and community life, but the effects of the tertiary activity of social and community life made to them indirectly should not be ignored. It is also noted that the spectra of social and community life be not kept untouched by several important social factors such as the effects of urbanization, the formation and composition of family

8) Johan Huizinga, [1955], whose work sheds a fresh light and gives deep insight on the multi-dimensional aspects of the play-concept in human life and history.

and housing and other living conditions, which are further surrounded by the social environment and protected by public order. Moreover, the spectra of social and community life in the contemporary industrialized society can not be absolutely separated from the ecology of material flow which is the unavoidable product of brisk economic activities. It is the deterioration of the quality of life that the emerging interests in industrialized societies have been growing in the past decade.[9]

The structure of SESS is illustrated by Diagram 1 below. In the diagram, the spectra of social and community life are arranged in the vertical direction begining with the structure of and changes in population which are placed on the upper panel of the diagram succeeded by the structure of and changes in man-power and the basic activities. Five dimensions of measurement which are indicated in the diagram are distinguished. They are: (1) the framework of national accounts, (2) the framework of demographic accounting, (3) the man-power balance, (4) the time budgets and (5) the system of social indicators. In what follows we shall give brief comments on the component dimensions of measurement. Much will not be said about the framework of national accounts, because some explanations of it have been given in the preceding articles. The framework of demographic accounting is for the illustration of the structure of and changes in population which are governed by demographic factors like birth, death and fertility rates as well as together with by social factors like urbanization and housing conditions. Utilizing the framework of demographic accounting, it is conceivable to construct a variety of Markovian stochastic models for explaining changes in population flow, as

9) SSES is closely associated with the balance of material flow which is left untouched in this article. The design of the balance of material flow has been attempted in my Japanese article. See, Kurabayashi [1974].

the United Nations report has put it. The man-power blance with which we shall be concerned in greater detail in section 4 plays the major part for illustrating the importance of the secondary activity in the spectra of social and community life. Particularly, it should be pointed out that the advancement of education, both in breadth and in depth, substantially contributes to the quality of man-power and its earning capacity which govern the structure of and changes in man-power. Owing to the increase of leisure hours arising out of shortening of working hours in industrialized countries, considerable attention has recently been devoted to the allocation of time between work and leisure. In particular, the diversified and multiform uses of the growing leisure hours must constitute one of the most important aspects in the spectra of social and community life in post-industrialized societies. We shall take up the aspect in the following section especially placing stress on the design of data-base that is appropriate for the quantitative analysis of the time budgets. Socalled 'social indicators movement' has formed one of the prevailing orientation of statistical developments since the end of sixties. These measures are relevant for providing a measuring rod of social activities, for which it is not always easy to find a common and unified unit of measurement. Being each social indicator individualized in the sense that it is only interested in a particular aspect of social activities, disregarding the inextricable interrelation between them, the system of social indicators acquires a special significance in the measurement dimensions of SESS for supplementing other component dimensions.[10)]

Having briefly reviewed the component dimensions of measure-

10) An attempt to develop social indicators in Japan with their measurement has been made by Economic Planning Agency, [1974].

ment in SESS, we must again return to the framework of national accounts. Undoubtedly, the primary purpose of the framework of national accounts is the collection, compiling and processing of economic data in a coherent and unified system. But, the framework of national accounts is likewise relevent for the measurement of SESS, because the production and the formation of income and its distribution both of which form the basic activities in the economy are closely associated with the seconday activity in the spectra of social and community life as well as the structure of and changes in man-power. A detailed system of the distribution of income and wealth that accomodates the information concerning the distribution of personal income and wealth proves to be essential not only for the analysis of economic inequality but also for the clarification of social justice. In this regard, it should be noted that the dynamics of man-power balance exercises strong effects on the personal distribution of income and wealth.[11)]

We have noted in the preceding discussions that such factors as the progress of urbanization, the formation and composition of family and housing and other living conditions are surrounded with and governed by social and public order. In concluding with this section, a few words must be spent to these social and political surroundings. First, the order and the safety of the citizens must be effectively protected against offences and delinquencies in order to maintain the spectra of social and community life in normal

---

11) The development of a detailed system of the distribution of consumption, income, and wealth has long been the concern of expert statisticians jointly cooperated with the development of SNA. One of their attempts making a step forward to the development of the system can be seen in United Nations [1972]. The attempt attracts our attention for the reason that the system paves the new way towards structuring a system of micro-economic accounting which should be indispensable for clarifying quantitatively the meaning of social justice. In this respect, see Jean Bénard [1972].

conditions. In particular, the safety of the citizens in industrialized societies is often jeopardized by criminal offences and delinquencies which are substantially ascribed to the progress of urbanization and the inequality of earnings and opprtunities resulting from material progress. Together with these factors, it is also pointed out by notable social scientists that the rise of urban population and the age-profile of its population and man-power positively contribute to the rising trend of crimes in industrialized societies. It is not unusual to observe throughout industrialized societies that potential sources of these crimes concentrate on those who belong to relatively young age groups. It is essential for taking decisive measures against increasing offences in industrialized societies to know the quantitative information about the number, types and ages of those who commit them. Another measuring rod for the order and safety of citizens is the statistical information about those who are victimized by offences and delinquencies. Such information is especially relevant for measuring undesirable but unavoidable costs that any society must pay for maintaining public order.[12)]

In the second place, the essential viewpoints at the issue of social environment are the structure and mobility of social groups in a society. It is generally recognized that several factors contribute to the formation of the structure and mobility of social groupings. They are: (i) the origin and history of families to which the members of a society belong, (ii) the evaluation of social

---

12) These points have already been made by criminology experts. For example, see Norval Morris and Cordon Hawkins [1970]. The construction of necessary data bases for feeding them into electronic computer systems which are effective device for the enforcement of law has attracted considerable attention, particularly, in the United States. The information incorporated into the data bases may be utilized for our purpose of quantitative analysis, though they are primarily intended for administrating criminal justice.

(Diagram 1) The Structure of SESS

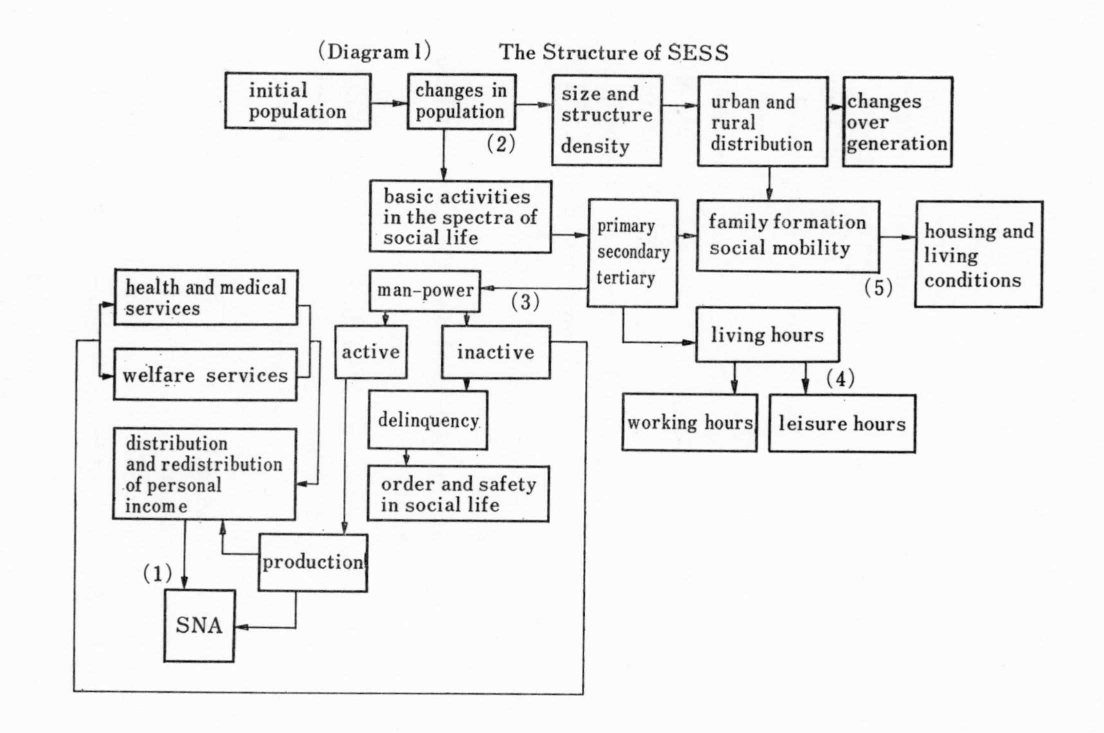

prestige in the occupational status to which the members of a society are ascribed and (iii) the economic and social power which the members of a society possess. The development of overall indicator(s) still remains a matter of future elaboration because of the difficulty of measurement and of the absence of available data. Yet, partial approaches to individual aspects of the social environment are possible to carry out, as preceding attempts have suggested. It is interesting to see from these attempts that there exists some social hierarchy which symbolizes the structure of occupational prestige even in industrialized societies. In particular, it is the matter of further consideration whether such social hierarchy is stable or not and what are determing factors to reach the stability of social hierarchy, if any of it exists. The point seemingly assumes great relevance for our study, because the progress of "the technological society" suggests the growing predominance of a handful groups of professinals consisting of so-called technocrats.[13]

3. The "Basic Survey of Social and Community Life" as a Data-base for SESS

In the foregoing section we have discussed in some detail the structure of a Socio-Economic Statistical System that is proposed for measuring a society's social and economic performance. In what follows of this section we shall turn our attention to the measurement of SESS taking into consideration of the usefulness of establishing a data-base for the measurement. In doing this, we shall refer to the "Basic Survey of Social and Community Life" that is initiated and carried out by the Bureau of Statistics of the Prime

13) For changing aspects of social hierarchy and social conflict in the progress of industrialized societies, see Jacques Ellul [1964] and Raymond Aron [1962], [1964].

Minister's Office of the Japanese Government with the intention of providing appropriate information for structuring social and community life making a point that the Survey should be utilized as a data-base for the measurement of SESS.[14] Before we proceed to the measurement of SESS, a few remarks deserve to be made for the nature and significance of a data-base for the collection, compilation, processing and storage of statistical information.

The powerful potential of a data-base structured on micro-economic units, such as individuals, households and business establishments etc., not only for the empirical studies of their economic and social behaviour but also a wide variety of its applications for the linkage of social and economic data has been rapidly acclaimed in the past few years. The growing recognition of the potential and of the impetus was motivated by a number of reasons. First of all, the data-base directly refers to the micro-economic behaviour of individual economic units the empirical study of which is not always possible to carry out by the ready-made statistics which are processed out of huge amounts of data assembled from censuses and sample surveys. By maintaining the original data in the form of a data-base, special tabulations which necessarily meet a wide variety of demands for the empirical studies could be produced as needed. The cause for structuring such data-base should be common to the empirical studies in social behaviour by individual units. In the second place, the construction of such data-base makes it easy to link the economic data with the social data on a consistent and unified basis. The objective of developing a socio-economic statistical system for the measurement of social and eco-

14) The first of the Survey was carried out in the week begining with October 17, 1976. The results of the Survey is under the process of collection, compilation and processing. It is expected that initial results of compilation be available by the end of April 1977. It is also understood that the Survey will be continued at regular intervals.

nomic performance in a society will not be attained, unless it becomes possible to link the basic social information with the basic economic information. Lastly, the increase in the power and capacity of computer must be noted. The construction of such a data-base and its manipulation for the objective of developing a socio-economic statistical system would not be possible without the advances which have been made in computer technology, both of ' hardware ' and of ' software '.

A data-base is a device for entering and processing data in a computer system performing various functions by a sequence of controlled computations. Data are organized within a data-base in units called files. Basically, a set of files consists of three bodies of the collection of statistical figures and other sources of information, both numerical and non-numerical. They are: (i) the descriptor of files, (ii) the key directory and (iii) filed data. The *descriptor of files* is a set of information which describes the general characteristics of statistical figures stored in files and drawn out for the sequence of data processing and computation. It may be often the case that the characteristics of statistical figures entered in the descriptor of files are supplemented by a set of information called the *key directory*, which serves for the efficient compilation of data characteristics. A set of information recorded in the form of data files is called *filed data* which constitute one of the major components of a data-base. The structure of a set of files may be constituted by a form of sequential files, in which the filed data are essentially listed by a linear list, but if the amounts of information contained in a set of files are sufficiently large then a form of randomized files may be effective for use.[15]

---

15) Further details for structuring data bases and data files are discussed in Ura [1973]. The idea of individual data files for the application to socio-demographic studies and the data linkage for the compilation of a system of

Returning to give accounts of the " Basic Survey of Social and Community Life ", which will be shortened as SSCL for simplification, the chief objectives of SSCL to collect statistical information concerning the basic activities in the spectra of social and community life that receive the primary consideration in the foregoing section in order to meet the growing concern in industrialized societies for the quality of social and community life. *A Manual for SSCL,* which is specially prepared for 1976 SSCL that inaugurates the first of this kind of survey in Japan, states that " in carrying out the Survey, the communities' response to and the people's demands for the basic activities getting along such social changes as the progress of ' the old aged society ', the dominance of nucleus family in the family composition, the shortening of working hours and changes in occupational structure will be disclosed. Such information is indispensable for policy making that gives priorities in social issues concerning the advances of lifelong education, the improvement of welfare for workers and the provision and upkeep of public facilities in local communities such as parks, athletic fields, libraries, museums, theatres and orchestras." The objects of SSCL refer to both individuals and households to which each individual belongs drawing about 75,000 sample households out of approximately 350 survey districts all over Japan prescribed by the Bureau of Statistics on the basis of 1975 Census of Population. Hence, the samples include the resident foreigners, but exclude official diplomatic and consular representatives and members of the armed forces of a foreign country who are stationed in Japan.

The contents of SSCL are structured in a matrix form and dis-

---

national accounts receives thorough consideration in their articles by Svein Nordbotten [1971], Odd Aukrust and Svein Nordbotten [1973] and Richard and Nancy Ruggles [1970].

played in Table 1. In the matrix, rows are classified according to the basic activities in the spectra of social and community life, which are constituted by the primary, secondary and tertiary activities respectively. They are further sub-divided by characteristic components. Thus, the primary activity is constituted by (I.1) domestic life and (I.2) living conditions, whereas the secondary activity consists of (II.1) learning and (II.2) earning. The specific characteristic of the tertiary activity is indicated by (III.1) leisure. The classification of columns refers to the units of measurement. The first two columns classify the objects of SSCL according to

Table 1. The Contents and Structure of SSCL

	Households	Individual	Disposable Hours
I. Primary Activity			
Domestic Life	Sex, Age, Marital Status, Household Composition, Relation to Household Head		Sleeping, Personal Cares, Meals, Housekeeping, Shopping, Resting, Others
Living Conditions	Housing Conditions and Spaces	Medical and Hospital Cares	Medical and Hospital Cares
II. Secondary Activity			
Learning	School Career	Learning outside of School	Learning and Studies
Earning	Working Status and Occupations, Working Hours, Holidays in a week, Annual income		Commuting, Working
III. Tertiary Activity			
Leisure		Entertainment, Recreational and Cultural Activities, Voluntary Activities Uses of Public Facilities	Entertainment, Recreational and Cultural Activities Voluntary Activities

households and individuals, and the last column specifies disposable hours for individuals. The specific inquiries entered in SSCL are expressed as the elements of the matrix. For example, those inquiries which refer to the domestic life of households get a factual survey according to categories of sex, age, marital status, household composition and the relation to the household head.

Independent inquiries are carried out for the member of a household according to the classification of those who are aged over 15 and those who are less than 15 years old. It is interesting to note that those who constitute the man-power population are distinguished from the rest of the population by the classification. Accordingly, the learning activity in the secondary activity is substantially relevant for those who are aged less than 15, even though the extension of schooling years in the recent decade in Japan has strongly influenced the composition and age-profile of the active man-power. The earning activity in the secondary activity, on the other hand, essentially refers to those who are aged over 15.

A variety of information is collected from the inquiries concerning those who are aged over 15. The set of information is itemized and indicated below:

+15 (1), sex; +15 (2), relation to the household head;
+15 (3), age; +15 (4), marital status, +15 (5), school career, which is broadly categorized by (i) elementary education, (ii) intermediary education and (iii) advanced education;
+15 (6), working status, which is categorized by the headings (i) working for earnings, (ii) domestic work, (iii) schooling and (iv) others;
+15 (7), occupations, which is sub-divided into the categories (i) those who are employed and (ii) the self-employed proprietors (iii) those working at home and (iv) the family employed. (i)

is divided into sub-categories: (i.1) manual workers, (i.2) professional practices, (i.3) clerical work, (i.4) administrative work, (i.5) sales and services, (i.6) transportation, communication and security work. (ii) is also broken down into the sub-categories: (ii.1) agriculture, forestry and fishing, (ii.2) manufacturing and services and (ii.3) independent professional works.

+15 (8), size of enterprises in which those who are working for earnings are employed. The item is categorized by the size of employees according to the classes (i) 1–4, (ii) 5–29, (iii) 30–99, (iv) 100–299, (v) 300–499, (vi) 500–999, (vii) over 1,000 employees and (viii) government institutions.

+15 (9), weekly working hours, which are divided into classes, (i) less than 15, (ii) 15–34, (iii) 35–42, (iv) 43–48, (v) 49–59, (vi) over 60 hours respectively and (vii) not fixed constantly.

+15 (10), holidays in a week.

[Note] In the classification, +15 denotes those who are aged over 15. And the number in the parenthesis indicates the number of inquiries.

As for those who are aged less than 15, a set of information is revealed from independent inquiries as indicated below:

−15 (1), sex; −15 (2), relation to the household head; −15 (3), age;

−15 (4), schooling status, which is categorized by the headings (i) children's nursery, (ii) nursery-school, (iii) primary school, (iv) secondary school and (v) no schooling.

−15 (5), lessons outside school, which is further classified by (i) types of institutions and (ii) types of lessons. (i) is classified into sub-categories (i.1) teaching institutions, (i.2) private teachers, (i.3) others and (i.4) no lessons. (ii) is also classified into sub-categories (ii.1) supplementary learning, (ii.2) abacus calculation, (ii.3) art of calligraphy, (ii.4) foreign languages, (ii.5) music, (ii.6) sports and (ii.7) others.

[Note] In the classification, −15 denotes those who are aged less than 15. The number in the parenthesis indicates the number of inquiries.

Inquiries concerning housing conditions and space refers to households. Housing conditions are categorized by (i) owner-occupied dwellings, (ii) rental dwellings owned by public corporations, (iii) privately owned rental dwellings, (iv) rental dwellings furnished by institutions for their employees, (v) rental rooms and (vi) boarding dwellings. Space is measured by the number of rooms in the dwellings. Annual earned income is also measured by individual household as a unit and is classified into 12 income classes: (i) less than 1, (ii) 1.00–1.49, (iii) 1.50–1.99, (iv) 2.00–2.49, (v) 2.50–2.99, (vi) 3.00–3.49, (vii) 3.50–3.99, (viii) 4.00–4.99, (ix) 5.00–5.99, (x) 6.00–7.99, (xi) 8.00–9.99, and (xii) over 10 million yen respectively.

One of the outstanding characteristics of SSCL is that the substantial part of its inquiries is addressed to the behaviour of individuals who constitute the spectra of social and community life. Their participation contained in the inquiries comprises all facets of the basic activities in the spectra of social and community life ranging from the primary activity to the tertiary activity. Thus, in connection with the living conditions of the primary activity (Table 1), inquiries on medical and hospital cares are carried out according to (i) types of medical establishments, which are subdivided into (i.1) hospitals, (i.2) medical clinics, (i.3) medical clinics attached to their workplace, (i.4) dental clinics and (i.5) other medical establishments, and (ii) the use of medical services and its frequency. The use of medical services is subdivided into the sub-categories: (ii.1) inpatients and (ii.2) outpatients. The classification of frequency differs according to the cases of inpatients and outpatients. In the case of inpatients, the classification of frequency is made by (1) not hospitalized, (2) less than one week, (3) over one week but less than one month, (4) over one month but less than three months and (5) over three months. In the case of outpatients, the classification is similarly made according to the duration of medical treatments, i.e. (1) no medical treatments, (2) 1–2, (3) 3–5, (4) 6–10, (5) 10–30 and (6) over 30 days respectively.

A question arises whether lessons outside of schools are exactly associated with the learning of the secondary activity or not, for it may be possible to consider that lessons outside of schools are the outcome of leisure to which the tetriary activity essentially refers. The contents of inquiries concerning lessons outside of schools definitely explain my standpoint that they constitute one of the important aspect of learning as an integral part in the secondary activity. The inquiries concerning lessons outside of schools for general education are constituted by (i) types of learning facilities with cross-classification by (ii) its frequency, (iii) aims and (iv) subjects. The types of learning facilities are subdivided by (i.1) vocational and training schools, (i.2) open classes and lectures, (i.3) lectures for the public, (i.4) educational programmes by radio and TV and (i.5) others. The frequency of learning is subdivided into categories: (i) every days a week, (ii) 2–3 days a week, (iii) 1 day a week, (iv) 2–3 days a month, (v) 1 day a month, (vi) more than 30 days in a year but intermittently, (vii) 15–30 days in a year but intermittently, (viii) less than 10 days but intermittently. The aims of learning are subdivided into (i) making a living (ii) changing or finding occupation, (iii) the preparation for entrance examination, (iv) obtaining some qualifications, (v) the utilization for living and (vi) others. The subjects of learning are categorized by (i) technology and electronics, (ii) business practices and commercial businesses, (iii) education and welfare, (iv) medical and health services, (v) domestic services and home economics, (vi) foreign languages, (vii) current affairs and (viii) liberal arts and others.

In order to inquire about the individual's association with his leisure in the tertiary activity, different items of questionnaire are designed for SSCL. They are inquiries on (1) entertainment and cultural activities, (2) sports, (3) voluntary activities and (4) travelling. Inquiries on entertainment and cultural activities are arranged so as to give cross-divisions according to (i) types of entertainment and cultural services, on the one hand, and (ii) their frequency, (iii) the individual's association with the community and (iv) facilities they are exercised, on the other. The types of entertainment are further itemized including such headings as flower arrangement, tea ceremony, going to cinema, performing music instruments and gardening etc. The categories given in the classification of the frequency of entertainment and cultural activities are the same as those in the frequency of learning mentioned before. The individual's association with the community in the enjoyment of entertainment and cultural activities is categorized under the headings in association with (i) his family, (ii) the people of his workplace, (iii) the people of his school, (iv) the people of the neighbourhood, (v) friends, (vi) others and (vii) himself alone. An inquiry is also made whether the individual belongs to particular clubs or groups for entertainment and cultural activities. It is apparent to us that these classifications are intended for collecting the information to what extent communities are involved in the entertainment and cultural activities of the people. The inquiry concerning the individual's association with the community in the enjoyment of entertainment and cultural activities is also made from a different aspect. The aspect is what sort of facilities is utilized for the entertainment by the people. The facilities are classified according to (i) the individual's home and the surroundings,

(ii) facilities in his workplace, (iii) facilities in his school, (iv) public facilities, (v) private facilities and (vi) others.

Similar sorts of information on sports are collected from inquiries concerning (i) categories of sporting with the cross-divisions of (ii) the frequency of its enjoyment, (iii) the individual's association with the community and (iv) the facilities where different sorts of sport are exercised. The categories of sporting are classified, for example, by base-ball, volley-ball, table-tennis, judo, swimming, hiking and golf etc. The classification of the frequency of sporting, the individual's association with the community and the facilities where different sorts of sport are exercised is formulated as same as corresponding inquiries concerning the enjoyment of entertainment and cultural activities.

In the collection of information on voluntary activities, they are defined as the provision of individual's efforts, skills and time for the advancement for the community's welfare without seeking his earnings. The categories of voluntary activities are classified by (i) social services, (ii) community services, (iii) the participation in the administration of community organizations, (iv) the participation in the administration of PTA (parents and teachers associations), (v) the participation in the administration of other social organizations, (vi) public activities of social and community services and (vii) others. The information on voluntary activities is augmented, in addition to the categories of voluntary activities, by the cross-divisions of their frequency and the individual's association with the community in carrying out the voluntary activities. The sub-classification of their frequency is formulated as same as the inquiries made for entertainment and cultural activities and sporting. It is also easy to see that the individual's association with the community in carrying out the voluntary activities is classified according to the categories used in the inquiries concerning the entertainment and cultural activities and sport.

Independent inquiries on travelling is particularly significant for collecting the information on the employment of leisure, because travelling far and frequently has become more and more popular recently, owing to the rising standard of living. The categories of travelling in the inquiries are classified according to its purposes, i.e. (i) travelling for sightseeing and recreation and (ii) others. The categories of travelling are supplemented with the information doubly classified by the frequency of travelling that was made in the past one year and by the size of party. The frequency of travelling is further subdivided into 6 classes which are (1) once in the year, (2) twice in the year, (3) three times in the year, (4) four times in the year, (5) 5–9 times in the year and (6) more than 10 times in the year. The categories of those who were travelling with the respondent are (1) his family, (2) people from his workplace, (3) people from his school, (4) people from his community, (5) his friends, (6) others and (7) himself alone. In addition to the information about the categories, frequency and companions of his travelling, the inquiry is made for the facilities he used during the travelling. The facilities are classified in the categories: (1) national lodgings, (2) youth hostels, (3) lodgings owned and operated by government and private institutions, (4) hotels and inns, (5) private pensions and (6) others.

It is noted in the last item of the column for individuals in Table 1 that an independent inquiry on uses of public facilities be indicated. The inquiry is for the purpose of disclosing the frequency of the individual's utilization of private and public facilities in participation with various cultural and community activities. The private and public facilities used are classified into the categories: (i) public halls and public cultural centres, (ii) libraries,

(iii) museums and cultural display centres, both private and public owned, and (iv) youth centres. The frequency of their utilization is inquired on annual basis of uses with the groupings: (i) 1–2 days, (ii) 3–5 days, (iii) 6–10 days, (iv) 10–30 days, (v) more than 30 days.

One of the most important aspect of SSCL is that it marks a great leap forward in compiling the individual's time budgets making inquiries concerning the use of time and his motivations. As is noted in the column for disposable hours of Table 1, the disposal of time can be arranged for according to basic activities of the individual in the spectra of social and community life. Explaining the point in further detail, the objects of inquiries concerning the disposal of time in SSCL refer to the individual aged over 15. The motivation of the disposal of time is related to the aforementioned basic activities and is classified into the following 17 headings, given here with their definition:

Headings	*Contents and Definition*
(1) Sleeping	The item includes not only a sleep in the night but also a nap.
(2) Personal cares	The item includes washing one's face and hand, bathing and dressing etc.
(3) Meals	Meals outside home for personal and social purposes or relations with others are included in item (12).
(4) Housekeeping	Cooking, washing, cleaning, taking care of children and other works that are necessary for managing one's household are included here.
(5) Shopping	
(6) Commuting to	

	work and school	
(7)	Other short trips	The item includes any movement from one place to another by means of transportation excluding commuting to school and work. Trips for work purposes, in the case of salesman, are excluded.
(8)	Working	The item is defined as working for compensation, but it also includes unpaid work for proprietors.
(9)	Learning and study	Education in schools and other educational facilities and lessons received outside schools are included here. Learning and studies outside workplaces for enhancing worker's capability and approved by the employer is excluded here and included in (8).
(10)	Cultural and entertainment activities	
(11)	Sport	
(12)	Social life	Included here are activities aimed of maintaining good personal and social relations to others such as receiving guests, attending parties and meetings.
(13)	Voluntary activities	
(14)	TV, radio and newspapers	The item includes watching and listening TV and radio, reading newspapers and magazines for recreation.
(15)	Resting and relaxing	Included here are resting and relaxing at one's home and workplace.
(16)	Receiving	

medical cares

(17) Others

The questionnaire requests the individual to fill in the printed form of time-table showing his disposal of time for two scheduled days in a particularly fixed week for SSCL. In the course of collecting the answer forms of the questionnaire, examinations are made by collectors of the forms so that total hours may sum up 24 hours. The questionnaire of time budget refers to two days so that it can take into account different patterns of behaviour which reflect the difference between weekdays and Sunday.

So far we have given some accounts of the contents and structure of SSCL. In order to use the information contained in SSCL as a data base for SESS, it is important that additional information for registering sample households be incorporated into a set of data files which is constituted of aforementioned inquiries for respective sample households. The additional information for the registers in the descriptor of files is supplemented with (i) the number of sample districts, (ii) the number of households and (iii) the number of household members. In the case of SSCL, the number of sample districts is indicated by 5 digits and is easily translated into the number of the survey district which was used for 1975 Population Census. It is conceivable by the translation that this set of data files could be linked with the grid-coordinate system code which provides detailed regional breakdowns for data linkage. The grid-coordinate system code has been developed by the Bureau of Statistics of the Prime Minister's Office on the occasion of the compilation of 1970 Census of Population and is widely recognized as a powerful tool for detailed regional studies and data linkage. The standard area of the grid-coordinate system is constituted by a unit district of 1 km^2 but, for particular regions, much detailed breakdowns, e.g. districts of $\frac{1}{2}$ km^2 and $\frac{1}{4}$ km^2, are given. It deserves to be noted that the set of data files acquires strong impetus for enlarging the amounts of information by establishing linkage with other sources of statistical information which is made possible by the help of the grid-coordinate system. In the case of SSCL data files, the number of household and the assigned number for each member of household are given by 2 digits and 1 digit respectively and are readily identifiable by the parallel use of the umber of sample districts.[16)]

4. The Structure of Man-power Balance as a Sub-system of SESS

In section 2, we have already noted the part and significance of the man-power balance in connection with the exposition of bsaic activities in the spectra of social and community life. In what follows of this section, we shall be concerned with the design and structure of the man-power balance. In so doing, we shall focus our attention on the recent drastic change in the demographic structure in Japan, which may be characterized by the ‘ advent of the old-aged society ’, and its implications for the structure of the man-power balance.

Before proceeding with the discussion of the structure of the man-power balance, it is convenient to look over the recent change in the demographic structure in Japan, which is portrayed in

16) A fairly detailed account of the grid-coordinate system is given in Bureau of Statistics [1974]. An experiment to make a match between the sample households and those are obtained from Family Budget Survey on the basis of the grid-coordinate system will be conducted upon being the data of SSCL available. As the Family Budget Survey contains valuable information on households' income, consumption and saving, the linkage of the two sorts of data will provide an essential data base for the construction of SESS.

Diagram 2. The Diagram 2.1. displays the long-term change in the composition of three major age groups of the population in Japan. The major age groups of the population are constituted by (I) those who are aged less than 15, (II) those who are aged 15–64 and (III) those who are aged over 65. Those who fall into the age groups of II and III constitute the man-power, although the substantial portion of those who are in the age group III have retired from labour and constitutes the hard core of the old aged. Diagram 2.1. clearly shows the drastic change in demographic structure that has occurred after the mid-fifties which is sharply contrasted with the marked stability in the demographic structure that was prevailing over one generation before 1950. Particularly notable is the drastic decrease of those who are in I-age group and the steady rising of those who are in III-age group. The rising trend in the composition of III-age group after the fifties is shown in Diagram 2.2. magnifying the scale of composition. It is observed from the diagram that the rising trend is further accelerated after mid-sixties. For this reason we may conclude that the demography of Japan just stands at the threshold of the old-aged society.

The man-power balance is a stastistical scheme that shows the sources and uses of man-power, which is defined as human resources aged over 15. The definition of man-power is broader in scope than both the concept of labour force which is usually defined as " all those who have been in employment for some part of a recent interval of time " and the concept of ' gainfully occupied ' whose usual definition is given as " all those who have had some earnings during, say, past years ".[17] The sources of

17) A reference to the terminology for ' labour force ' and ' gainfully occupied ' should be consulted in United Nations [1975]. The structure of labour force and its changes in the past decades has been dealt with acknowledged experitise by Umemura [1971].

Diagram 2. Deonographic changes in Japan

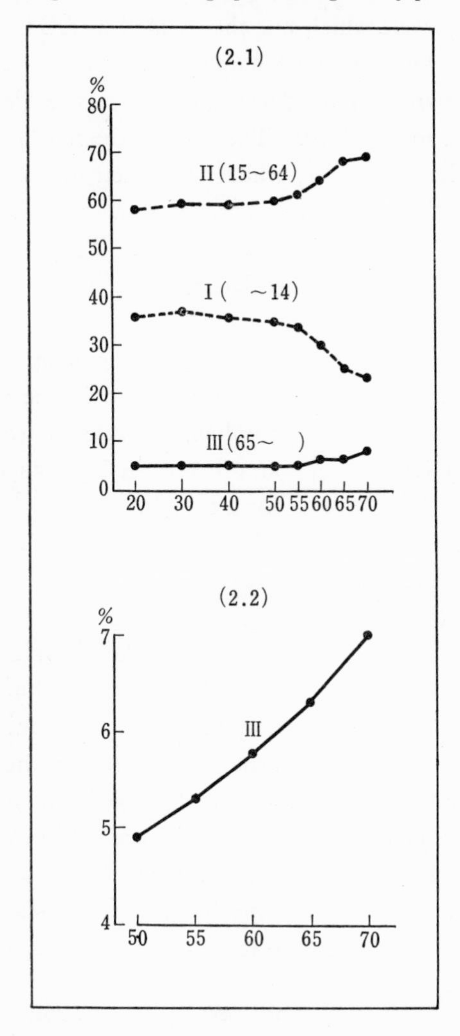

the man-power is sub-divided into (i) active man-power and (ii) inactive man-power, which are abbreviated as ACT and IN ACT respectively, according to its employment status. The changing states of employment have decisive effect on the classification of the uses of the man-power. The uses of the man-power are sub-divided into five categories, which have their own counterparts in the sources of the man-power, according to the changing states of employment in a certain interval of time. They are listed below with their definition and abbreviation:[18]

	Categories	*Definition*
(i)	Those who are continuously employed (CONT).	Those who are in the same state of employment both at the initial and at the terminal points of time in a fixed time interval.
(ii)	Those whose state of employment has changed (TRANS).	Those whose state of employment at the terminal point of time is different from that at the initial point of time in a fixed time interval.
(iii)	Those who are new comers entering into the state of employment (NEW).	Those who are in the state of employment at the terminal point of time but are not at the initial point of time in a fixed time interval.
(iv)	Those who have left from employment (LEAV).	Those who are not in the state of employment at the terminal point of time but are in the state of employment at the initial point of time in a

18) The changing states of employment has attracted particular attention in United Nations [1975]; for the construction of a coefficient matrix that represents the transition probability of changing states of employment, referring to the data of Japan's *Employment Status Survey*.

		fixed time interval.
(v)	Those who are not in the state of employment in continuation (CONT IN).	Those who are not in the state of employment both at the initial and at the terminal points of time in a fixed time interval.

It is readily seen from the classification that the first three categories correspond with the active man-power in the sources and that the remaining two correspond with the inactive man-power. It is also not unreasonable to consider that a fixed time interval for the definition of categories is determined by one year interval looking backward.

As another way of classification of the uses of the man-power it is conceivable that its industrial uses are taken into account. Although much detailed classification may be conceivable, the subdivisions of the uses into (i) the use for the primary industry and ii) that for non-primary industry are basic. They are abbreviated as PRIM and NON PRIM respectively. It is of particular relevance for the analysis of the man-power that the industrial uses be combined with the uses according to the changing states of employment as we shall see the point later.

A number of factors exercise strong influence on the sources of the man-power. They are: (1) demographic factors and (2) the educational level of the man-power. The demographic factors are primarily characterized by the sex composition and the age structure, whereas the educational level may be reflected by the stages of educational achievements of the man-power. The demographic structure in the sources of man-power can be composed of age groups as follows: (I) those who are 15–19 years old, (II) those who are 20–24 years old, (III) those who are 25–39 years old, (IV) those who are 40–54 years old and (V) those who are over 55. It is of some convenience for detailed studies in the demography of the old aged that the age group of V be further broken down into (VI) those who are aged 55–64 and (VII) those who are aged over 65. It is particularly notable to point out that these five age groups (I–V) distinguish major turning points in individual life cycles. Broadly speaking, the age groups of I and II correspond with the age of the entry into the state of employment seeking for earnings whereas the age group III is related to the formation of nucleus family and such age as one's youngest children may reach the age of receiving of compulsory education. The age group IV corresponds with such age that one's employment nears the age of retirement, whereas the age group V is generally regarded as the age of one's retirement from working. Stages of education are broadly categorized by (i) elementary education, ELE in abbreviation, (ii) intermediary education, INT in abbreviation, and (iii) advanced education, ADV in abbreviation, respectively. The category of ELE stands for such educational level that falls into the compulsory school education, whereas the category of INT refers to such educational level that is equivalent to high school education. The category of ADV includes all stages of education that are equivalent to and higher than the level of junior college. It deserves to be noted here that these categories of the stages of education are exactly parallel with the classification of school career in the inquiries for the aged over 15 of SSCL.

The structure of the man-power balance is displayed in Diagram 3, where the rectangular and diamond shaped boxes indicate the sources and uses of the man-power respectively. The man-power balance has two different time dimensions for measurement. First, it measures out the existing state of human resources and their sources and uses. The stock of human resources at a par-

Diagram 3. Structure of man-power balance

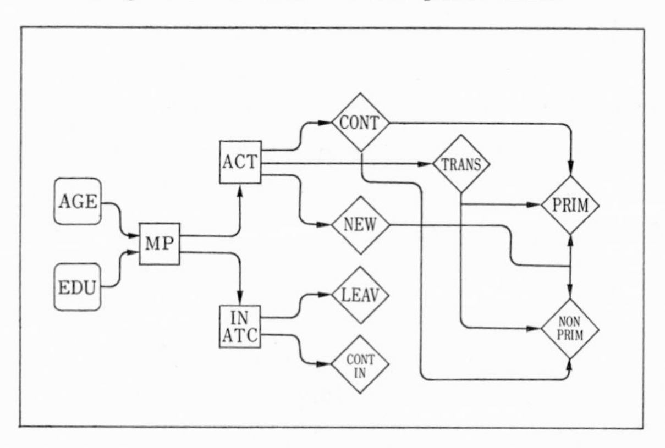

ticuar date is the primary concern for the measurement. The aspect is referred to the stock measurement of the man-power balance. Second, the changes in human resources in a certain period are figured out in the man-power balance. In this aspect, the flow of human resources in a certain period is the ultimate objective of the measurement. The aspect is referred to the flow measurement of the man-power balance. In the analysis of the man-power balance that follows, data are taken from the *Employment Status Survey* which is concerned with the stock of human resouces as of July 1st for each sample year. Hence, the stock measurement of the man-power balance is given throughout the analysis that follows. In the analysis, a comparison is made for three consecutive sample years, 1965, 1968 and 1971.[19] As the striking changes

19) Emoloyment Status Survey, which is carried out by the Bureau of Statistics every three years begining with 1956, contains abundant amounts of information not only referring to the status of the man-power but also making use of the derivation of the size distribution of earned income on the basis of approximately 300,000 sample households drawn out of the nation-wide survey districts used in the Population Census.

in the demographic structure are taking place in the period that are covered by the sample years, additional interest is gained from an experimental analysis of the man-power balance for the period.

Table 2.1. shows the age composition of the man-power, among which the uses of the active man-power are displayed in Table 2.2. It is readily seen that a marked declining tendency in the composition of the young aged (15–24 years old) is contrasted with the gradual rising in the composition of the middle and the old aged. A haphazard looking on Table 2.2. may tempt us to conclude that the persistent stability is maintained in the structure of uses of the man-power. But, the following tables, which display the age profile for the uses of the man-power of both sex, provides a full and detailed account that the conclusion may not necessarily be the case.

Table 2. Man-power and its active uses (unit: %)

(2.1) Man-power by Age			
	1965	1968	1971
15-24	27.6	26.0	24.9
25-39	32.6	32.7	31.9
40-54	21.3	22.0	23.2
55-	18.6	19.1	19.9
55-64	10.1	10.2	10.4
65	8.5	9.0	9.5
(2.2) Active Uses of Man-power			
	1965	1968	1971
CONT	92.3	91.7	92.1
TRANS	3.3	3.6	3.7
NEW	4.4	4.7	4.2

Table 3. Age-profile of active man-power (unit: %)

	CONT			TRANS			NEW		
AGE	1965	1968	1971	1965	1968	1971	1965	1968	1971
15-19	5.2	5.5	3.5	12.9	12.3	6.5	56.7	53.4	41.1
20-24	14.5	13.2	14.7	30.0	29.1	32.5	18.3	20.7	28.1
25-39	38.7	37.7	36.2	36.0	37.5	37.2	13.7	16.5	19.3
40-54	26.6	27.9	29.5	13.9	14.1	16.1	5.9	6.7	8.3
55-	15.0	15.7	15.9	7.2	7.0	7.7	2.3	2.7	3.2
55-64	10.5	10.6	10.6	6.3	6.1	6.7	1.8	2.0	2.5
64-	4.5	5.1	5.0	0.9	1.0	1.0	0.5	0.7	0.7

Table 4. Age-profils of active man-power by sex (unit: %)

unit : %

AGE		CONT			TRANS			NEW		
		1965	1968	1971	1965	1968	1971	1965	1968	1971
MALE	I	4.0	4.3	2.9	10.4	9.3	5.2	64.6	61.9	48.6
	II	12.8	11.7	13.0	25.0	23.7	26.1	21.1	23.5	34.5
	III	41.6	41.2	39.9	41.0	43.1	42.3	8.1	8.2	8.4
	IV	25.3	26.4	27.9	14.1	14.5	16.0	3.0	2.9	4.1
	V	16.3	16.5	16.4	9.5	9.3	10.5	3.2	3.6	4.1
	VI	11.1	10.9	10.8	8.2	8.0	9.0	2.4	2.5	3.1
	VII	5.2	5.6	5.6	1.3	1.3	1.5	0.8	1.1	1.0
FEMALE	I	7.2	7.4	4.9	18.0	17.0	8.7	55.9	47.6	36.3
	II	17.6	15.9	17.7	39.8	39.4	43.9	16.1	18.8	23.8
	III	33.6	31.9	29.8	25.8	27.0	28.5	18.1	22.2	26.2
	IV	28.8	30.6	32.3	13.3	13.3	16.4	8.2	9.4	10.9
	V	12.8	14.3	15.2	3.1	2.6	3.8	1.6	2.1	2.8
	VI	9.4	10.2	11.1	2.7	2.3	2.5	1.3	1.7	2.2
	VII	3.4	4.1	4.1	0.4	0.3	0.3	0.3	0.4	0.6

I (15~19), II (20~24), III (25~39), VI (40~54), V (55~), VI (55~64), VII (65~)

Table 3 shows the age profile of the uses of the active man-power concerning the total of both sex, whereas its breakdown according to sex is displayed in Table 4. It is interesting to see from the observation of Table 3 that the there seems to be a steady rise in the composition of the middle and the old aged (those who are

Table 5. The structure of enrolled scoolboys (girls) and students according to stages of education (unit: %)

	ELE	INT	ADV
1930	90.8	7.8	1.4
1940	91.7	6.8	1.5
1950	87.6	10.3	2.1
1960	82.3	14.5	3.2
1970	70.4	21.6	8.0

Source: Ministry of Education, *A Century of Educational Statistics*, April 1971 (in Japanese).

in age groups IV and V) in the uses of the active man-power. The steady rise in the composition of the middle and the old aged in the uses of the active man-power is sharply contrasted with the variation in the composition of the young age group. Especially notable is the dramatic declining of the composition of the young aged (those who are in the age group I) in the new entry into the active man-power, which shows a 12% decrease in three years between 1968 and 1971. Basically, two factors contribute to this startling declining in the composition. Firstly, the declining is caused by the changing structure in demography to which I have already referred. In the second place, the rising trend of shooling years that necessarily results in the advancement of one's school career, which delays his early entry into the employment, must be noted. The rising trend of schooling years is faithfully reflected in Table 5, which displays the structure of schoolboys and students according to different stages of education.

Table 6 illustrates the growing number of those who are graduated from advanced educational institutions by their types in the past two decades. It is interesting to see from the table that an exploding rise in the flow of graduates from advanced educational institutions takes place after the sixties. Particularly spectacular is

Table 6. Growth of the graduates from advanced educational institutions

	Colleges, universities	Junior colleges	Graduate schools MC	Graduate schools DC
				(persons)
1955	107,867	31,117	(2,310)	
1960	121,979	32,892	3,109	1,413
1965	162,349	55,728	4,790	2,061
1969	217,805	111,091	9,350	2,945
				(%)
1960/1955	113.08	105.71	—	—
1965/1960	133.10	169.42	154.07	145.86
1969/1965	134.16	199.35	195.20	142.89

Note: MC and DC stand for the courses for Master's and Doctor's degree.
Source: Same as Table 5.

the rise of graduates from junior colleges in the late sixties which are doubling in five years after 1965.[20] The rise of those who are out of MC which can only parallel with the rise of graduates from junior colleges in the late sixties should also be noted, although we must take into account an important factor in the comparison that the rise in MC case starts with an intially low level Then a question arises how the prolonged schooling years affects the pattern of the man-power balance and where those graduates find a place in the uses of man-power. We shall come back to the point later. In the meantime, we shall follow the age profile of the active man-power according to different sex.

Turning our attention to Table 4, a couple of marked differences

20) In this regard, it should be noted that the overwhelming portion of the enrolled students of junior colleges-approximately 90%-is occupied by female students.

in the age profile of the uses of the active man-power is easily detected from the inspection of the table. First, in the category of CONT, a steady rising trend in the composition of the old aged (the age group V) for female is observed, whereas the composition of the same age group for male stays strictly stable. Although we do not provide here the figures of the age profile cross-tabulated with the breakdown by industry, it is possible to make a point that the difference by sex is more clearly discerned in the primary industry than in the non-primary industry. Second, in the category of NEW, the rising of the composition of the age group II for female in the 1965–1971 period stays in the size of 8%, which is greatly superseded by 14% rising of the composition of the age group II for male in the corresponding period. The significant difference in the rise of the composition of the age group II, whose age is equivalent to that of those who are graduated from

Table 7. Age-profile of inactive man-power

unit : %

		LEAV			CONT IN		
		1965	1968	1971	1965	1968	1971
	I	5.6	6.4	4.2	58.7	53.7	47.6
	II	12.7	12.7	14.7	11.5	13.2	16.4
	III	17.3	19.5	18.1	3.2	3.3	3.1
	IV	12.7	12.4	14.1	2.3	2.8	2.9
	V	51.6	49.2	48.7	24.3	27.0	29.9
	VI	23.8	25.4	24.3	5.7	6.3	26.4
	VII	27.8	23.8	24.4	18.6	20.7	3.5
	I	3.7	3.6	2.4	17.5	16.4	13.9
	II	25.9	30.8	34.5	6.7	6.2	7.2
	III	33.3	41.4	38.0	31.4	32.1	31.9
	IV	14.8	13.0	13.3	18.9	18.1	18.4
	V	22.3	11.2	12.1	25.5	27.4	28.3
	VI	11.0	6.4	7.3	11.3	11.6	11.6
	VII	11.3	4.8	4.9	14.2	15.8	16.7

advanced educational institutions, according to sex is further explained by the following Table 7 which exhibits the age profile of the uses of the inactive man-power according to sex. It is interesting to see from Table 7 that the rising of the composition of the age group II for female concerning the category of LEAV in the period 1965–1971 amounts to 10% which is compared with a corresponding rise for male of only 2%. It would not be wrong to make reasoning that the retirement from the active part of man-power for female in the age group II be essentially motivated by marriage. Such reasoning would support the theory that female's work in the active man-power has not yet given women their due place in the permanent and lifelong work system. It may not be groundlus to say that most of female graduates from advanced educational instituitons, currently in Japan, would not always seek their permanent job and that they would be ready to withdraw from the labour force longing for a happy home.
The fact is confirmed by the inspection of the following Table 8 which portrays the cross-divisions of those who fall into the category of LEAV according to age groups and stages of education by sex, for the two sample years of 1968 and 1971. In the case of female, the composition of those who are in the age group of 15–24 years old and are graduated from advanced educational institutions of the category LEAV has increased by 4% in three years between 1968 and 1971. But, the direction of the movement for the corresponding composition concerning the case of male has been opposite showing a little decrease by 1%. Thus, it may be concluded from the reasoning associated with Tables 4, 7 and 8 that those women who actively take part in the man-power having received advanced education and in relatively young age group (up till 24 years old) are more and more inclined towards early retirement from their working by indulging in their personal hap-

piness.[21]

Returning again to Table 7, it is illuminating to learn from the examination of the table that the composition of the uses of the inactive part of the man-power bears the mark of the advent of the old aged society. First, it is reflected in the rising composition of the category of CONT IN, which amounts to 5% rise for male and 3% for female in the 1965–1971 period. It is apparent to us that the rising composition of the category of CONT IN is caused by the increasing weight of the old aged occupied in the age structure of the man-power. Second, it is noted from the table that the composition of the category of LEAV shows a declining trend for both sex. Particularly notable is a sharp decrease observed in the case of female. Against the case of female, the composition of the category of LEAV for male indicates a mild declining. The different pattern appeared in the composition of the category of LEAV by different sex may be explained by looking into the following Table 9. It is interesting to see that the direction of the movement of the composition for both sex and both age groups becomes different according to different industries. It is true that a remarkable rising in the composition of the non-primary industry (NON PRIM) is observed, but the corresponding composition declines for the primary industry (PRIM). It is also noted that the variation of the composition for both industries simultaneously occurs in the 1965–1968 period and that the magnitude of variation is greater in the over 65 age group for male but it is greater in 55–64 age group for female. It appears that a sharp declining of the share of LEAV for female may be explained by a startling decrease in the share of the same sex for PRIM occurred

21) As the reasoning is based upon the observation of the period 1968–1971, it would be dangerous to generalize the conclusion drawn from the reasoning for the future projection without further qualification.

in 1965–1968 period. On the other hand, in the case of male, a considerable increase in the share of LEAV for NON PRIM seems to be counterbalanced by the increase in the corresponding share for PRIM resulting in a mild declining trend for male as a whole. The reasoning advanced here suggests that the advent of the old aged society has complex impact not only on the structure of the man-power balancebut also on the distribution of personal income through earning activities. One aspect of the

Table 8. Composition or LEAV by educational stages

unit: %

	1968					1971				
	Σ	15~24	25~34	35~54	55~	Σ	15~24	25~34	35~54	55~
GRA	95.5	77.4	98.6	100.0	100.0	94.8	74.7	98.5	100.0	99.9
ELE	63.3	39.3	48.3	63.8	76.5	61.2	31.6	43.1	66.3	83.4
INT	23.4	35.7	35.0	26.3	14.8	25.5	41.0	40.0	25.5	10.6
ADV	8.8	3.4	13.3	10.0	9.7	8.1	2.1	15.4	8.2	5.9
SCH	4.5	22.6	1.4	0	0	5.2	25.3	1.5	0	0.1
GRA	99.3	98.1	99.8	100.0	100.0	99.2	98.1	100.0	100.0	99.9
ELE	50.6	38.5	42.9	64.3	88.5	45.0	29.7	36.5	62.0	84.3
INT	41.9	52.0	49.1	30.7	8.6	45.0	56.8	52.2	33.0	12.9
ADV	6.8	7.6	7.8	5.0	3.0	9.2	11.6	11.3	5.0	2.7
SCH	0.7	1.9	0.2	0	0	0.8	1.9	0	0	0.1

Table 9. Industrial Composition of LEAV

		PRIM			NON PRIM		
	Age	1965	1968	1971	1965	1968	1971
M	55-64	20.8	10.7	10.7	79.2	84.3	89.3
	65-	56.4	39.0	32.6	43.6	61.0	67.4
FE	55-64	60.0	29.1	24.5	40.0	70.9	75.5
	65-	78.9	60.0	55.9	21.1	40.0	44.1

(Note) M: Male, FE: female

impact of the advancement of the old aged society on the size distribution of earned income will be discussed in its association with the economic status of the old aged in an article that follows.

REFERENCES

Raymond Aron, *Dix-huit leçon sur la société industrielle*, Paris 1962.

Raymond Aron, *La lutte de classes, nouvelles leçon sur les sociétés industrielles*, Paris 1964.

The Asahi Press, *Kutabare GNP* (GNP in the dust), Tokyo 1971, (in Japanese).

Odd Aukrust and Svein Nordbotten, " Files of Individual Data and their Potential for Social Research ", *Review of Income and Wealth*, July 1973.

Jean Bénard, *Comptabilité nationale et modeles de politique économique*, Paris 1972.

Bureau of Statistics, Prime Minister's Office, *Chiki Mesh Tokei no Kaisetsu* (Explanatory Notes of National Grid-Coordinate System), Tokyo 1974, (in Japanese).

Economic Planning Agency, Council for National Standard of Living, *Shakai Shihyo*, (Social Indicators), Tokyo 1974, (in Japanese).

Economic Planning Agency, *NNW: Measuring Net National Welfare of Japan*, Tokyo 1973.

Jacques Ellul, *The Technological Society*, New York 1964.

Johan Huizinga, *Homo Ludens: A Study of the Play-Element in Culture*, Boston 1955.

Y. Kurabayashi, " National Economic Accounts and a System of Social Statistics ", *Keizai Kenkyu*, May 1974, (in Japanese).

Siegfried Lörcher, *Zur Quantfizierung der " Sozialen Wohlfahrt " in Japan*, Hamburg 1976.

Norval Morris and Gordon Hawkins, *The Honest Politicians Guide to Crime Control*, Chicago 1970.

T. Mizoguchi, " An Estimation of Income Distribution of Total Household in Japan ", *Keizai Kenkyu*, July 1976, (in Japanese).

Svein Nordbotten, *Two Articles of Statistical Data Files and their Utilization in Socio-demographic Model Building*, Artikler fra Statistisk Sentralbyra, Nr 40, Oslo 1971.

Milton Moss, ed., *The Measurement of Economic and Social Performance*, New York 1973.

William Nordhaus and James Tobin, *Is Growth Obsolete?*, New York 1972.

Richard and Nancy Ruggles, *The Design of Economic Accounts*, New York 1970.

M. Umemura, *Rodoryoku no Kozo to Koyo Mondai*, (The Structure of Labour

Force and its Implications to Issues of Employment), Tokyo 1971, (in Japanese).

United Nations, *A System of National Accounts*, New York 1968.

United Nations, *Towards a System of Social and Demographic Statistics*, New York 1975.

United Nations, A Draft System of the Distribution of Income, Consumption and Accumulation, E/CN. 3/425, 1972.

U.S. Department of Health, Education an Welfare, *Toward a Social Report*, Washington D.C. 1969.

S. Ura, *Data Kozo*, (The Structure of Data Bases and Files), Tokyo 1973, (in Japanese).

Elenor B. Sheldon and Wilbert E. Moore, ed., *Indicators of Social Change and Measurement*, New York 1968.

8

DEMOGRAPHIC FACTORS IN THE DISTRIBUTION OF EARNED INCOME AND THE ECONOMIC STATUS OF THE OLD AGED DEPENDENTS

1. Introduction

In what follows the author will be concerned with the part of demographic factors in the explanation of the distribution of earned income and their implications for the economic status of the old aged. The author will attempt to exploit the information squeezed out of *Sample Survey of Recipients of Health Insurance*, which has been unduly ignored as a statistical source for the analysis of size distribution in earned income. As the samples of the Survey are drawn out of the population that is constituted of earners of wages and salaries who participate in specific schemes of health insurance, a brief sketch of the institutional background of health insurances in Japan will be discussed in section 2. Following this introductory sketch I shall illustrate, in the same section, the nature and characteristics of the *Sample Survey of Recipients of Health Insurance* on which our empirical works rest as statistical source. It is important for the effective use of any statistical information that the nature and characteristics of the information be fully understood. In section 3, the author will show that demographic factors such as sex and age contribute to the formation of the pattern of size distribution in earned income by presenting the distribution of the earners of wages and salaries tabulated according to different schemes of health insurance, sex, income and age groups. It is uncovered from the tabulation that marked differences of the distribution pattern in the earners of wage and salaries according to different size of enterprises are distinguished in relation to different age groups. The measurement of Gini coefficient by different age groups will present different features according to different sex. In section 4, the author will take up the economic status of the old aged dependents over 65. It is interesting to explore the economic status of the old aged dependents that is reflected in their distribution in relation to the distribution of the earners of wages and salaries who support them. The distribution of the old aged dependents is tabulated according to income and age groups of those who support them by different sex and categories of health insurance schemes. The statistical analysis applied to the tabulation will show that the variation of the distribution for the old aged dependents is largely explained by the effect of age groups with the implication that the effect of income groups plays a less essential part. Such an analysis seems to have a definite importance for the policy making of social welfare in that the advent of "the old aged society" should make it necessary to collect quantitative information on the old aged dependents in relation to those who support them. The author hopes his attempt will be a step forward in this direction.[1]

1) The present article is an outgrowth of the author's joint research with Pro-

2. Health and Medical Insurance in Japan; the system and its institutional background

As we have noted before, the statistical information on which most of our research rely is obtained from the *Sample Survey of Recipients of Health Insurance* by the Social Insurance Agency of Ministry of Welfare. A few remarks on the system and institu-

Table 1. Number and distribution of persons covered by different categories of H.I. system in Japan for March, 1974

(1,000 persons)

Categories	Total number	Insured persons	Dependents
Self Employed H.I.	44,125 (40.3)		
Government Managed H.I.	27,411 (25.0)	13,490	13,921
Society Managed H.I.	24,640 (22.5)	10,857	13,783
Day Labourers' H.I.	845 (0.8)	528	317
Seamen's H.I.	737 (0.7)	257	480
National Public Services M.A.A.	3,004 (2.8)	1,158	1,846
Public Corporations Staff Members M.A.A.	2,166 (2.0)	785	1,381
Local Public Services M.A.A.	6,090 (5.6)	2,496	3,594
Private Schools Teachers M.A.A.	409 (0.4)	222	187

Note: Figures in parenthesis stand for percentage. H.I. and M.A.A. stand for health insurance and mutual assistance association respectively.

---

fessor H. Ichikawa on the cause and effect of the income distribution in lower income classes.

In this article, we do not intend to furnish details of works related to the size distribution of income and wealth in Japan. Such attempt has been made by Mizoguchi using extensively Japanese data with much wider scope in the works of Mizoguchi [1974, 1975]. In the subsequent analysis of this article attention is drawn to the part of demographic factors and family composition played in the size distribution of income. In this connection, it should be noted that Mouer has thoroughly analyzed the importance of sociological factors using data of Family Budget Survey, which is reported in Mouer [1975].

tional background of Japanese health and medical insurance may be appropriate for understanding the characteristics of the statistical information.

Table 1 exhibits the number of persons covered by different categories of heath insurance system in Japan as of March 1974 and its percentage distribution. Table 1 readily shows that major categories of health insurance (H.I.) system in Japan are (i) self-employed H.I., (ii) government managed H.I. and (iii) society managed H.I.. The first of those major categories refers to those who are self-employed and independent professions, whereas (ii) and (iii) are related to wage and salary earners. The categories (ii) and (iii) are notably different in that (ii) consists of wage earners of small scale enterprises and their dependents and that

Table 2. Percentage distribution of employees of non-primary industries according to the size of enterprises[2)]
(number of employees)

Years	Total	0–29	30–299	300–999	1,000–	Public services
1962	100.0	29.3	23.8	7.8	23.8	14.8
1965	100.0	29.0	24.8	8.4	23.1	14.2
1968	100.0	30.3	24.7	8.6	23.5	12.7
1971	100.0	30.3	25.2	9.0	23.1	12.4

Source: Bureau of Statistics, Office of the Prime Minister of Japan, *Employment Status Survey*, 1962, 1965, 1968 and 1971 editions.

2) The *Employment Status Survey*, which is carried out by the Bureau of Statistics of Office of the Prime Minister of Japan every three years beginning with 1956, contains adequate amounts of information for deriving the size distribution of earned income which is comparable to those which are derived from other sources. An attempt has been made by R. Wada [1975] in his lengthy work to compare the patterns of income distribution in Post-War Japan that are obtainable from various sources placing its central focus on the data of the *Employment Status Survey*.

(iii) is made up of those who earn their wages and salaries at large scale enterprises.

According to the regulation on the establishment of the health insurance system, the health insurance society is usually organized by such enterprises that employ more than 300 employees.

It follows from the observation of Table 2 that the category of (ii) refers to approximately 2/3 of private non-primary workers and that (iii) is associated with the remaining 1/3 of private non-primary workers who are gainfully occupied in the large enterprises.

It is interesting to compare the distribution of those who are covered by three major categories of the health insurance system, i.e. the insured persons and their dependents, according to age, with that of total population. The comparison is made for 1972 in Table 3.

The *Sample Survey of Recipients of Health Insurance*, on which the subsequent analysis of this article substantially rests, refers to those who are covered by the categories of the health insurance (ii) and (iii), i.e. Government Managed H.I. and Society Managed

Table 3. Distribution of total population, insured persons and their dependents according to age

(10,000 persons)

(1) Age	(2) Total population	(3) Self Employed H.I.	(4) Goverment Managed H.I.	(5) Society Managed H.I.	(4) + (5)
Total	10,734	4,396	2,621	2,293	4,914
0–19	3,437	1,353	781	755	1,535
20–39	3,714	1,219	1,076	987	2,063
40–59	2,391	1,095	556	419	975
60–	1,191	729	208	132	340

Source: Social Insurance Agency of Ministry of Welfare, *1972 Sample Survey of Recipients of Health Insurance.*

H.I.. The total of the insured persons and their dependents covered by these categories of health insurance occupies approximately the half of total population in Japan as is readily seen by Table 3. The Social Insurance Agency of the Ministry of Welfare has initiated the Survey in 1966. The Survey has been substantially improved since 1972 introducing the scheme of collection of data according to the three-way classification of earned income of insured persons, age of insured persons and age of dependents. The Survey has been carried out on an annual basis and its information refers to October 1 every year. The information collected from the Survey contains such items as age, date of birth, sex, earned income of the insured person, categories of the health insurance, number of dependents, their age, date of birth, sex and relation to the insured persons. The number of samples for 1972 Survey is given below:

Table 4. Number of samples for 1972 survey

	Government Managed H.I.	Society Managed H.I.
Insured persons	53,125	51,480
Dependents	51,300	63,087

Source: *1972 Sample Survey of Recipients of Health Insurance.*
Population estimates are obtained from sample figures by blowing up the sample figures by 250.929 times for Government Managed H.I. and 200.139 for Society Managed H.I. respectively.[3]

3) Though it is unnecessary to give the details of the method of the Survey, its brief exposition is appropriate in this place. The universe population of the insured persons is listed and classified by District Social Insurance Office. By the district list of the insured persons each District Social Insurance Office draws uniform samples. After the drawing of samples it conducts a direct survey to the samples and reports them to the Ministry of Welfare. No direct recording by each sample is given. It is generally recognized from the method of survey and the numbers of samples that they provide sufficiently good representation of the universe population.

The Survey has two notable features. First, a marked difference in the pattern of the distribution of earned income is distinguished from the Survey according to different size of enterprises. As noted before, the members of Government Managed H.I. are working in small-scale enterprises less than 300 employees, whereas those who join Society Managed H.I. are employed by large enterprises with larger than 300 employees.

Second, the Survey contains the information on the economic status of the dependents supported by the insured workers. The distribution of the dependents is classified according to such characteristics as earned income of the supporting relative, his age, and the age of dependents. As we shall come back to the point in later sections, the information is especially pertinent to the analysis of the economic status of theold aged.[4)]

Prior to the statistical analysis of income distribution which is obtainable from the information of the Survey, it is appropriate to offer the definition of the teminology used in the Survey.

(i) The *insured persons* are those who are employed in the establishments which join either Government Managed H.I. or Society Managed H.I..

(ii) The *dependents* are defined as those who are registered on

---

4) As an exception to the additional information on the demographic factor of the dependents it should be refered to the three-way classification made by income classes and age groups of the head of family with types of family, whose information is offered in 1969 National Survey of Family Income and Expenditure of the Bureau of Statistics, the Prime Minister's Office of Japan. The types of family are classified by the status of earners such that (i) earner, family head, (ii) earners, family head and his (or her) spouse, (iii) earners, family head, and others (except spouse), (iv) earners, family head, his (or her) spouse and other. It is observed from the information that not all types of family significantly influence the difference in the income distribution, but that the income distribution is influenced for some type of family.

the health insurance as dependents of an insured person. Accordingly, a family in the ordinary sense does not necessarily consist of one insured person and its dependents if more than one members of the family are actively employed. In our definition a family in the ordinary sense could be considered as a set of insured persons and dependents. We shall come back to the topic later in section 4.

(iii) *Income* in this Survey is defined as the monthly permanent earnings estimated by the three-month average earned income of May, June and July. Bonus and other transitory incomings are excluded because they do not form the permanent part of earnings. Transfer income and property income are also excluded from the concept because they are not the payments for primary inputs. Therefore, the concept may be regarded as the earned income of primary distribution before the tranfer of factor incomes.

3. The Distribution of Income by Sex and Different Age Groups

Before we go into a detailed analysis of income distribution by sex and age groups, we shall make a brief sketch of the overall profile of earned income according to sex and different age groups. A comparison of average earnings between different categories of health insurance is provided by Table 5. It is observed from the table that the differential in earned income between sex apparently exists for the workers belonging to both categories of health insurance.

Table 6 shows the relative variation of income by age groups for the categories of workers distinguished by sex and types of health insurance, putting the average earned income for each category equal to 100.0. The classification of age groups roughly reflects

Table 5. Comparison of earned income per-capita according to age classes between different categories of health insurance

(unit : yen)

	0–19	20–24	25–34	35–44	45–54	55–64	65–
Government Managed H.I.							
Male	43670	58073	76710	83714	82295	72408	64404
Female	36751	41260	43184	42313	42869	40384	38115
Society Managed H.I.							
Male	49442	64662	86669	97200	97550	85236	73901
Female	43922	50743	55000	56553	59486	56384	52385

Notes : (i) Earned income in this table refers to monthly income.
(ii) Average per-capita income is shown below.

	Government Managed H.I.	Society Managed H.I.
Male	73623	84982
Female	42415	52303

Source : 1972 *Sample Survey of Recipients of Health Insurance.*

different stages of life cycles. Thus, the two age groups from the lowest age correspond to the participation in the man-power (or the working population). The two age groups next to the younger age groups extend to the life cycle that a new family may be formed by marriage and the age of its child may reach the beginning of the compulsory education. The age of 55 is general marked as the age of retirement from working.

Table 6. Relative variation of per-capita earned income by age from average per-capita income

	0–19	20–24	25–34	35–44	45–55	55–64	65–
Government Managed H.I.							
Male	59.3	78.9	104.2	113.7	111.8	98.3	87.5
Female	86.6	97.3	101.8	99.8	101.1	95.2	89.2
Society Managed H.I.							
Male	58.2	76.1	102.0	114.4	114.8	100.3	87.0
Female	84.0	97.0	105.2	108.1	113.7	107.8	100.2

Table 7 and Table 8 exhibit the distribution of the number of insured persons by different sex classified according to age and income groups. The groupings of income are formulated as quartiles by pooling the samples of Government Managed and Society Managed Health Insurance schemes distinguishing different sex.

Table 7. Percentage distribution of insured persons by age and income groups (Male)

Government Managed H.I.

	Age						
Income	0–19	20–24	25–34	35–44	45–54	55–64	65–
I	88.78	54.93	17.86	12.96	16.94	32.94	48.49
II	9.47	34.16	34.70	24.28	23.10	26.16	20.02
III	1.56	9.20	31.01	29.41	24.55	17.29	11.23
IV	0.19	1.71	16.43	33.35	35.41	23.61	20.26
I	14.46	30.84	18.94	10.26	7.76	11.45	6.29
II	1.56	19.37	37.17	19.40	10.69	9.18	2.62
III	0.32	6.43	40.96	28.98	14.01	7.49	1.82
IV	0.04	1.34	24.25	36.71	22.57	11.42	3.66

Society Managed H.I.

	Age						
Income	0–19	20–24	25–34	35–44	45–54	55–64	65–
I	80.97	34.69	4.20	2.01	3.35	14.54	33.20
II	17.39	49.50	25.92	6.76	6.16	20.25	19.72
III	1.59	13.56	41.17	25.26	17.36	19.87	14.89
IV	0.06	2.25	28.72	65.97	73.13	45.34	32.19
I	28.86	44.35	10.75	3.65	3.52	5.53	3.34
II	3.77	38.52	40.43	7.44	3.94	4.68	1.21
III	0.29	8.82	53.71	23.28	9.30	3.84	0.76
IV	0.01	0.98	25.09	40.71	26.23	5.87	1.10

Note: Following groups of income are used:
I under 56000 III 80000–98000
II 60000–76000 IV over 104000 (unit: yen)

It is readily seen that the differential in earnings between different sex apparently exists as indicated below:

	Male	*Female*
I	under 56000	under 33000
II	60000–76000	36000–42000
III	80000–98000	45000–52000
IV	over 104000	over 56000

The upper panel of each table shows the percentage distribution of insured persons for relevant age groups adding up to 100.0 with respect to each column, whereas the lower panel of the tables indicates the percentage distribution of insured persons for relevant income groups adding up to 100.0 regarding with each row.

Marked differences are observed in the pattern of the distribution of insured persons for different categories of health insurance schemes that reflect the different scale of enterprises.

(i) In the lowest income group of male, the workers participating in the Society Managed H.I. are concentrated by 73% on younger age groups who are under 24. The concentration on younger age groups of workers who belong to the Government Managed H.I. in the same income group is not so significant as the case cited above, indicating that 45% is occupied by those young workers who fall into the age groups less than 25.

(ii) Similarly, in the lowest income male group, the employment of the old aged over 55 shows a marked difference between those who belong to the Government Managed H.I. and those who are in the Society Managed H.I. Indeed, the old aged workers of the lowest income bracket who are in the Society Managed is approximately half in the percentage distribution of the old aged workers who belong to the Government Managed H.I.

(iii) There exists no significant difference in the percentage dis-

Table 8. Percentage distribution of insured persons by age and income groups (Female)

Government Managed H.I.

	Age						
Income	0–19	20–24	25–34	35–44	45–54	55–64	65–
I	38.00	24.79	21.63	39.26	38.81	46.33	53.57
II	43.81	36.40	35.67	24.67	24.79	23.54	18.96
III	16.50	29.54	23.09	16.94	16.87	15.37	13.74
IV	1.68	9.27	19.61	19.12	19.53	14.76	13.74
I	10.14	18.13	17.22	23.46	18.36	9.86	2.82
II	13.79	31.40	16.49	17.39	13.84	5.91	1.18
III	7.26	35.61	20.72	16.68	13.15	5.39	1.19
IV	1.06	15.97	25.15	26.93	21.77	7.41	1.17

Society Managed H.I.

	Age						
Income	0–19	20–24	25–34	35–44	45–54	55–64	65–
I	5.67	2.60	12.54	19.84	15.68	19.75	30.56
II	43.28	13.76	10.68	16.52	17.00	19.75	19.44
III	45.46	52.63	22.08	17.94	18.33	18.87	8.33
IV	5.59	31.01	54.70	45.70	48.99	41.62	41.67
I	10.02	10.62	22.29	28.31	18.67	8.43	1.66
II	37.30	27.42	9.26	11.50	9.89	4.12	0.51
III	20.57	55.05	10.05	6.56	9.60	2.06	0.12
IV	2.61	33.55	25.77	17.29	15.47	4.71	0.60

Note: Following groups of income are employed:
I under 33000   III 45000–52000
II 36000–42000   IV over 56000   (unit: yen)

tribution of the workers in the lowest income group between the Government Managed H.I. and the Society Managed H.I. for the case of female. But, the different pattern of the employment of female workers between the two categories of health insurance schemes becomes apparent if we compare the percentage distribu-

Table 9. Percentage distribution of income by age and income groups (Male)

Government Managed H.I.

Income	Age						
	0–19	20–24	25–34	35–44	45–54	55–64	65–
I	82.42	44.53	11.26	7.31	9.60	20.54	31.21
II	14.03	38.81	30.87	19.94	19.07	24.37	20.62
III	3.08	13.60	35.59	31.32	26.58	21.17	15.45
IV	0.46	3.07	22.28	41.43	44.75	33.91	32.72
I	12.80	31.71	20.01	10.57	7.91	11.29	5.70
II	1.49	18.88	37.47	19.71	10.73	9.15	2.57
III	0.31	6.25	40.78	29.22	14.12	7.51	1.82
IV	0.04	1.34	24.25	36.71	22.57	11.42	3.66

Society Managed H.I.

Income	Age						
	0–19	20–24	25–34	35–44	45–54	55–64	65–
I	74.33	27.40	2.45	0.96	1.53	7.93	19.43
II	22.81	50.99	20.84	4.86	4.39	16.03	17.97
III	2.75	17.99	42.24	23.60	16.11	20.73	17.29
IV	0.12	3.62	34.46	70.59	77.97	55.31	45.30
I	27.02	46.74	11.23	3.47	3.24	5.30	2.98
II	3.59	37.62	41.32	7.63	4.02	4.64	1.19
III	0.28	8.49	53.54	23.69	9.44	3.83	0.73
IV	0.01	0.98	25.09	40.71	26.23	5.87	1.10

Note: Following groups of income are used:
I under 56000 III 80000–98000
II 60000–76000 IV over 104000 (unit: yen)

tion of those who belong to the 20–24 age group. 89% of female workers in the age group who are in the Society Managed H.I. is occupied by the top two income groups, whereas 61% of the corresponding female workers who belong to the Government Managed H.I. concentrates on the bottom two income classes. 3% of female

Table 10. Percentage distribution of income by age and income groups (Female)

Government Managed H.I.

	Age						
Income	0–19	20–24	25–34	35–44	45–54	55–64	65–
I	30.03	17.58	20.42	25.48	24.82	30.65	34.55
II	46.14	34.44	23.09	22.58	22.39	22.45	19.20
III	21.13	34.32	25.81	19.30	19.30	18.35	17.47
IV	2.69	13.67	30.67	32.63	33.76	28.56	28.77
I	10.57	19.04	17.23	23.13	18.07	9.46	2.49
II	13.74	31.58	16.50	17.35	13.80	5.86	1.17
III	7.10	35.51	20.81	16.73	13.23	5.41	1.20
IV	0.89	13.87	24.25	27.75	23.03	8.26	1.94

Society Managed H.I.

	Age						
Income	0–19	20–24	25–34	35–44	45–54	55–64	65–
I	3.97	1.51	6.14	9.57	7.18	9.48	15.26
II	39.20	10.91	7.60	11.42	11.29	13.64	14.41
III	49.39	50.74	19.76	15.32	14.93	16.04	7.72
IV	7.55	36.83	66.50	63.69	66.60	60.83	62.62
I	11.09	11.29	21.63	27.84	18.35	8.23	1.56
II	37.37	27.78	9.14	11.33	9.84	4.04	0.50
III	20.19	55.40	10.18	6.51	5.57	2.04	0,12
IV	2.20	29.11	24.80	19.61	18.01	5.59	0.68

Note: Following groupings of income are employed:
I under 33000 III 45000–52000
II 36000–42000 IV over 56000 (unit: yen)

workers in the age group who belong to the Society Managed H.I. falls into the lowest income group, making a sharp contrast with the case of the Government Managed H.I., where 25% of female workers of the same age group are found in the lowest income group.

Table 11. Gini coefficient by age groups

	0–19	20–24	25–34	35–44	45–54	55–64	65–
Government Managed H.I.							
Male	0.304	0.205	0.152	0.143	0.147	0.171	0.204
Female	0.166	0.157	0.186	0.212	0.218	0.254	0.288
Society Managed H.I.							
Male	0.248	0.172	0.129	0.125	0.128	0.142	0.170
Female	0.130	0.126	0.148	0.181	0.179	0.194	0.200

(iv) As for the female workers of the old aged over 55, it is observed from the tables that the concentration on the lowest income is significantly the case for those who participate in the Government Managed H.I. The heavy concentration of the percentage distribution of female workers who belong to over 55 age groups of the Government Managed H.I. is compared with less significant concentration of the counterpart of the female workers who are in the Society Managed H.I.

These observations suggest the reasoning that the income-age profile of male workers is firmly associated with the hierarchy constituted by the small and large-scale enterprises. A part of workers who find employment in the large-scale enterprises in the younger age might be dropped out of the large-scale enterprises where they are hired, and be shifted to small-scale enterprises by the progress of age owing to their failure to climb up the ladder of social success or their pursuit of fresh opportunities. The pattern of the income-age profile in male workers is sharply contrasted with that of female workers. It appears in the case of female workers that the flow of active man-power is kept stable between the small and large-scale enterprises. The change in the flow of man-power along the income-age profile is essentially caused by marriage for the case of female workers.

Gini coefficient of income inequality is readily calculated from the information exhibited in Tables 7–10, which is shown in Table 11. As is observed from the table, in the case of male, the measure of income inequality first declines and then moves up hitting the bottom at the age group of 35–44. On the other hand, the measure of income inequality rises peristently with age for femal workers.[5)]

It is also noted in Table 11 that the measure of income inequality shows systematically higher values for the case of the Government Managed H.I. than for the case of the Society Managed H.I., regardless of sex.[6)]

4. Economic Status of the Old Aged in Relation to the Distribution of Earned Income of Those Who Support Them

Few attempts have been made so far to explore the economic status of the old aged in relation to economic and demographic chracteristics of those who support the old aged, largely because of

---

5) Gini coefficient is measured by applying the following formula to individual samples:

$$G(h) = \sum_{i=1}^{n}\sum_{j=1}^{n} |y_i(h)-y_j(h)|/(2n^2y^*(h))$$

where $G(h)$ is Gini coefficient of h-th age group, $y^*(h)$ and $y_i(h)$ are the mean earned income of those who belong to h-th age group and the earned income i-th sample which belongs to h-th age group respectively. n stands for the number of samples which belong to h-th age group. The meaning and value judgement implied in the use of Gini coefficient receive thorough and detailed consideration in Kurabayashi and Yatsuka [1975].

6) It is necessary for meaningful comparison of Gini coefficient that Lorenz curves lying behind the comparison are well-behaved in the sense that one of the curves lies inside to the other without cutting each other. The intersecting cases are observed in the comparison between the Government Managed H.I. and the Society Managed H.I. for the same sex if we draw Lorenz curves on the graph. For this point, see in particular, Atkinson [1973] and Sen [1973].

the meagre sources of necessary information. As we have noted in section 2, the *Sample Survey of Recipients of Health Insurance* on which our experimental work essentially depends contains valuable information for the purpose. Indeed, the distribution of the number of dependents classified by age and income groupings of those who support them is available from the Survey. Being short of the space for displaying the entire information concerning the distribution of the number of dependents which are subdivided by age groups, we show only the distribution of the old aged dependents over 65. Tables 12 and 13 show the result. As the form of tabulation is the same as in Tables 7 and 8, we need not to reiterate the explanation of the tables. The following observations can directly be made from the tables.[7)]

(i) Substantial portion of the old aged dependents, both male and female, are supported by the middle aged (between 35 and 54) insured persons. It appears that the distribution of the old aged dependents by age groups is not so significantly different between income groups of the insured persons.

(ii) But, the pattern of the distribution of the old aged depen-

---

7) In the context of this paper, it should be noted that the economic status of the old aged dependents only refers to their dependence on those who support them. It is quite true for thorough exploration of the economic status of the old aged that much wider aspects need be considered as the work of Morgan has already shown. But, his emphasis on distributional aspects rather than means or aggregates is fully taken into account in my work, even though the narrow concept of the economic status for the old aged is used here. For this point, see, in particular, Morgan [1965].

The implication of demographic aspects that affect the distribution of family income is the major concern of the article by Kuznets. But, the data handled by him essentially refer to such factors as sex and age of family heads. The dependence of the old aged on the earners of wages and salaries, dealt with in my work in greater details, is entirely outside of his scope of studies. For his work, see, in particular, Kuznets [1974].

Table 12. Percentage distribution of the dependents aged over 65 by the groupings of age and income of the insured persons who support them (Male)

Government Managed H.I.

	Age						
Income	0–19	20–24	25–34	35–44	45–54	55–64	65–
I	100.00	53.85	15.79	15.26	17.05	28.45	46.44
II	0.00	30.77	33.25	27.07	22.59	23.20	17.34
III	0.00	11.54	32.30	27.16	23.45	18.23	11.15
IV	0.00	3.35	18.56	30.52	36.81	30.11	25.08
I	0.30	2.09	9.87	26.46	23.47	15.40	22.42
II	0.00	0.99	17.16	38.77	25.30	10.37	6.91
III	0.00	0.39	17.51	40.86	28.02	8.56	4.57
IV	0.00	0.10	8.11	37.80	35.24	11.33	8.42

Society Managed H.I.

	Age						
Income	0–19	20–24	25–34	35–44	45–54	55–64	65–
I	100.00	26.53	2.19	1.48	3.07	6.78	30.33
II	0.00	40.82	19.12	7.19	3.73	13.56	18.03
III	0.00	26.53	45.22	22.10	15.58	19.07	9.84
IV	0.00	6.12	33.47	69.24	77.52	60.59	41.80
I	0.70	9.15	7.75	15.49	29.58	11.27	26.06
II	0.00	6.10	29.27	32.52	15.55	9.76	6.71
III	0.00	1.55	27.06	39.21	25.39	5.36	1.43
IV	0.00	0.12	6.84	41.96	43.18	5.82	2.08

Note: For the groupings of income, see the note of Table 7.

dents by income groupings of the insured persons within the same age group is marked by notable difference between the case of the Government Managed H.I. and that of the Society Managed H.I.. Let us take the age group of 45–54 for male as an example. In the case of the Government Managed H.I. 40% of the old aged dependents on the lower two (I and II) income groups of the

insured persons, whereas the counterpart of the case of the Society Managed H.I. only amounts to 7%. Correspondingly, in the case of the Society Managed H.I. 93% of the old aged dependents are found in the higher two (III and IV) income groups, making decided contrast with the case of the Government Managed H.I. where they occupy 60% of the old aged dependents.
(iii) Similar difference is discovered in the distribution of the old aged dependents for the case of female between different schemes of health insurance.

Preceding observations may be combined with the findings exhibited in Table 11, indicating that the measure of income inequality becomes greater in the case of the workers participating in the Government Managed H.I. than that of those who are in the Society Managed H.I. The difference in the institutional schemes of health insurance is the direct reflection of the difference in the scale of enterprises, and the old aged dependents supported by the small-scale enterprises suffer from double disadvantages. Substantial portion of the old aged, in the first place, is supported by those worker who earn relatively low income. Secondly, the earnings of the workers employed in small-scale enterprises are more unequally distributed than those of corresponding workers of the large-scale enterprises for different age groups. Thus, it follows from this reasoning that the economic status of the old aged dependents who are supported by the workers of small-scale enterprises is compelled to be unduly lower position by the combination of these unfavourable factors. Bearing in mind the preceding reasoning, we shall examine the factors that essentially contribute to the distribution pattern of the old aged dependents. We employ the following notations:

n^h_{ij}=the number of the old aged dependents who are supported by such insured persons that fall into i-th income and j-th

Table 13. Percentage distribution of the dependents aged over 65 by the groupings of age and income of the insured persons who support them (Female)

Government Managed H.I.

Income	Age						
	0–19	20–24	25–34	35–44	45–54	55–64	65–
I	0.00	25.00	5.26	15.85	21.51	44.44	20.00
II	0.00	0.00	26.32	7.32	15.05	18.52	0.00
III	0.00	25.00	5.26	31.71	19.35	22.22	60.00
IV	0.00	50.00	63.16	45.12	44.09	14.81	20.00
I	0.00	2.08	2.08	27.08	41.67	25.00	2.08
II	0.00	0.00	16.67	20.00	46.57	16.67	0.00
III	0.00	1.82	1.82	47.27	32.73	10.91	5.45
IV	0.00	2.06	12.37	38.14	42.27	4.12	1.03

Society Managed H.I.

Income	Age						
	0–19	20–24	25–34	35–44	45–54	55–64	65–
I	0.00	0.00	3.57	0.00	1.16	6.25	50.00
II	0.00	0.00	7.14	4.35	3.49	15.62	0.00
III	0.00	50.00	17.36	17.39	11.65	21.87	0.00
IV	0.00	50.00	71.43	78.26	83.72	56.25	50.00
I	0.00	0.00	20.00	0.00	20.00	40.00	20.00
II	0.00	0.00	15.38	23.08	23.08	38.46	0.00
III	0.00	5.56	13.89	33.33	27.78	19.44	0.00
IV	0.00	1.20	11.98	32.34	43.11	10.78	0.60

Note: For the groupings of income, see the note of Table 8.

age group of h-th category of health insurance schemes;

$n_{ij}^{h_0}$ = the number of all dependents who are supported by such insured persons that fall into i-th income and j-th age group of h-th category of health insurance schemes;

and

$$r_{ij}^{h} = n_{ij}^{h}/n_{ij}^{h_0} .$$

In other words, the distribution of the old aged dependents is normalized in terms of the distribution in the total population of dependents by r^h_{ij}. Supposing that the normalized distribution of the old aged is subject to the effects of both income and age in a form

$$r^h_{ij} = m^h + b^h_i + t^h_j + e^h_{ij},$$

where b_i and t_j differentiate the effects of i-th income and j-th age group of relevant insured persons for the old aged dependents, and e_{ij} are random variables representing residual effects. Using the data tabulated in Tables 12 and 13, the following analysis of variance tables are readily calculated.

It is readily seen from the comparison of Table 14 with Table 15 that in the case of male the variation of r_{ij} is essentially explained by the age effect. In fact, the age effect is significant at 1% level of significance for the case of male. The effect is not significant even at 5% level of significance for the case of female. It should also be noted in the comparison that the income effect is not a significant factor for the explanation of the variation of r_{ij} at 5% level of significance for both sex. It is not surprising that the variation of r_{ij} is essentially due to the demographic factor of male insured persons, because the old aged people supported by male insured persons are clustered around 35–54 age groups of the insured persons as Table 12 clearly indicates.

The reasoning and findings advanced in this section apparently suggest that the economic status of the old aged is intimately associated with and substantially governed by such demographic factors as age, sex, or other of workers who support the dependents. Following the information supplied from the *Special Survey of the Old Aged*, which was carried out for 1968 by the Ministry of Welfare, approximately half of the old aged over 60

Table 14. The analysis of variance of r^h_{ij} (Male)

Government Managed H.I.				Society Managed H.I.			
sources of variation	d.f.	sum of squares	mean square	sources of variation	d.f.	sum of squares	mean square
between income	3	0.01017	0.00339	between income	3	0.01072	0.00357
between age	6	0.21777	0.03630	between age	6	0.13281	0.02214
error	18	0.01764	0.00098	error	18	0.02498	0.00138

Note: 'd.f.' stands for the degree of freedom.

Table 15. The analysis of variance of r^h_{ij} (Female)

Government Managed H.I.				Society Managed H.I.			
sources of variation	d.f.	sum of squares	mean square	sources of variation	d.f.	sum of squares	mean square
between income	3	0.19899	0.06633	between income	3	0.07907	0.02636
between age	6	0.65813	0.10959	between age	6	0.57189	0.09532
error	18	0.54755	0.03043	error	18	0.84376	0.04688

Note: 'd.f.' stands for the degree of freedom.

Table 16. Distribution of number of families by types

(unit: percent)

types		1965	1968	1970	1971
the old aged	I	86.1	84.0	81.4	81.4
	IV	4.2	5.7	4.8	4.9
single parent	I	75.9	69.7	73.6	71.2
	IV	2.3	1.4	2.8	3.3
others	I	22.0	22.2	21.8	21.8
	IV	26.1	26.1	26.2	26.2

Source: Ministry of Welfare, *National Survey of Living*, respective years.
Note: I and IV stand for the lowest and highest income quartiles of all families.

is supported by their relatives. Facing the growing importance of the old aged in the total population, which is often called " the old aged society ", the major concern of the policy making for social welfare should be directed to explore thoroughly the actual status of the old aged. The dependence of the old aged on those who support them certainly forms one of the important aspect that deserves further detailed analysis, in view of the fact that relatively unfavourable standards of living of the old aged families prevail, as can be seen in Table 16 below.

5. Acknowledgements

Earlier version of this paper was presented to 14th General Conference of International Association for Research in Income and Wealth held at Aulanko, Finland in August 1975. The author extends his appreciation for helpful comments raised by Messrs. Jean-Pierre Poullier, J. L. Nicholson and other participants. He also wishes to thank Professor H. Ichikawa who has made the basic statistical materials accessible that are used in this paper. Mrs. Ayako Sugiyama has substantially contributed to the computational work. He appreciates for her continuous assistance. Thanks are also due to an anonymous referee of *Behaviormetrika* for his helpful comments. Any shortcomings that may arise in this paper, needless to say, are author's own.

6. Additional Remarks

In connection with the subject that I have dealt with in this paper, the following works have appeared after I had sent the final version of this paper to printing. They are:

(i) Takayama, N. (April 1976). Factors Governing the Inequality of Income and Monetary Assets Distributions in Japan, Keizai Kenkyu (*The Economic Review*), (in Japanese).

(ii) Mizoguchi, T. (July 1976). An Estimate of Income Distribution of Total Household in Japan, Keizai Kenkyu (*The Economic Review*), (in Japanese).

(iii) Takayama, N. and Yoshioka, S. (July 1976). Factors Determining the Size Distribution of Income in Japan—A Comparative Analysis of NFIE with FIES, Working Paper, J-4, Income and Assets Distribution Research Project, Institute of Economic Research, Hitotsubashi University.

In these works, Takayama and Yoshioka draw a conclusion from the comparative statistical analysis of the Family Income and Expenditure Survey and National Survey of the Family Income and Expenditure, both of which are carried out by the Bureau of Statistics of the Prime Minister's Office of Japan, that the predominant factors that govern the income distribution of worker's households are the size of enterprises which employ the workers, the categories of their occupation and the age of household's head. Their conclusion seems well fitted in the observations that are drawn from this paper, although the unit of observation is different in their and my works. It should also be noted that the analysis of the economic status of the old aged dependents that is made in section 4 of my paper is entirely outside the scope of their analysis in spite of the fact that they stress the importance of the old aged in the formation of the size distribution of household's income.

REFERENCES

A. B. Atkinson, " On the Measurement of Inequality ", *Wealth, Income and Inequality*, ed. by A. B. Atkinson, Harmondsworth 1973.

Y. Kurabayashi, and A. Yatsuka. Redistribution of Income and Measures of Income Inequality, Discussion Paper No. I, Economic Welfare Studies

Group, Institute of Statistical Research, Tokyo 1975.

S. Kuznets. " Demographic Aspects of the Distribution of Income among Families: Recent Trends in the United States ", *Econometrics and Economic Theory, Essays in Honour of Jean Tinbergen*, ed. by W. Sellekaerts, New York 1974.

T. Mizoguchi. " Size Distribution of Income and Wealth in Post-War Japan," Keizai Kenkyu (The Economic Review), (in Japanese) 1974.

T. Mizoguchi. " Size Distribution of Household Income in Post-War Japan ", *Income Distribution, Employment and Economic Development in Southeast and East Asia*, Vol. II, The Japan Economic Research Center and The Council for Asian Manpower Studies 1975.

J. N. Morgan. " Measuring the Economic Status of the Aged ", *International Economic Review* 1965.

R. E. Mouer, " A Subsystems Approach to Income Distribution in Japan Using the FIES Data ". *Economic Studies Quarterly* (in Japanese) 1975.

A. Sen, *On Economic Inequality*, Oxford 1973.

R. O. Wada, " Impact of Economic Growth on the Size Distribution of Income: The Postwar Experience of Japan ". *Income Distribution, Employment and Economic Development in Southeast and East Asia*, Vol. II, The Japan Economic Research Center and The Council for Asian Manpower Studies 1975.

Name Index

Subject Index